HANDBOOK TO COMPANY DIRECTORS

FOR OPTIMUM EFFECTIVENESS

RAM K NARAYAN

ISBN 979-8-89363-890-5

Index

Note from the Author

Greetings to dear Readers.

Joining the board of directors of successful companies is an aspiration and matter of pride for not only senior employees of the company but also many outside professionals.

The Board of Directors play a vital role in shaping up and guiding the destiny of an organization. They are also the legal trustees of the assets held by the organization. The courts have used various terms to define directors, such as agents, trustees, and managing partners to act as representatives of the shareholders to, carry out their will and objective.

Among the directors, the role of Independent Directors (IDs) who are truly independent are most crucial and challenging in the corporate world. The IDs who are also Non-Executive Directors (NEDs have to effectively govern and not manage the companies.

There is ever increasing requirement for high performing, effective directors who can make a difference in governance. NEDs are required to dedicate their time and skills in overseeing the company's executive management's performance, effectively participate in committee meetings and board meetings. They add immense value by providing a broad perspective of the company's issues to ultimately protect the interests of shareholders. They are expected to objectively review the policies and plans framed by the executive management and offer guidance as may become necessary.

NEDs share the responsibility of developing frameworks and controls for accessing and regulating risks. They assure the stakeholders that the financial information is reasonably accurate, and the financial controls and risk management systems are robust and secure. When required, the NEDs should not fear to challenge the performance of the executive management team and the promoters.

It is imperative that the board prepares the skills to secure and evaluate information received, ask penetrating and insightful questions. They must have the strategic foresight to explore and evaluate changing business conditions - technological, marketing or financial and how they may impact adversely the Company so that the needed corrective /defensive measures can be taken by the board collectively to reduce the impact and incidence on the Company.

Proficient board members think about the values that drive policies. They are able to articulate why a specific action is imprudent, what is the underlying risk, and why it is a risk. Since board members are not always present at the organization, they delegate accountability for the achievement of intended results within the established boundaries of ethics and prudence. There must be a **Commitment to adhere to the board's written code of conduct and to respect decisions of the board.**

Barring, may be, few dozens of blue chip companies in the country, most NEDs of companies are perceived to be relatives, friends, employees or past connections of the promoters. The trend is for the promoters to appoint known Accountants, Lawyers, Retired Civil Servants; Retired Defense Service personnel; Medical professionals; Post graduates; Engineers; Management Executive; luminaries etc. on their boards. Most do not possess any special domain experience to discharge their expected responsibilities. Many of them do not recognize the onerous responsibilities that attaches to the office of directors. They seldom have the knowledge on board process and how to protect themselves from liabilities for acts of omissions and commissions by others who manage the affairs of the company.. **They are unaware of the expectations cast on them by the Companies Act, 2013; Rules framed thereunder; the SEBI LODR, 2015 Regulations; the Secretarial Standards. etc.**

The general in-house training programs for directors in Companies are considered to be grossly inadequate to meet the professional development needs of the directors.

The objective of this book is to act as a personal guide to the NEDs and other directors through twelve Chapters. Every critical requirement contained in the Companies Act, 2013, its Rules, applicable Secretarial Standards and the SEBI Listing Regulations, 2015 has been covered extensively so that every Director can discharge his responsibilities as knowledgeable professionals and escape befalling consequences for non-compliances or contraventions.

The applicable sections of the Companies Act, 2013 Act has been mentioned only with the section numbers followed by applicable relevant Rule number and SEBI LODR, 2015 requirements under the word "Reg".

It is hoped that the book will be of use to the fraternity of directors and those who are aspiring to be inducted on the board of directors of companies in India.

This is the fifth book of the author. Earlier books being -

(1)   Management of Risks under the Companies Act, 2013;

(2)   Corporate Governance in India-Challenges;

(3) *Reservoir of Central Acts of Parliament-for all;*

(4) *Business-Ethics, Failures, Scams, Frauds, Punishments.*

Ram K Narayan

ram7883@gmail.com

April 22, 2024

Essence of the Twelve Chapters of the Book

Chapter I:

Some of the critical definitions under the Companies Act, 2013/ SEBI (LODR). 2015:

Associate.	Books of Account.	Control.
Document.	Electronic mail.	Electronic Mode.
Financial Statement.	Free Reserves.	Interested Director.
Key Managerial Personnel.	Material Subsidiary.	Net Worth.
Officer.	Officer who is Default.	Promoter.
Promoter Group.	Related Party.	Relative.
Related Party Transactions.	Small Company.	Subsidiary.

Senior Management

The Chapter also lists sections which specify punishment by Imprisonment along with fine to Directors for contraventions of the Act which may be over and above that have been provided under the respective Sections under various Chapters of the Companies Act, 2013.

These are:

Punishment for-

Fraud.   False Statements.   False Evident.   Repeated Defaults.

Wrongful withholding of property. Where no specific punishment has been provided.

Chapter II:

Kinds of Directors

First.	Additional.	Alternate.	Casual.
De facto.	Proportional Representation.	Executive.	Independent.
Managing.	Nominee.	Non-Executive.	Resident.	Rotational
Shadow.	Small Shareholder.	Woman.	

Chapter III:

Composition, Appointment, Retirement, Vacation, Disqualification, Resignation, Removal of Directors.

Related requirements under the Companies Act, 2013, the Rules thereto and the SEBI (LODR) 2015 have been covered.

Note:

MCA has, of late, started invoking prosecution actions for contravention of the requirements under this Chapter – both against the company and the individuals.

Chapter IV:

Independent Directors, NEDs and their Liabilities {Under the Act and SEBI}

Who is an ID?   Provisions related to ID.

Schedule IV covering:

Code for IDs. {*Guidelines on professional conduct:; Roles and Functions; Duties; Manner of appointment; Re-appointment; Resignation; Separate meetings; Evaluation Mechanism*}.

Data Bank of IDs;

Obligations with respect to IDs (SEBI Regulations}.

Liabilities for acts of omissions and commissions by managements?

Extra care that may be taken by IDs.

Chapter V:

Duties, Functions, Responsibilities and Powers of Directors

Both under the Companies Act, 2013 & SEBI (LODR) Regulations, 2015 have been covered.

Chapter VI:

The chapter covers:

Meetings of the Board; Committees of the Board under the Act; the Rules thereto; and SEBI (LODR);

Board Process as contained in the Mandatory Secretarial Standards **(SS-1)**-ICSI;

Recommendatory Standard **SS-4** on Report of Board of Directors.

Chapter VII:

Management & Administration; and Mandatory Secretarial Standards (SS-2) for General Meetings of ICSI.

Statutory Registers to be maintained; Requirements related to holders of Beneficial Interest in Company;

Inspection of registers;

Annual Return;

Resolutions by shareholders;

Minutes; AND

Mandatory Secretarial Standards on General Meetings (SS-2) ICSI.

Chapter VIII:

Declaration and Payment of Dividends

Under the Companies Act, 2013; Declaration and Payment of Dividend Rules, 2014 & the Recommendatory Secretarial Standards (SS-3) by ICSI

Chapter IX:

Accounts of Companies under Companies Acct, 2013; Companies (Accounts) Rules, 2014 & Financial Statements and Board's Report

Books of Accounts and relevant Documents which shall be maintained;

Expectations from Financial Statements; Features of Financial Statements and Board's Report to Shareholders,

CSR Compliance Requirements.

Chapter X:

Audit, and Auditors

Appointment; Reappointment; Removal; Resignation; eligibility; Qualifications;

Disqualifications; Remuneration; Powers; Duties; Reporting of Frauds by Auditors;

Services not to be rendered by auditors.

Chapter XI:

Appointment and Remuneration of Managerial Personnel; Related Rules & Schedule V to Companies Act, 2013:related to –

Appointments.

Reappointments,

Remuneration without Central Government's approval etc.

Chapter XII:

Potential Risk Areas to be cautious of by NEDs, non-promoter; non-whole-time directors to avoid classification as:

"Officer of the Company who is in Default"

Relevant Sections of the Companies Act, 2013.

Introduction, Key Definitions and Severe Punishments for certain offences

A. Introduction

Company is a juristic, artificial, legal person. It can, *inter alia*, enter into contracts, own assets in its own name, sue and be sued by others.

In essence, it is not human but acts through body of persons, to whom powers of management are delegated in terms of the provisions contained in the Memorandum and Articles of Association of the Company with necessary safeguards to protect primarily the Company's interests and those of the shareholders.

Such body of persons is called the **"Board of Directors."** The directors are not only agents of the company but more importantly they are their trustees. Only an individual can act as director of a company.

For discharging their duties and responsibilities towards the company, its' shareholders and others, the board of directors are primarily governed by the provisions of the Companies Act, 2013, the Company's Rules framed thereunder and the SEBI enactments including SEBI (Listing Obligations and Disclosures Requirements) Regulations, 2015.

The board of directors of companies are constituted of whole-time directors, Non-Executive Directors, and Nominee Directors. The board of directors are vested with powers of management by the Articles of Association of the Company, the Companies Act, 2013; the Rules framed thereunder and in the case of Listed Company's additionally, by the SEBI LODR, 2015 Regulations.

The Whole-Time directors are responsible and answerable for the day-to-day activities of companies. Non-executive directors may be independent or non-independent.

Any Return that has to be filed before the Registrar of Companies of appropriate jurisdiction shall be e-filed and on payment of applicable fee payable pursuant to section 403 of the act and Rule 12 of the Companies (Registration of Offices and Fees) Rules, 2014.

Part A of the Table provide for payment of normal fee for different categories of companies;

Part B additional fee for delays in filing of the forms which is "x" times of normal filing fee.

Chapter XXIX of the Act provide for punishment to any person who is found to be guilty of certain offences. These punishments are over and above the specific punishments such persons may be subject to, under respective sections. These have been stated in this **Paragraph C of this Part.**

B. Some Important Definitions

Sec 2(6) Associate company, in relation to another company, means a company in which that other company has a significant influence, but which is not a subsidiary company of the company having such influence and includes a joint venture company.

Explanation —For the purpose of this clause,—

(a)   the expression **"significant influence"** means control of at least twenty per cent. of total voting power, or control of or participation in business decisions under an agreement;

(b)   the expression **"joint venture"** means a joint arrangement whereby the parties that have joint control of the arrangement have rights to the net assets of the arrangement;

Regulation 2 (b)

"associate" shall mean any entity which is an associate under sub-section (6) of section 2 of the Companies Act, 2013 or under the applicable accounting standard

Provided that this definition shall not be applicable for the units issued by mutual fund which are listed on a recognized stock exchange(s) for which the provisions of the Securities and Exchange Board of India (Mutual Funds) Regulations, 1996 shall be applicable

Sec 2(10) Board of Directors - or - Board - in relation to a company, means the collective body of the directors of the company.

Sec 2(12) Book and paper and Book or paper include books of account, deeds, vouchers, writings, documents, minutes and registers maintained on paper or in electronic form;

Sec 2(13) books of account includes records maintained in respect of—

(*i*)   all sums of money received and expended by a company and matters in relation to which the receipts and expenditure take place;

(*ii*)   all sales and purchases of goods and services by the company;

(*iii*) the assets and liabilities of the company; and

(*iv*)   the items of cost as may be prescribed under section 148 in the case of a company which belongs to any class of companies specified under that section;

Sec 2(18) Chief Executive Officer means an officer of a company, who has been designated as such by it;

Sec 2(19) Chief Financial Officer means a person appointed as the Chief Financial Officer of a company;

Reg 2(f) Chief financial officer" or "whole time finance director" or "head of finance", by whatever name called, shall mean the person heading and discharging the finance function of the listed entity as disclosed by it to the recognized stock exchange(s) in its filing under these regulations;

Sec 2(27) Control shall include the right to appoint majority of the directors or to control the management or policy decisions exercisable by a person or persons acting individually or in concert, directly or indirectly, including by virtue of their shareholding or management rights or shareholders agreements or voting agreements or in any other manner;

Sec 2(34) Rule 2(c)Director - means a director appointed to the Board of a company..

Digital signature- means the digital signature as defined under clause (p) of sub-section (1) of section 2 of the Information Technology Act, 2000 (21 of 2000);

Rule 2(e) Director Identification Number- (DIN) means an identification number allotted by the Central Government to any individual, **intending to be appointed** as director or to any existing director of a company, for the purpose of his identification as a director of a company;

Provided further that (DIN) includes the Designated Partnership Identification Number (DPIN) issued under section 7 of the Limited Liability Partnership Act, 2008 (6 of 2009) and the rules made thereunder;

Sec 2{36) "Document" includes summons, notice, requisition, order, declaration, form and register, whether issued, sent or kept in pursuance of this Act or under any other law for the time being in force or otherwise, maintained on paper or in electronic form;

Rule 2(f) e-Form - means a form in the electronic form as prescribed under the Act or the rules made thereunder and notified by the Central Government under the Act;

Rule 2(g) Electronic Mail - means the message sent, received or forwarded in digital form using any electronic communication mechanism that the message so sent, received or forwarded is storable and retrievable;

Rule 2(h) Electronic mode - for the purposes of clause (42) of section 2 of the Act, means carrying out electronically based, whether main server is installed in India or not, including, but not limited to-

(i)   business to business and business to consumer transactions, data interchange and other digital supply transactions;

(ii)   offering to accept deposits or inviting deposits or accepting deposits or subscriptions in securities, in India or from citizens of India;

(iii)   financial settlements, web based marketing, advisory and transactional services, database services and products, supply chain management;

(iv)   online services such as telemarketing, telecommuting, telemedicine, education and information research; and

(v)   all related data communication services, whether conducted by e-mail, mobile devices, social media, cloud computing, document management, voice or data transmission or otherwise;.

Rule 2(i)- Electronic record means the electronic record as defined under clause (t) of sub-section (1) of section 2 of the Information Technology Act, 2000.

Rule 22(k)- Executive Director means "a whole-time director..

Sec 2(40) Financial Statement in relation to a company, includes—

(i)   a balance sheet as at the end of the financial year;

(ii)   a profit and loss account, or in the case of a company carrying on any activity not for profit, an income and expenditure account for the financial year;

(iii)   cash flow statement for the financial year;

(iv)   a statement of changes in equity, if applicable; and

(v)   any explanatory note annexed to, or forming part of, any document referred to in sub-clause (*i*) to sub-clause (*iv*):

Provided that the financial statement, with respect to One Person Company, small company and dormant company, may not include the cash flow statement;

Sec 2 (43) Free Reserves means such reserves which, as per the latest audited balance sheet of a company, are available for distribution as dividend:

Provided that—

(*i*)   any amount representing unrealized gains, notional gains or revaluation of assets, whether shown as a reserve or otherwise, or

(*ii*)   any change in carrying amount of an asset or of a liability recognized in equity, including surplus in profit and loss account on measurement of the asset or the liability at fair value,

   shall not be treated as free reserves;

Sec 2(46) Holding company, in relation to one or more other companies, means a company of which such companies are subsidiary companies;

Explanation —For the purposes of this clause, the expression "company" includes any- body corporate;

Sec 2(47) Independent Director: - means an independent director as referred to in sub-section (6) of section 149.

Sec 2(49) interested director - means a director who is in any way, whether by himself or through any of his relatives or firm, body corporate or other association of individuals in which he or any of his relatives is a partner, director or a member- interested in a contract or arrangement, or proposed contract or arrangement, entered into or to be entered into by or on behalf of a company.

Sec 2(51) Key managerial personnel - in relation to a company, means—

(i)   the Chief Executive Officer or the managing director or the manager;

(ii)   the company secretary;

(iii)   the whole-time director;

(iv)   the Chief Financial Officer;

(v)   such other officer, not more than one level below the directors who is in whole-time employment, designated as key managerial personnel by the Board; and

(vi)   such other officer as may be prescribed;

Sec 2(53) Manager - means an individual who, subject to the superintendence, control and direction of the Board of Directors, has the management of the whole, or substantially the whole, of the affairs of a company, and **includes a director** or any other person occupying the position of a manager, by whatever name called, whether under a contract of service or not;

Sec 2(54) Managing Director - means a director who, by virtue of the articles of a company or an agreement with the company or a resolution passed in its general meeting, or by its Board of Directors, is entrusted with substantial powers of management of the affairs of the company and **includes a director** occupying the position of managing director, by whatever name called.

Reg 2(e): chief executive officer" or "managing director" or "manager" shall mean the person so appointed in terms of the Companies Act, 2013;

Reg 16 (1) (c) "material subsidiary" shall mean a subsidiary, whose income or net worth exceeds ten percent of the consolidated income or net worth respectively, of the listed entity and its subsidiaries in the immediately preceding accounting year.

Explanation.-The listed entity shall formulate a policy for determining 'material' subsidiary.

(1) (d) "senior management" shall mean the officers and personnel of the listed entity who are members of its core management team, excluding the Board of Directors, and shall also comprise all the members of the management one level below the Chief Executive Officer or Managing Director or Whole Time Director or Manager (including Chief Executive Officer and Manager, in case they are not part of the Board of Directors) and shall specifically include the functional heads, by whatever name called and the Company Secretary and the Chief Financial Officer.

Sec 2(57) Net worth means the aggregate value of the paid-up share capital and all reserves created out of the profits, securities premium account and debit or credit balance of profit and loss account, after deducting the aggregate value of the accumulated losses, deferred expenditure and miscellaneous expenditure not written off, as per the audited balance sheet, but does not include reserves created out of revaluation of assets, write-back of depreciation and amalgamation.

Sec 2(59) Officer - includes any **director**, manager or key managerial personnel or any person in accordance with whose directions or instructions the Board of Directors or any one or more of the directors is or are accustomed to act;

Sec 2(60) Officer who is in default - for the purpose of any provision in this Act which enacts that an officer of the company who is in default shall be liable to any penalty or punishment by way of imprisonment, fine or otherwise, means any of the following officers of a company, namely:—

(i)   **whole-time director;**

(ii)   key managerial personnel;

(iii)   where there is no key managerial personnel, such **director or directors** as specified by the Board in this behalf and who has or **have given his or their consent in writing to the Board to such specification, or all the directors, if no director is so specified;**

(iv)   **any person who, under the immediate authority of the Board or** any key managerial personnel, is charged with any responsibility including maintenance, filing or distribution of accounts or records, authorizes, actively participates in, knowingly permits, or knowingly fails to take active steps to prevent, any default;

(v)   **any person in accordance with whose** advice, directions or instructions the Board of Directors of the company is accustomed to act, other than a person who gives advice to the Board in a professional capacity;

(vi)   **every director, in respect of a contravention of any of the provisions of this Act, who is aware of such contravention by virtue of the receipt by him of any proceedings of the Board or participation in such proceedings without objecting to the same, or where such contravention had taken place with his consent or connivance;**

(vii)   in respect of the issue or transfer of any shares of a company, the share transfer agents, registrars and merchant bankers to the issue or transfer;

Sec 2(69) promoter - means a person—

(a)   who has been named as such in a prospectus or is identified by the company in the annual return referred to in section 92; or

(b)   who **has control over the affairs of the company, directly or indirectly** whether as a shareholder, **director or otherwise;** or

(c)   in accordance with whose advice, directions or instructions the Board of Directors of the company is accustomed to act:

Provided that nothing in sub-clause (c) shall apply to a person who is acting merely in a professional capacity;

SEBI (Issue of Capital and Disclosure Requirements) Regulations, 2018

Reg. 2 (oo)

"promoter" shall include a person:

(i)   who has been named as such in a draft offer document or offer document or is identified by the issuer in the annual return referred to in section 92 of the Companies Act, 2013; or

(ii)   who has control over the affairs of the issuer, directly or indirectly whether as a shareholder, director or otherwise; or

(iii)   in accordance with whose advice, directions or instructions the board of directors of the issuer is accustomed to act:

Provided that nothing in sub-clause (iii) shall apply to a person who is acting merely in a professional capacity;

Provided further that a financial institution, scheduled commercial bank, foreign portfolio investor other than Category III foreign portfolio investor, mutual fund, venture capital fund, alternative investment fund, foreign venture capital investor, insurance company registered with the IRDA of India or any other category as specified by the Board from time to time, shall not be deemed to be a promoter merely by virtue of the fact that twenty per cent. or more of the equity share capital of the issuer is held by such person unless such person satisfy other requirements prescribed under these regulations;

(pp) "promoter group" includes:

(i)   the promoter;

(ii)   an immediate relative of the promoter (i.e. any spouse of that person, or any parent, brother, sister or child of the person or of the spouse); and

(iii)   in case promoter is a body corporate:

(A)   a subsidiary or holding company of such body corporate;

(B)   anybody corporate in which the promoter holds twenty per cent. or more of the equity share capital; and/or any-body corporate which holds twenty per cent. or more of the equity share capital of the promoter;

(C)   anybody corporate in which a group of individuals or companies or combinations thereof acting in concert, which hold twenty per cent. or more of the equity share capital in that body corporate and such group of individuals or companies or combinations thereof also holds twenty per cent or more of the equity share capital of the issuer and are also acting in concert; and

(iv)   in case the promoter is an individual:

(A)   anybody corporate in which twenty per cent. or more of the equity share capital is held by the promoter or an immediate relative of the promoter or a firm or

Hindu Undivided Family in which the promoter or any one or more of their relative is a member;

(B)   Anybody corporate in which a body corporate as provided in (A) above holds twenty per cent. or more, of the equity share capital; and

(C)   any Hindu Undivided Family or firm in which the aggregate share of the promoter and their relatives is equal to or more than twenty per cent. of the total capital;

(v)   all persons whose shareholding is aggregated under the heading "shareholding of the promoter group":

Provided that a financial institution, scheduled bank, foreign portfolio investor other than Category III foreign portfolio investor, mutual fund, venture capital fund, alternative investment fund, foreign venture capital investor, insurance company registered with the IRDA of India or any other category as specified by the Board from time to time, shall not be deemed to be promoter group merely by virtue of the fact that twenty per cent. or more of the equity share capital of the promoter is held by such person or entity:

Provided further that such financial institution, scheduled bank, foreign portfolio investor other than Category III foreign portfolio investor, mutual fund, venture capital fund, alternative investment fund and foreign venture capital investor insurance company registered with the IRDA of India or any other category as specified by the Board from time to time shall be treated as promoter

group for the subsidiaries or companies promoted by them or for the mutual fund sponsored by them;

Sec 2(70) Prospectus – means any document described or issued as a prospectus and includes a red herring prospectus referred to in section 32 or shelf prospectus referred to in section 31 or any notice, circular, advertisement or other document inviting offers from the public for the subscription or purchase of any securities of body corporate.

Sec 2 (71) – public company – means a company which—

(a)   is not a private company;

(b)   has a minimum authorized capital of one lakh rupees

Provided that a company which is a subsidiary of a company, **not being a private company, shall be deemed to be public company** for the purposes of this Act even where such subsidiary company continues to be a private company in its articles ;

Sec 2(76) Related party, with reference to a company, means—

(i)   a **director** or his relative;

(ii)   a key-managerial personnel or his relative;

(iii)   a firm, in which a **director**, manager or his relative is a partner;

(iv)   a private company in which a **director** or manager is a member or director;

(v)   a public company in which a director or manager is a director or holds along with his relatives, **more than two per cent.** of its paid-up share capital;

(vi)   anybody corporate whose Board of Directors, managing director or manager is accustomed to act in accordance with the advice, directions or instructions of a director or manager;

(vii)   any person on whose advice, directions or instructions a **director** or manager is accustomed to act:

Provided that nothing in sub-clauses (vi) and (vii) shall apply to the advice, directions or instructions given in a professional capacity;

(viii)   any company which is –

(A)   a holding, subsidiary or an associate company of such company; or

(B)   a subsidiary of a holding company to which it is also a subsidiary;

(C)   a director, or key managerial personnel of the holding company or his relative with reference to a company, shall be deemed to be a related party. **{R3}**

(ix)   such other person as may be prescribed;

Sec 2 (77) & Rule 4: Relative – with reference to any person, means anyone who is related to another, if —

(i)   they are members of a Hindu Undivided Family;

(ii)   they are husband and wife; or

(iii)   one person is related to the other as:

(1)   **Father:** {the term includes step-father}.

(2)   **Mother:** {the term includes the step-mother}.

(3)   **Son:** (the term includes the step-son}.

(4)   Son's wife.

(5)   Daughter.

(6)   Daughter's husband.

(7)   **Brother:** {the term includes the step-brother};

(8)   **Sister:** {the term includes step-sister}.

Reg 2(zc): Related Party Transaction – means a transfer of resources, services or obligations between a listed entity and a related party, regardless of whether a price is charged and a "transaction" with a related party shall be construed to include a single transaction or a group of transactions in a contract:

Provided that this definition shall not be applicable for the units issued by mutual funds which are listed on a recognized stock exchange(s);

Sec 2(85) Small Company – means a company, other than a public company,—

(i)   **paid-up share capital** of which does not exceed fifty lakh rupees or such higher amount as may be prescribed which shall not be more than ten crore rupees and

(ii)   **turnover** of which as per profit and loss account for the immediately preceding financial year does not exceed two crore rupees or such higher amount as prescribed which shall not be more than one hundred crore rupees:

Provided that **nothing in this clause shall apply** to—

(A)   a holding company or a subsidiary company;

(B)   a company registered under section 8; or

(C)   a company or body corporate governed by any special Act;

Sec 2(87) Subsidiary company or subsidiary - in relation to any other company (that is to say the holding company), means a company in which the holding company—

(i)   controls the composition of the Board of Directors; or

(ii)   exercises or controls more than one-half of the 5[total voting power] either at its own or together with one or more of its subsidiary companies:

Provided that such class or classes of holding companies as may be prescribed shall not have layers of subsidiaries beyond such numbers as may be prescribed.

Explanation —For the purposes of this clause,—

(a)   a company shall be deemed to be a subsidiary company of the holding company even if the control referred to in sub-clause (i) or sub-clause (ii) is of another subsidiary company of the holding company;

(b)   the composition of a company's Board of Directors shall be deemed to be controlled by another company if that other company by exercise of some power exercisable by it at its discretion can appoint or remove all or a majority of the directors;

(c)   the expression "company" includes any-body corporate;

(d)   "layer" in relation to a holding company means its subsidiary or subsidiaries;

Sec 2 (94) Whole-time director – includes a director in the whole-time employment of the company;

C. Chapter XXIX of the Act, 2013 – Severe Punishments for certain offences

Sec 447. Punishment for fraud —

Without prejudice to any liability including repayment of any debt under this Act or any other law for the time being in force, any person who is found to be guilty of fraud, **shall be punishable** with **imprisonment** for a term which shall not be less than six months but which may extend to ten years and shall also be liable to fine which shall not be less than the amount involved in the fraud, but which may extend to three times the amount involved in the fraud:

Provided that where the **fraud in question involves public interest,** the term of imprisonment shall not be less than three years.

Provided further that where the fraud involves an amount less than ten lakhs or one per cent of the turnover of the company whichever is lower, and **does not involve public interest**, any person guilty of such fraud shall be punishable with imprisonment for a term which may extend to five years or with fine which may extend to fifty lakh rupees or with both.

Explanation —For the purposes of this section—

(i)   **fraud** in relation to affairs of a company or any-body corporate, **includes** any act, omission, concealment of any fact or abuse of position committed by any person or any other person with the connivance in any manner, with intent to deceive, **to gain undue advantage** from, or to injure the interests of, the company or its shareholders or its creditors or any other person, whether or not there is any wrongful gain or wrongful loss;

(ii)   **wrongful gain** means the gain by unlawful means of property to which the person gaining is not legally entitled;

(iii)   **wrongful loss** means the loss by unlawful means of property to which the person losing is legally entitled.

Sec 448. Punishment for false statement —

Save as otherwise provided in this Act, if **in any return, report, certificate, financial statement, prospectus, statement or other document** required by, or for, the purposes of any of the provisions of this Act or the rules made thereunder, any person makes a statement,—

(a)   which **is false in any material** particulars, knowing it to be false; or

(b)   which omits any material fact, **knowing it to be material**, he **shall be liable** under section 447.

Sec 449. Punishment for false evidence —

Save as otherwise provided in this Act, **if any person intentionally** gives false evidence—

(a)   upon any examination on oath or solemn affirmation, authorized under this Act; or

(b)   in any affidavit, deposition or solemn affirmation, in or about the winding up of any company under this Act, or otherwise in or about any matter arising under this Act, he **shall be punishable with imprisonment** for a term which shall not be less than three years but which may extend to seven years and with fine which may extend to ten lakh rupees.

Sec 450. Punishment where no specific penalty or punishment is provided —

If a **company or any officer of a company or any other person contravenes any of the provisions of this Act or the rules made thereunder, or any condition,** limitation or restriction subject to which any approval, sanction, consent, confirmation, recognition, direction or exemption in relation to any matter has been accorded, given or granted, and for which no penalty or punishment is provided elsewhere in this Act, **the company and every officer of the company** who is in default or such other person shall be liable to a penalty of ten thousand rupees, and in case of continuing contravention, with a further penalty of one thousand rupees for each day after the first during which the contravention continues, **subject to a maximum** of two lakh rupees in case of a company and fifty thousand rupees in case of an officer who is in default or any other person" shall be substituted

Sec 451. Punishment in case of repeated default —

If a **company or an officer of a company** commits an offence punishable **either with fine or with imprisonment** and where the same offence is committed for the second or subsequent occasions **within a period of three years**, then, that company and every officer thereof who is in default **shall be punishable with twice** the amount of fine for such offence in addition to any imprisonment provided for that offence.

Sec 452. Punishment for wrongful withholding of property —

(1)   If **any officer or employee** of a company—

      (a)   **wrongfully obtains** possession of any property, including cash of the company; or

      (b)   having any such property including cash in his possession, **wrongfully withholds** it or knowingly applies it for the purposes other than those expressed or directed in the articles and authorized by this Act, he shall, on the complaint of the company or of any member or creditor or contributory thereof, be **punishable with fine** which shall not be less than one lakh rupees but which may extend to five lakh rupees.

(2)   The Court trying an offence may also order such officer or employee to deliver up or refund, within a time to be fixed by it, any such property or cash wrongfully obtained or wrongfully withheld or knowingly misapplied, the **benefits that have been derived from such property or cash or in default,** to undergo imprisonment for a term which may extend to two years.

"Provided that the imprisonment of such officer or employee, as the case may be, **shall not be ordered** for wrongful possession or withholding of a dwelling unit, if the court is satisfied that the **company has not paid** to that officer or employee, as the case may be, any amount relating to—

(a)   provident fund, pension fund, gratuity fund or any other fund for the welfare of its officers or employees, maintained by the company;

(b)   compensation or liability for compensation under the Workmen's Compensation Act, 1923 in respect of death or disablement.".

Sec 453. Punishment for improper use of – Limited or – Private Limited—

If any person or persons trade or carry on business under any name or title, of which the word -Limited or the words - Private Limited or any contraction or imitation thereof is or are the last word or words, that person or each of those persons shall, unless duly incorporated with limited liability, or unless duly incorporated as a private company with limited liability, as the case may be, punishable with fine which shall not be less than five hundred rupees but may extend to two thousand rupees for every day for which that name or title has been used.

454A. Penalty for repeated default

Where a **company or an officer of a company or any other person** having already been subjected to penalty for default under any provisions of this Act, **again commits such default within a period of three years** from the date of order imposing such penalty passed by the adjudicating officer or the Regional Director, as the case may be, it or **he shall be liable for the second or subsequent defaults** for an amount equal to **twice** the amount of penalty provided for such default under the relevant provisions of this Act

Sec 455. Dormant company —

(1) Where a company is formed and registered under this Act for a future project or to hold an asset or intellectual property and has

no significant accounting transaction, such a company or an inactive company may make an application to the Registrar in the manner prescribed under Rule 3 of Companies {Miscellaneous} Rules, 2014 for obtaining the status of a dormant company.

Explanation —For the purposes of this section,—

(i)   inactive company - means a company which has not been carrying on any business or operation, or has not made any significant accounting transaction during the last two financial years, or has not filed financial statements and annual returns during the last two financial years;

(ii)   significant accounting transaction - means any transaction other than—

    (a)   payment of fees by a company to the Registrar;

    (b)   payments made by it to fulfil the requirements of this Act or any other law;

    (c)   allotment of shares to fulfil the requirements of this Act; and

    (d)   payments for maintenance of its office and records.

Rule 3. Application for obtaining status of dormant company.

A company may make an application in Form MSC-1 to the Registrar for obtaining the certificate of status of a Dormant Company in Form Misc-2, after passing a special resolution to this effect in the general meeting of the company or after issuing a notice to all the shareholders of the company for this purpose and obtaining consent of at least 3/4th shareholders (in value):

Provided that:

(i)   no inspection, inquiry or investigation has been ordered or taken up or carried out against the company;

(ii)   no prosecution has been initiated and pending against the company under any law;

(iii) the company is neither having any public deposits which are outstanding nor the company is in default in payment thereof or interest thereon;

(iv)   the company is not having any outstanding loan, whether secured or unsecured: Else prior concurrence of the lender obtained shall be enclosed with Form MSC-1;

(v)   there is no dispute in the management or ownership of the company and a certificate in this regard is enclosed with Form MSC-1;

(vi)   the company does not have any outstanding statutory taxes, dues, duties etc. payable to the Central Government or any State Government or local authorities etc.;

(vii) the company has not defaulted in the payment of workmen's dues;

(viii) the securities of the company are not listed on any stock exchange within or outside India.

Sec 460. Condonation of delay in certain cases—

(a)   where any application required to be made to the Central Government under any provision of this Act in respect of any matter is not made within the time specified therein, that Government may, for reasons to be recorded in writing, condone the delay; and

(b)   where any document required to be filed with the Registrar under any provision of this Act is not filed within the time specified therein, the Central Government may, for reasons to be recorded in writing, condone the delay.

Sec 463. Power of court to grant relief in certain cases —

(1)   If in any proceeding for negligence, default, breach of duty, misfeasance or breach of trust against an officer of a company, it appears to the court hearing the case that he is or may be liable in respect of the negligence, default, breach of duty, misfeasance or breach of trust, **but that he has acted honestly and reasonably,** and that having regard to all the circumstances of the case, including those connected with his appointment, **he ought fairly to be excused, the court may relieve him, either wholly or partly,** from his liability on such term, as it may think fit:

Provided that **in a criminal proceeding** under this sub-section, **the court shall have no power** to grant relief from any civil liability which may attach to an officer in respect of such negligence, default, breach of duty, misfeasance or breach of trust.

(2)   Where any such officer has reason to apprehend that any proceeding will or might be brought against him in respect of any negligence, default, breach of duty, misfeasance or breach of trust, **he may apply to the High Court for relief** and the High Court on such application shall have the same power to relieve him as it would have had if it had been

a court before which a proceedings against that officer for negligence, default, breach of duty, misfeasance or breach of trust had been brought under sub-section (1).

(3)   No court shall grant any relief to any officer under sub-section (1) or sub-section (2) unless it has, by notice served in the manner specified by it, required the Registrar and such other person, if any, as it thinks necessary, to show cause why such relief should not be granted.

Chapter II

Kinds of Directors

1. **First Director –**

    (a)   Person named as first director in the Articles {*Sec. 152(1)*} shall be the first director.

    (b)   If not named, subscribers to the Memorandum who are individuals shall be deemed to be the first directors of the company, until directors are duly appointed by the shareholders.

1. Additional Director –

(a)   Articles of the company must permit such an appointment.

(b)   When the Board considers it necessary to appoint a person as a director of the company outside its' general meeting, it may do so at any time as may be deemed necessary under *section 161 (1)* of the Act.

(c)   A person who fails to get appointed as a director in a general meeting cannot be appointed as additional director.

(d)   The additional director shall hold office up to the date of the next annual general meeting or the last date on which the annual general meeting of the company should have been held, whichever is earlier.

(e)   Directors may appoint Additional Director by passing a resolution in a Board Meeting or by Circular Resolution.

(f)   The number of directors and additional directors taken together shall not exceed the number specified in the Articles.

(g)   The duties and liabilities of the additional director are the same as that of the other directors appointed at general meetings.

2.   **Alternate Director –**

   (a)   Articles of the company must permit such an appointment.

   (b)   Such a person cannot be the one who fails to get appointed as a director in a general meeting.

   (c)   *The* board of directors may appoint alternate director by a resolution in board meeting or by circular resolution.

   (d)   The appointment is made during the temporary absence from India of the director for a period of not less than three months. Both the original and his alternate shall be counted as one for all purposes under the Act.

   (e)   Such an appointee cannot be a person holding any alternate directorship for any other director in the company.

   (f)   Such as appointee cannot be a Director in the Company.

(g)   No person shall be appointed as an alternate director for an Independent Director unless he is qualified to be appointed as an independent director under Companies Act.

(h)   No alternate director shall hold office for a period longer than that is permissible to the director in whose place he has bene appointed.

(i)   The alternate director shall vacate the office when the director in whose place he has been appointed returns to India or the tenure of the Original Director expires.

(j)   The provisions of the Act for the re-appointment of a retiring director shall apply only to the original director and not to the Alternate Director. {*Sec 161*}

(k)   In the absence of the principal director, the alternate director has the same power as the principal director

(l)   The alternate director should receive all meeting and committee notes that

(m)   the principal director would receive.

(n)   In the same way as any regular director, the alternate director is personally

(o)   responsible for their actions.

3.   **Casual Vacancy Director-** Sec. 161(4) of the Act –

(a)   The regulations of the Articles for filling casual vacancy may be followed.

If articles is silent –

(b)   The board of directors may appoint another persona s director **at a board meeting** to fill up the vacancy arising in the office of a director before his term of office expires in the normal course.

(c)   The appointment shall be subsequently approved by members in the **immediate next** general meeting.

(d)   The casual director so appointed shall hold office only up to the date up to which the director in whose place he is appointed would have held office if it had not been vacated.

The vacancy may arise due to death, resignation or disqualification under section 164 of the Act.

4.   **Chief Executive Officer (CEO)**

(a)   Section 2 (18) of the Act defines CEO as an officer of a company, who has been designated as such by it;.

(b)   The Act does not defines the qualification, experience, role, functions, term and conditions of appointment etc., of CEO.

(c)   Section 203 of the Act requires that **every listed company; every other public company having a paid-up share capital of ten crore rupees or more shall appoint a CEO.**

(d)   CEO is considered to be the highest-ranking executive of an organization. They make all significant decisions for the company and report directly to the board of directors.

On the other hand, a **Managing Director (MD)** is a high-ranking executive in charge of a specific business division or product. They report to the CEO and are responsible for ensuring that all business operations run fairly, effectively, and efficiently .

In summary, the primary role of the CEO is to oversee all major decisions for the company, while the primary role of an MD is to oversee all day-to-day business operations within a specific division of the company.

5.   **De facto director:**

(a)   A *de facto* director is a person who assumes to act as a director.

(b)   He is held out as a director by the company, and claims and purports to be a director, although never actually or validly appointed as such. For example, they sign contracts, make decisions, and appear to third parties as a director on behalf of the company.

A de facto director has the same responsibilities toward the company as a regular director.

To establish that a person was a *de facto* director of a company it is necessary to prove that he undertook functions in relation to the company which could properly be discharged only by a director or that the board of directors of the company is accustomed to act in accordance with his advice, instructions or directions though he did not act in his capacity as a professional advisor.

6. **Directors appointed by principle of proportional representation {Sec 163}.**

(a) Where the articles of a company provide for the appointment of **not less than two-thirds of the total number of the directors** of a company in accordance with the principle of proportional representation, whether by the single transferable vote or by a system of cumulative voting or otherwise and such appointments may be made once in every three years and casual vacancies of such directors shall be filled.

(b) This mode of appointment provides an opportunity for the minority shareholders to constitute a BOD by way of proportional representation

(c) The Board constituted can be for a tenure of three years.

(d) After span of three years, it has to be reconstituted.

(e) The directors appointed through Section 163 cannot be removed by the procedure enunciated under Section 169 of the Companies Act, 2013.

(f) Under Cumulative voting, each shareholder is entitled to one vote per share multiplied by the number of directors to be elected. In cases, where multiple candidates are being considered for multiple positions each shareholder has the option of placing all of his votes towards one seat or he can choose to split his votes across multiple candidates.

7.   **Executive Director {ED}**

(a)   {Rule 22(k) of the Companies (Specification of definitions details} Rules, 2014-

ED means "a whole- time director as defined.

(b)   EDs are responsible for running the business, recruitment, managing people, and entering into contracts.

(c)   EDs are internal professionals involved in the daily functions of the company.

(d)   Any person who is a full-time employee of the company (i.e. whole-time director) or who is responsible for the day-to-day operations of the company (i.e. managing director) may be called an Executive Director.

(e)   An Executive Director can be designated as CEO or/ Managing Director; whole-time Director.

(f)   He is usually responsible for the executive functions in the management and administration of the company.

8.   **Independent Director**

1.   Section 2(47), defines "independent director" as an independent director referred to in sub-section (5) of section 149; *{Read Chapter IV}*

9.   **Managing Director**

(a)   Section 2 (54) of the Companies Act, 2013, defines Managing Director as a director who by virtue of the articles of a company or an agreement with the company or a resolution passed in its general meeting, or by its Board of Directors, is entrusted with substantial powers of management of the affairs of the company and includes a director occupying the position of managing director, by whatever name called.

(b)   The explanation to section 2(54) excludes administrative acts of a routine nature when so authorized, by the Board such as the power to affix the common seal of the company to any document or to draw and endorse any cheque on the account of the company in any bank or to draw and endorse any negotiable instrument or to sign any certificate of share or to direct registration of transfer of any share, from the substantial powers of management.

(c)   Managing director or a whole-time director can be appointed for a maximum period of 5 (five) years.

(d)   They are eligible for re-appointment. The re-appointment can be done for the next term but not before one year of the expiry of the current term

(e)   **The minimum age** of a director {*including MD, WTD, Manager*} should be 21 years. The **maximum age** is 70 years. For appointment or continuation in office of a person above 70 years, shareholder's approval by special resolution in the General meeting or ordinary resolution with Central Government permission is required.

(f)   A manager cannot be appointed by a company along with a managing director. But, it may appoint a whole-time director along with a managing director or manager.

10. Nominee Director –

A. The Articles of the company may provide for appointment of nominee director.{Sec 161(3)}

B. The Board may appoint any person as a director nominated by any financial institution or an agency in pursuance of an agreement or the provisions of any law for the time being in force or any agreement or by the Central Government or the State Government under its shareholding in a Government company.

C. The nominee director would represent the stakeholders on the board of directors to protect the stakeholder's interest that the company does not function in a manner detrimental to the interest of the stakeholders they represent.

D. Nominee Director cannot be considered as an independent director.

E. The appointee shall have an active Director Identification Number.

F. On appointment of nominee director, total number of Directors in the Company cannot exceed the maximum limit.

G. The appointment may be made by a resolution in board meeting or by resolution passed by circulation.

11. **Non-Executive Directors {NED}**

    (a)   **NEDs** are generally external professionals.

    (b)   The Companies Act, 2013 has not defined NED.

    (c)   NEDs are not involved in the day-to-day functions or activities of the Company.

    (d)   NEDs are appointed by board of directors to offer expertise from an 'outsider's' perspective.

    (e)   Independent Directors fall in this category.

Regulation 17(1A) of SEBI LODR, 2015 requires that the Company should not appoint or continue the appointment of any person as a NED **who has attained the age of 75 years unless Special Resolution is passed** to that effect in which case the explanatory statement annexed to the notice for such motion shall indicate the justification for appointing such a person

12. **Resident Director** –

    (a)   Section 149(3) of the Act specifies that every company shall have **at least one director** who has stayed in India for a total period of not less than one hundred and eighty-two days in the previous calendar year.

    (b)   This provision applies to all companies, both private and public.

13. **Rotational Directors:** {Sec 152(6)(a)} –

    (a)   Rotational directors are those directors who fall in the two-third of the total number of directors of a **public company** who shall be persons whose period of office is liable to determination by retirement of directors by rotation.

(b)   In case the Articles provide for the retirement of all the directors at every annual general meeting, the company shall not have rotational directors.

(c)   At the first annual general meeting of a public company held next after the date of the general meeting at which the first directors are appointed and at every subsequent annual general meeting, **one-third** of such of the directors for the time being as are liable to retire by rotation, or if their number is neither three nor a multiple of three, then, the number nearest to one-third, shall retire from office.

(d)   The directors to retire by rotation at every annual general meeting shall be those who have been longest in office since their last appointment, but as between persons who became directors on the same day, those who are to retire shall, in default of and subject to any agreement among themselves, be determined by lot.

(e)   At the annual general meeting at which a director retires as aforesaid, the company may fill up the vacancy by appointing the retiring director or some other person thereto.

Nominee director, Independent Director, Directors appointed by proportional representation, Small shareholder director, are not reckoned in total number of directors for determining the two-thirds of directors liable to retire by rotation.

14. **Shadow Director –**

(a) Shadow director is one, though not appointed to the Board, but on whose directions the Board is accustomed to act.

(b) Sec 2(59} of the Act while defining **"Officer"** includes within its fold **any person in** accordance with whose directions or instructions the Board of Directors or any one or more of the directors is or are accustomed to act-not being a professional advisor.

15. **Small Shareholder Director –**

(a) Section 151 read with Rule 7 of Companies (Appointment and Qualification of Directors) Rules, 2014 provide that a listed company, **may,** upon receipt of notice, of not less than one thousand small shareholders or one-tenth of the total number of such shareholders, whichever is lower, have a small shareholders' director elected by the small shareholders.

(b) The company may *suo moto* appoint a director representing small shareholders

(c) Under Rule 7 (Appointment and qualification of directors) Sub rule (1), a listed company , may upon a notice of at least 1000 small shareholders or 1/10th of total number of 'such' shareholder (.i.e.1/10th of total no. of small shareholders) whichever is lower, have a director elected by the small shareholders

(d)   The small shareholders intending to propose a person as a candidate for the post of small shareholder shall leave a notice of their intention with the company at least 14 days before the meeting under their signatures specifying the name, address, shares held, folio no. of the person whose name is being proposed for the post of director and of the small shareholders who are proposing such person for the office of director.

(e)   Sub rule (4) states that if the director elected by small directors fulfills the criteria of independent director laid down under section 149(6) and gives the declaration of his independence in accordance with section 149(7) then such director shall be considered as independent director.

(f)   All the provision of section 152 shall apply for the appointment of small shareholders' director except that - such director shall not be liable to retire by rotation;

(g)   Sub rule (6) – A person shall not be appointed as small shareholders' director if person is not eligible for appointment in terms of section 164.

(h)   Tenure of such director shall not exceed three consecutive years and On the expiry of the tenure, such director shall not be eligible for re-appointment, directly or indirectly for a period of 3 years.

(i)   Explanation of section 151(1) defines 'small shareholder' as a shareholder holding shares of nominal value of **not more than twenty thousand.**

The person elected by small shareholder as 'director' may or may not be a shareholder of a company but a person electing such 'director' shall be the 'small shareholders'

(j)   Sub rule (8) – No person shall hold office of small shareholders' director in more than two companies at same time.

16.   **Woman Director –**

Second proviso to Sec 149(1) of the Act stipulates that it is mandatory for certain companies to appoint at least one woman director.

Rule 3 of the Companies (Appointment & Qualification of Directors) Rules, 2014 requires the following companies to appoint women director –

1. Every listed company.

A.   Every public company having paid-up share capital of Rs. 100 crores or more.

B.   Every public company which has a minimum turnover of Rs. 300 crores or more.

The duties of a woman director are similar to the general duties and responsibilities of the other directors that have been provided under Section 166 of the Companies Act.

In the event of an intermittent vacancy of a woman director, the board must fill it as soon as possible, but not later than the next board meeting or three months from the date of the vacancy, whichever is earlier.

There is no specific provision that provides punishment for the non-appointment of a woman director.

Therefore, the general penal provisions under Sectio 172 of the Act will be applicable. The section states: "that both the company and every officer of the company who is in default shall be punishable with fine of no less Rs 50,000 (fifty thousand) which may extend to Rs 5,00,000 (five lakhs) in case of any contravention of the provisions regarding appointment of directors.

According to research from Prime Database, the ratio was one woman director for every eight board members in 2018, while a decade ago, it stood at one woman director for every 20 members. Out of 4,783 directors, there are 885 women that cumulatively sit on the boards of Nifty-500 companies.

A decade after the implementation of the Companies Act 2013, which mandated at least one woman director on company boards, Nifty-500 companies have an average of one in five board members being women – 223 Nifty-500 companies have only one woman director.

Per **reporting** in the *Economic Times*, globally, one in three S&P 500 company board directors are women, driven not by legal mandates but by investor pressure and company initiatives for increased gender diversity. The UK-backed Hampton-Alexander Review has proposed a target of 40% women representation on FTSE-350 company boards by the end of 2025.

Under SEBI LODR regulations, for the top 500 listed entities, it has been obligatory to have at least one **independent** woman director starting April 1, 2019, and for the top 1000 listed entities, this requirement extends to at least **one independent woman director** since April 1, 2020.

Chapter III

Composition, Appointment, Reappointment, Retirement, Vacation, Disqualifications for appointment, Number of Directorship, Resignation, Removal of Directors

A. COMPOSITION

(a)   **Under the Companies Act, 2013 {Sec 149} & Companies (Appointment and Qualification of Directors) Rules, 2014**

(1)   Every company shall have a Board of Directors consisting of individuals as directors and shall have—

    (a)   a **minimum number** of three directors in the case of a **public company**, two directors in the case of a **private company,** and one director in the case of a **One Person Company**; and

    (b)   a **maximum** of fifteen directors:

A company may appoint **more than fifteen** directors after passing a **special resolution:**

Every listed company ; every other public company having paid-up capital of one hundred crores or more or turnover of three hundred crore or more **shall have at least one woman director.**

(3)   Every company shall have **at least one director who has stayed in India for a total period of not less than one hundred and eighty-two days** in the previous calendar year.

(4)   **Every listed public company shall have at least one-third of the total number of directors as independent directors** and the Central Government may prescribe the minimum number of independent directors in case of any class or classes of public companies.

B. Composition of Directors [SEBI LODR, 2015]

Reg 17. Board of Directors.

(1)   The composition of board of directors of the listed entity shall be as follows:

(a)   board of directors shall have an optimum combination of executive and non-executive directors with **at least one woman director and not less than fifty per cent. of the board of directors shall comprise of non-executive directors;**

Provided that the Board of directors of the top 500 listed entities shall have at least one independent woman director by April 1, 2019 and the Board of directors of the top 1000 listed entities **shall have at least one independent woman director by April 1, 2020;**

(b)   where the **chairperson of the board of directors is a non- executive director, at least one-third of the board of directors shall comprise of independent directors** and where the listed entity **does not have a regular non-executive chairperson, at least half of the board of directors shall comprise of independent directors:**

Provided that where the regular **non-executive chairperson is a promoter** of the listed entity or is **related to any promoter or person occupying management positions at the level of board** of director or at one level below the board of directors, **at least half of the board of directors of the listed entity shall consist of independent directors.**

Explanation

For the purpose of this clause, the expression "related to any promoter" shall have the following meaning:

(i)   if the promoter is a listed entity, its directors other than the independent directors, its employees or its nominees shall be deemed to be related to it;

(ii)   if the promoter is an **unlisted** entity, its directors, its employees or its nominees shall be deemed to be related to it.

(c)   The board of directors of the top 1000 listed entities with effect from April 1, 2019 and the top 2000 listed entities with effect from April 1, 2020 **shall comprise of not less than six directors.**

(d) where the listed company has **outstanding SR equity shares, at least half of the board of directors shall comprise of independent directors.**

(1A) No listed entity shall **appoint a person or continue** the directorship of any person as a **non-executive director who has attained the age of seventy five years unless a special resolution** is passed to that effect,

in which case the explanatory statement annexed to the notice for such motion shall indicate the justification for appointing such a person.

(1C). The listed entity shall ensure that approval of shareholders for appointment or re-appointment of a person on the Board of Directors or as a manager is taken at the next general meeting or within a time period of three months from the date of appointment, whichever is earlier:

A **public sector company** shall ensure that the approval of the shareholders for appointment or re-appointment of a person on the Board of Directors or as a Manager is taken at the next general meeting:

The appointment or a re-appointment of a person, including as a managing director or a whole-time director or a manager, who was **earlier rejected** by the shareholders at a general meeting, shall be done only with the **prior approval of the shareholders:**

The statement **annexed to the notice** to the shareholders, for considering the appointment or re-appointment of such a person earlier rejected by the shareholders shall **contain a detailed explanation and justification** by the Nomination and Remuneration Committee and the Board of directors for recommending such a person for appointment or re-appointment.

(1D) With effect from April 1, 2024, the continuation of a director serving on the board of directors of a listed entity shall be **subject to the approval by the shareholders in a general meeting at least once in every five years from the date of their appointment or reappointment,** as the case may be:

Continuation of the director serving on the board of directors of a listed entity as on March 31, 2024, **without the approval of the shareholders for the last five years** or more shall be subject to the **approval of shareholders** in the first general meeting to be held after March 31, 2024:

Exception being the Whole-Time Director, Managing Director, Manager, Independent Director or a Director retiring as per the sub-section (6) of section 152 of the Companies Act, 2013, if the approval of the shareholders for the reappointment or continuation of the aforesaid directors or Manager is otherwise provided for by the provisions of these regulations or the Companies Act, 2013 and has been complied with:

The requirement specified in this regulation shall not be applicable to the director appointed pursuant to the order of a Court or a Tribunal or to a nominee director of the Government on the board of a listed entity, other than a public sector company, or to a nominee director of a financial sector regulator on the board of a listed entity:

The requirement specified in this regulation shall not be applicable to a director nominated by a financial institution registered with or regulated by the Reserve Bank of India under a lending arrangement in its normal course of business or nominated by a Debenture Trustee registered with the Board under a subscription agreement for the debentures issued by the listed entity.

(IE) Any vacancy in the office of a director shall be filled by the listed entity at the earliest and in any case **not later than three months from the date such vacancy**:

If the listed entity becomes non-compliant with the requirement of this regulation, due to expiration of the term of office of any director, the resulting vacancy shall be filled by the listed entity not later than the date such office is vacated:

This sub-regulation shall not apply if the listed entity fulfils the requirement of this regulation without filling the vacancy.

B. Appointment/ Reappointment of Directors Sec 152

(2) Every director **shall be appointed by the company in general meeting.**

(3) **No person shall be appointed** as a director of a company **unless** he has been allotted the **Director Identification Number.**

Every individual intending to be appointed as director of a company shall make an application in **Form DIR-3** for allotment of Director Identification Number to the Central Government. **{Sec 153}**

Under Rule 9: Form DIR-3 shall be signed and submitted electronically by the applicant using his or her own Digital Signature Certificate and shall be verified digitally in **Form DIR-4** by –

(i)   a chartered accountant in practice or a company secretary in practice or a cost accountant in practice; or

(ii)   a company secretary in full time employment of the company or by the managing director or director of the company in which the applicant is to be appointed as director.

The Central Government shall, within one month from the receipt of the application, **allot a Director Identification Number**. *{Sec 154}*

Rule 10:

Provisional DIN shall be generated by the system automatically which shall not be utilized till the DIN is confirmed by the Central Government.

[Final DIN shall be allotted after verification of the information submitted and after satisfaction of the queries].

Rule 11: Cancellation or surrender or Deactivation of DIN.

The Central Government or Regional Director (Northern Region), Noida or any officer authorised by the Regional Director may, upon being satisfied on verification of particulars or documentary proof attached with the application received from any person, cancel or deactivate the DIN in case –

(a)   the DIN is found to be duplicated in respect of the same person provided the data related to both the DIN shall be merged with the validly retained number;

(b)   the DIN was obtained in a wrongful manner or by fraudulent means;

(c)   of the death of the concerned individual;

(d)   the concerned individual has been declared as a person of unsound mind by a competent Court;

(e)   if the concerned individual has been adjudicated an insolvent:

(f)   on an application made in Form DIR-5 by the DIN holder to surrender his or her DIN along with declaration that he has never been appointed as director in any company and the said DIN has never been used for filing of any document with any authority, the Central Government may deactivate such DIN: Provided that before deactivation of any DIN in such case, the Central Government shall verify e-records

No individual, who has already been allotted a Director Identification Number under section 154, shall apply for, obtain or possess another Director Identification Number. *{Sec 155}*

Every individual who has been allotted a Director Identification Number under these rules shall, **in the event of any change in his particulars** as stated in Form DIR-3, **intimate such change(s) to the Central Government** within a period of thirty days of such change(s) in Form DIR-6 *{Rule 12}*

Every existing director shall, **within one month of the receipt of Director Identification Number** from the Central Government, **intimate** his Director Identification Number **to the company or all companies wherein he is a director.** *{Sec 156}*

(1)   Every company shall, within fifteen days of the receipt of intimation under section 156, furnish the Director Identification Number of all its directors to the Registrar or any other officer or authority as may be specified by the

Central Government with such fees as may be prescribed or with such additional fees as may be prescribed within the time specified under section 403 and every such intimation shall be furnished in such form and manner as may be prescribed.

(2) If any company fails to furnish the Director Identification Number, such company shall be liable to a penalty of twenty-five thousand rupees and in case of continuing failure, with a further penalty of one hundred rupees for each day after the first during which such failure continues, subject to a maximum of one lakh rupees, **and every officer who is in default** shall be liable to a penalty of not less than twenty-five thousand rupees and in case of continuing failure, with a further penalty of one hundred rupees for each day after the first during which such failure continues, subject to a maximum of one lakh rupees.".{*Sec 157*}

Every person or company, while furnishing any return, information or particulars as are required to be furnished under this Act, shall mention the Director Identification Number in such return, information or particulars in case such return, information or particulars relate to the director or contain any reference of any director. {*Sec 158*}

Sec 152 (4) Every **person proposed to be appointed** as a director by the company in general meeting or otherwise, **shall furnish his Director Identification Number** and a **declaration that he is not disqualified** to become a director under this Act.

Sec 152 (5) A person appointed as a director shall not act as a director **unless he gives his consent to hold the office as**

director and such consent has been **filed with the Registrar** within thirty days of his appointment.

***Rule 8. Consent to act as director.**- Every person who has been appointed to hold the office of a director shall on or before the appointment furnish to the company a consent in writing to act as such in Form DIR-2:*

Provided that in the case of **appointment of an independent director** in the general meeting, **an explanatory statement** for such appointment, annexed to the notice for the general meeting, shall include a **statement that in the opinion of the Board, he fulfils the conditions specified in this Act for such an appointment.**

Sec 152 (6) (a) Unless the articles provide for the retirement of all directors at every annual general meeting, **not less than two-thirds of the total number of directors of a public company** shall—

(i)   be persons whose period of office is liable to **determination by retirement of directors by rotation;** and

(ii)   save as otherwise expressly provided in this Act, **be appointed by the company in general meeting.**

(b)   The remaining directors in the case of any such company shall, in default of, and subject to any regulations in the articles of the company, also be appointed by the company in general meeting.

(c)   At the **first annual general meeting** of a public company held next after the date of the general meeting at which the first directors are appointed in accordance with clauses (a) and (b) and at every subsequent annual general meeting, **one-third of such of the directors** for the time being as are liable to retire by rotation, or if their number is neither three nor a multiple of three, then, the number nearest to one-third, shall retire from office.

(d)   The directors to retire by rotation at every annual general meeting shall be those who have been longest in office since their last appointment, but as between persons who became directors on the same day, those who are to retire shall, in default of and subject to any agreement among themselves, be determined by lot.

(e)   At the annual general meeting at which a director retires as aforesaid, the company may fill up the vacancy **by appointing the retiring director or some other person thereto.**

Explanation — For the purposes of this sub-section, "total number of directors" shall not include independent directors, whether appointed under this Act or any other law for the time being in force, on the Board of a company.

(7) (a) If the vacancy of the retiring **director** is not so filled-up and the meeting has not expressly resolved not to fill the vacancy, the meeting shall stand adjourned till the same day in the next week, at the same time and place, or if that day is a national holiday, till the next succeeding day which is not a holiday, at the same time and place.

(b)   If at the adjourned meeting also, the vacancy of the retiring director is not filled up and that meeting also has not expressly resolved not to fill the vacancy, the retiring director shall be deemed to have been re-appointed at the adjourned meeting, unless—

(i)   at that meeting or at the previous meeting a resolution for the re-appointment of such director has been put to the meeting and lost;

(ii)   the retiring director has, by a notice in writing addressed to the company or its Board of directors, expressed his unwillingness to be so re-appointed;

(iii)   he is not qualified or is disqualified for appointment;

(iv)   a resolution, whether special or ordinary, is required for his appointment or re-appointment by virtue of any provisions of this Act; or

(v)   section 163 is applicable to the case.

Reg 24 SEBI LODR, 2015

(1) At least one independent director on the board of directors of the listed entity shall be a director on the board of directors of an unlisted material subsidiary, whether incorporated in India or not.

Explanation — For the purposes of this provision, notwithstanding anything to the contrary contained in regulation 16, the term "material subsidiary" shall mean a subsidiary, whose income or net worth exceeds twenty percent of the consolidated income or net worth respectively, of the listed entity and its subsidiaries in the immediately preceding accounting year.

Sec 159. If any **individual or director of a company makes any default** in complying with any of the provisions of **section**

152, section 155 and section 156, such individual or director of the company **shall be liable to a penalty** which may extend to fifty thousand rupees and where the default is a continuing one, with a further penalty which may extend to five hundred rupees for each day after the first during which such default continues.".

Sec 160. Right of persons other than retiring directors to stand for directorship —

(1)   A person who is not a retiring director in terms of section 152 shall, subject to the provisions of this Act, be eligible for appointment to the office of a director at any general meeting, if he, or some member intending to propose him as a director, has, **not less than fourteen days before the meeting, left at the registered office of the company, a notice** in writing under his hand signifying his candidature as a director or, as the case may be, the intention of such member to propose him as a candidate for that office, along with the deposit of one lakh rupees or such higher amount as may be prescribed which shall be refunded to such person or, as the case may be, to the member, if the person proposed gets elected as a director or gets more than twenty-five per cent. of total valid votes cast either on show of hands or on poll on such resolution.

(2)   The company shall at least seven days before the general meeting inform its members of the candidature of a person for the office of director.

Sec 162. Appointment of directors to be voted individually —

unless a proposal to move such a motion has first been agreed to at the meeting without any vote being cast against it.

Sec 163. Option to adopt principle of proportional representation for appointment of not less than two-thirds of the total number of the directors of a company- whether by the single transferable vote or by a system of cumulative voting or otherwise and such appointments may be made once in every three years and casual vacancies of such directors shall be filled.

C. Disqualifications for appointment to the office of Director

Sec 164:

(1)   A person shall not be eligible for appointment as a director of a company, if —

    (a)   he is of unsound mind and stands so declared by a competent court;

    (b)   he is an undischarged insolvent;

    (c)   he has applied to be adjudicated as an insolvent and his application is pending;

    (d)   he has been convicted by a court of any offence, whether involving moral turpitude or otherwise, and sentenced in respect thereof to imprisonment for not less than six months and a period of five years has not elapsed from the date of expiry of the sentence:

Provided that if a person has been convicted of any offence and sentenced in respect thereof to imprisonment for a period of seven years or more, he shall not be eligible to be appointed as a director in any company;

(e)   an order disqualifying him for appointment as a director has been passed by a court or Tribunal and the order is in force;

(f)   he has not paid any calls in respect of any shares of the company held by him, whether alone or jointly with others, and six months have elapsed from the last day fixed for the payment of the call;

(g)   he has been convicted of the offence dealing with related party transactions under section 188 at any time during the last preceding five years; or

(h)   he has not been allotted DIN under Section 154. *{Sec 152(3)}*

(i)   He is a director in more than twenty companies or more than ten public companies in compliance with Sec 165(1).

(2) No person who is or has been a director of a company which—

(a)   has not filed financial statements or annual returns for any continuous period of three financial years; or

(b)   has failed to repay the deposits accepted by it or pay interest thereon or to redeem any debentures on the due date or pay interest due thereon or pay any dividend declared and such failure to pay or redeem continues for one year or more, shall be eligible to be re-appointed as a director of that company or appointed in other company for a period of five years from the date on which the said company fails to do so.

Rule 14: Disqualification of directors sub-section (2) of section 164

(1)   Every director shall inform to the company concerned about his disqualification in **Form DIR-8** before he is appointed or re-appointed.

(2)   Whenever a company fails to file the financial statements or annual returns, or fails to repay any deposit, interest, dividend, or fails to redeem its debentures, the company shall immediately file **Form DIR-9,** to the Registrar furnishing therein the names and addresses of all the directors of the company during the relevant financial years.

(3)   When a company fails to file the Form DIR-9 within thirty days of the failure that would attract the disqualification under sub-section (2) of section 164, officers of the company specified in clause (60) of section 2 of the Act **shall be the officers in default.**

D. Number of Directorships

Sec 165.

(1)   **No person, shall hold office as a director, including any alternate directorship, in more than twenty companies at the same time:**

Within the overall twenty, the **maximum number of public companies in which a person can be appointed as a director shall not exceed ten.**

Explanation — For reckoning the limit of public companies directorship in private companies that are either holding or subsidiary company of a public company shall be included.

(2)   The members of a company may, **by special resolution, specify any lesser number** of companies in which a director of the company may act as directors.

"(6) If a person accepts an appointment as a director in violation of this section, he shall be liable to a penalty of two thousand rupees for each day after the first during which such violation continues, subject to a maximum of two lakh rupees.".

Maximum number of directorships

Reg 17A. The directors of listed entities shall comply with the following conditions with respect to the maximum number of directorships, including any alternate directorships that can be held by them at any point of time -

(1)   A person shall not be a director in more than eight listed entities with effect from April 1, 2020:

Provided that a person shall not serve as an independent director in more than seven listed entities.

(2)   Notwithstanding the above, any person who is serving as a whole time director/managing director in any listed entity shall serve as an independent director in not more than three listed entities.

Explanation — For the purpose of this regulation, the count for the number of listed entities on which a person is a director /

independent director shall be only those whose equity shares are listed on a stock exchange.

E. Vacation of Office

{Sec 167}

(1)   The office of a director shall become vacant in case—

(a)   he incurs any of the disqualifications specified in section 164;

(b)   he absents himself from all the meetings of the Board of Directors held during a period of twelve months with or without seeking leave of absence of the Board;

(c)   he acts in contravention of the provisions of section 184 relating to entering into contracts or arrangements in which he is directly or indirectly interested;

(d)   he fails to disclose his interest in any contract or arrangement in which he is directly or indirectly interested, in contravention of the provisions of section 184;

(e)   he becomes disqualified by an order of a court or the Tribunal;

(f)   he is convicted by a court of any offence, whether involving moral turpitude or otherwise and sentenced in respect thereof to imprisonment for not less than six months:

Provided that the office shall be vacated by the director even if he has filed an appeal against the order of such court;

    (g)   he is removed in pursuance of the provisions of this Act;

    (h)   he, having been appointed a director by virtue of his holding any office or other employment in the holding, subsidiary or associate company, ceases to hold such office or other employment in that company.

(2)   If a person, functions as a director even when he knows that the office of director held by him has become vacant on account of any of the disqualifications, **he shall punishable with** fine of five lakh rupees.

(3)   Where all the directors of a company vacate their offices under any of the disqualifications, the promoter or, in his absence, the Central Government shall appoint the required number of directors who shall hold office till the directors are appointed by the company in the general meeting.

(4)   A private company may, by its articles, provide any other ground for the vacation of the office of a director in addition to those specified.

F. Resignation from Office of Director

Sec 168.

(1)   A director may resign from his office **by giving a notice in writing to the company** and the Board shall on receipt of such notice take note of the same and the **company shall intimate the Registrar** in Form DIR-12 and shall also place the fact of such resignation in the report of directors laid in the immediately following general meeting by the company: The company will also post the information on its website.

Provided that a **director shall also forward a copy of his resignation in Form DIR-11 along with detailed reasons** for the resignation to the Registrar **within thirty days** of resignation. *{Rule 16}*

(2)	The resignation of a director shall take effect from the date on which the notice is received by the company or the date, if any, specified by the director in the notice, whichever is later:

G. Removal of Directors

Sec 169

(1)	A company may, by ordinary resolution, remove a director, not being a director appointed by the Tribunal, before the expiry of the period of his office after giving him a reasonable opportunity of being heard:

Provided that nothing contained in this sub-section shall apply where the company has availed itself of the option given to it under section 163 to appoint not less than two-thirds of the total number of directors according to the principle of proportional representation.

(2)	A special notice shall be required of any resolution, to remove a director under this section, or to appoint somebody in place of a director so removed, at the meeting at which he is removed.

(3)	On receipt of notice of a resolution to remove a director, the company shall forthwith send a copy thereof to the director concerned, and the director, whether or not he is a member of the company, shall be entitled to be heard on the resolution at the meeting.

(5)   A vacancy created by the removal of a director under this section may, if he had been appointed by the company in general meeting or by the Board, be filled by the appointment of another director in his place at the meeting at which he is removed, provided special notice of the intended appointment has been given.

(6)   A director so appointed shall hold office till the date up to which his predecessor would have held office if he had not been removed.

(7)   If the vacancy is not filled, it may be filled as a casual vacancy in accordance with the provisions of this Act:

Provided that the director who was removed from office shall not be re-appointed as a director by the Board of Directors.

Punishment for contravention

If a company is in default in complying with any of the provisions of this Chapter and **for which no specific penalty or punishment is provided** therein, the company and **every officer of the company who is in default** shall be liable to a penalty of fifty thousand rupees, and in case of continuing failure, with a further penalty of five hundred rupees for each day during which such failure continues, subject to a maximum of three lakh rupees in case of a company **and one lakh rupees in case of an officer who is in default. {Sec 172}**

Chapter IV

Independent Directors, Non-Executive Directors & their Liabilities

A. Who is an Independent Director?

1. **Sec. 149(6) of the Companies Act, 2013:**

    An independent director in relation to a company, **means a director other than a managing director or a whole-time director or a nominee director,—**

(a)   who, in the opinion of the Board, is a **person of integrity and possesses relevant expertise and experience;**

(b)   (i)   who is or was **not a promoter** of the company or its holding, subsidiary or associate company;

       (ii)   who is **not related to promoters or directors** in the company, its holding, subsidiary or associate company;

(c)   who **has or had no pecuniary relationship** with the company, its holding, subsidiary or associate company, or their promoters, or directors, during the two immediately preceding financial years or during the current financial year;

(d) **none of whose relatives has or had pecuniary relationship** or transaction with the company, its holding, subsidiary or associate company, or their promoters, or directors, **amounting to two per cent. or more of its gross turnover or total income or fifty lakh rupees** or such higher amount as may be prescribed, whichever is lower, during the two immediately preceding financial years or during the current financial year;

(e) who, **neither himself nor any of his relatives—**

    (i) **holds or has held the position of a key managerial personnel or** is or has been employee of the **company or its holding, subsidiary or associate company** in any of the **three financial years** immediately preceding the financial year in which he is proposed to be appointed;

    (ii) is or has been an **employee or proprietor or a partner,** in any of the three financial years immediately preceding the financial year in which he is proposed to be appointed, of—

(A) a **firm of auditors** or company secretaries in practice or cost auditors of the company or its holding, subsidiary or associate company; or

(B) any **legal or a consulting firm** that has or had any transaction with the company, its holding, subsidiary or associate company amounting to ten per cent. or more of the gross turnover of such firm;

(iii)   **holds** together **with his relatives two per cent. or more of the total voting power of** the company; or

(iv)   is a **Chief Executive or director**, by whatever name called, of **any nonprofit organisation that receives twenty-five per cent. or more of its receipts from the company, any of its promoters, directors** or its holding, subsidiary or associate company or that holds two per cent. or more of the total voting power of the company; or

(f)   **An independent director shall possess** appropriate skills, experience and knowledge in one or more fields of **finance, law, management, sales, marketing, administration, research, corporate governance, technical operations or other disciplines** related to the company's business. {*Rule 5*}

2.   **Reg. 16 (1)(b) of SEBI (LODR), 2015**

"**independent director**" **means a non-executive director, other than a nominee director** of the listed entity-

(i)   who, **in the opinion of the board of directors, is a person of integrity and possesses relevant expertise and experience;**

(ii)   who is or was **not a promoter of the listed entity or its holding, subsidiary or associate company or member of the promoter** group of the listed entity;

(iii)   who is **not related to promoters or directors in the listed entity, its holding, subsidiary or associate company;**

(iv)   who, apart from receiving director's remuneration, has or had no material pecuniary relationship with the listed entity, its holding, subsidiary or associate company, or their promoters, or directors, during the three immediately preceding financial years or during the current financial year;

(v)   **none of whose relatives –**

(A) is holding securities of or interest in the listed entity, its holding, subsidiary or associate company during the three immediately preceding financial years or during the current financial year of **face value in excess of fifty lakh rupees or two percent of the paid-up capital of** the listed entity, its holding, subsidiary or associate company, respectively, or such higher sum as may be specified;

(B) is indebted to the listed entity, its holding, subsidiary or associate company or their promoters or directors, in excess of such amount as may be specified during the three immediately preceding financial years or during the current financial year;

(C) has given a guarantee or provided any security in connection with the indebtedness of any third person to the listed entity, its holding, subsidiary or associate company or their promoters or directors, for such amount as may be specified during the three immediately preceding financial years or during the current financial year; or

(D) has any other pecuniary transaction or relationship with the listed entity, its holding, subsidiary or associate company amounting to two percent or more of its gross turnover or total income:

Provided that the pecuniary relationship or transaction with the listed entity, its holding, subsidiary or associate company or their promoters, or directors in relation to points (A) to (D) above **shall not exceed two percent of its gross turnover or total income or fifty lakh rupees or** such higher amount as may be specified from time to time, whichever is lower.

(vi)   who, neither himself/herself, nor whose relative(s) –

(A) holds or has **held the position of a key managerial personnel or is or has been an employee** of the listed entity or its holding, subsidiary or associate company or any company belonging to the promoter group of the listed entity, in any of the **three financial years** immediately preceding the financial year in which he is proposed to be appointed:

Provided that in case of a relative, who is an employee other than key-managerial personnel, the restriction under this clause shall not apply for his / her employment.

(B) is or has **been an employee or proprietor or a partner,** in any of the **three financial years** immediately preceding the financial year in which he is proposed to be appointed, of —

(1)   a firm of **auditors** or company secretaries in practice or cost auditors of the listed entity or its holding, subsidiary or associate company; or

(2)   any **legal or a consulting firm** that has or had any transaction with the listed entity, its holding, subsidiary or associate company amounting to **ten per cent or more of the gross turnover** of such firm;

(C) **holds together with his relatives two per cent** or more of the total **voting power** of the listed entity; or

(D) is a **chief executive or director,** by whatever name called, of any **non-profit organisation** that receives **twenty-five per cent** or more of its **receipts** or corpus from the listed entity, any of its promoters, directors or its holding, subsidiary or associate company or that holds **two per cent** or more of the total **voting power** of the listed entity;

(E) is a **material supplier, service provider or customer or a lessor or lessee** of the listed entity;

(vii)   **who is not less than 21 years of age.**

(viii)   who is not a non-independent director of another company on the board of which any non-independent director of the listed entity is an independent director

B. Provisions related to Independent Directors under section 149:

(4) Every **listed public company** shall have **at least one-third of the total** number of directors **as independent directors.**

The minimum number of **independent directors** shall **be at least two independent directors** in case of

(i)   the **Public Companies** having paid up share capital of ten crore rupees or more; or

(ii)   the **Public Companies** having turnover of one hundred crore rupees or more; or

(iii)   the **Public Companies** which have, in aggregate, outstanding loans, debentures and deposits, exceeding fifty crore rupees: *{Rule 4}*

Any **intermittent vacancy** of an independent director shall be filled-up by the Board at the earliest but not later than immediate next Board meeting or three months from the date of such vacancy, whichever is later:

Where a company ceases to fulfil any of three conditions mentioned in (4) above, for three consecutive years, it shall not be required to comply with these provisions until such time as it meets any of such conditions; *{Rule 4}*

(7) Every independent director **shall at the first meeting of the Board** in which he **participates as a director** and thereafter at the **first meeting of the Board in every financial year or whenever there is any change** in the circumstances which may affect his status as an independent director, **give a declaration that he meets the criteria of independence as provided** in definition. [(sub-section (6)].

(8) **The company and independent directors shall abide by the provisions specified in Schedule IV.**

If a company **has no profits or its profits are inadequate, an independent director may receive remuneration,** exclusive of any fees payable **under sub-section (5) of section 197**, in accordance with the provisions of **Schedule V.**".

(10) An independent director **shall hold office for a term up to five consecutive years** on the Board of a company, **but shall be eligible for reappointment** on passing of a **special resolution**

by the company **and disclosure** of such appointment in the **Board's report.**

(11) **No independent director shall hold** office **for more than two consecutive terms,** *but* such independent director **shall be eligible** for appointment after the **expiration of three years of ceasing** to become an independent director:

Provided that an independent director shall not, during the said three years, be appointed in or be associated with the company in any other capacity, either directly or indirectly.

(12) **Notwithstanding anything contained in this Act,—**

(i)   **an independent director;**

(ii)   **a non-executive director not being promoter or key managerial personnel, shall be held liable, only in respect of such acts of omission or commission by a company which had occurred with his knowledge, attributable through Board processes, and with his consent or connivance or where he had not acted diligently.**

(13) The provisions in respect of **retirement of directors by rotation shall not be applicable** to appointment of independent directors.

SCHEDULE IV
[Section 149(8)]

Code for Independent Directors

The Code is a guide to professional conduct for independent directors. Adherence to these standards by independent directors and fulfilment of their responsibilities in a professional and faithful manner will promote confidence of the investment community, particularly minority shareholders, regulators and companies in the institution of independent directors.

I. Guidelines of professional conduct:

An independent director shall:

(1)   uphold ethical standards of integrity and probity;

(2)   act objectively and constructively while exercising his duties;

(3)   exercise his responsibilities in a *bona fide* manner in the interest of the company;

(4)   **devote sufficient time and attention to his professional obligations for informed and balanced decision making;**

(5)   not allow any extraneous considerations that will vitiate his exercise of objective independent judgment in the paramount interest of the company as a whole, while concurring in or dissenting from the collective judgment of the Board in its decision making;

(6)   not abuse his position to the detriment of the company or its shareholders or for the purpose of gaining direct or indirect personal advantage or advantage for any associated person;

(7)   **refrain from any action that would lead to loss of his independence;**

(8)   where circumstances arise which make an independent director lose his independence, the independent director must immediately Inform the Board accordingly;

(9) assist the company in implementing the best corporate governance practices.

II. Role and functions:

The independent directors **shall**:

(1)   help in **bringing an independent judgment to bear on the Board's deliberations** especially on issues of strategy, performance, risk management, resources, key appointments and standards of conduct;

(2)   bring an objective view in the evaluation of the performance of board and management;

(3)   scrutinize the performance of management in meeting agreed goals and objectives and monitor the reporting of performance;

(4)   satisfy themselves on the integrity of financial information and that financial controls and the systems of risk management are robust and defensible;

(5)   safeguard the interests of all stakeholders, particularly the minority shareholders;

(6)   balance the conflicting interest of the stakeholders;

(7)   determine appropriate levels of remuneration of executive directors, key managerial personnel and senior management and have a prime role in appointing and where necessary recommend removal of executive directors, key managerial personnel and senior management;

(8)   **moderate and arbitrate in the interest of the company as a whole, in situations of conflict between management and shareholder's interest.**

III. Duties:

The independent directors **shall—**

(1)   undertake appropriate induction and regularly update and refresh their skills, knowledge and familiarity with the company;

(2)   seek appropriate clarification or amplification of information and, where necessary, take and follow appropriate professional advice and **opinion of outside experts at the expense of the company;**

(3)   strive to attend all meetings of the Board of Directors and of the Board committees of which he is a member;

(4)   participate constructively and actively in the committees of the Board in which they are chairpersons or members;

(5)   strive to attend the general meetings of the company;

(6)   **where they have concerns about the running of the company or a proposed action, ensure that these are addressed by the Board and, to the extent that they are not resolved, insist that their concerns are recorded in the minutes of the Board meeting;**

(7)   keep themselves well informed about the company and the external environment in which it operates;

(8)   not to unfairly obstruct the functioning of an otherwise proper Board or committee of the Board;

(9)   **pay sufficient attention and ensure that adequate deliberations are held before approving related party transactions and assure themselves that the same are in the interest of the company;**

(10)   **ascertain and ensure that the company has an adequate and functional vigil mechanism and to ensure that the interests of a person who uses such mechanism are not prejudicially affected on account of such use;**

(11)   report concerns about unethical behavior, actual or suspected fraud or violation of the company's code of conduct or ethics policy;

(12)   act within their authority, assist in protecting the legitimate interests of the company, shareholders and its employees;

(13)   not disclose confidential information, including commercial secrets, technologies, advertising and sales promotion plans, unpublished price sensitive information, unless such disclosure is expressly approved by the Board or required by law.

IV. Manner of Appointment

(1)   Appointment process of independent directors shall be **independent of the company management;** while selecting independent directors the Board shall ensure that there is appropriate balance of skills, experience and

knowledge in the Board so as to enable the Board to discharge its functions and duties effectively.

(2)   The appointment of independent director(s) of the company shall be approved at the meeting of the shareholders.

(3)   The explanatory statement attached to the notice of the meeting for approving the appointment of independent director **shall include a statement that in the opinion of the Board, the independent director proposed to be appointed fulfils the conditions specified in the Act and the rules made thereunder and that the proposed director is independent of the management.**

(4)   The appointment of independent directors shall be formalized through a letter of appointment, which shall set out :

    (a)   the term of appointment;

    (b)   the expectation of the Board from the appointed director; the Board-level committee(s) in which the director is expected to serve and its tasks;

    (c)   the fiduciary duties that come with such an appointment along with accompanying liabilities;

    (d)   provision for Directors and Officers (D & O) insurance, if any;

    (e)   **the Code of Business Ethics that the company expects its directors and employees to follow;**

    (f)   the list of actions that a director should not do while functioning as such in the company; and

(g)   the remuneration, mentioning periodic fees, reimbursement of expenses for participation in the Boards and other meetings and profit related commission, if any.

(5)   The terms and conditions of appointment of independent directors shall be open for inspection at the registered office of the company by any member during normal business hours.

(6)   The terms and conditions of appointment of independent directors shall also be posted on the company's website.

V. Re-appointment:

The re-appointment of independent director shall be on the basis of report of performance evaluation.

VI. Resignation or removal:

(1)   The resignation or removal of an independent director shall be in the same manner as is provided in sections 168 and 169 of the Act.

(2)   An independent director who resigns or is removed from the Board of the company shall be replaced by a new independent director within three months from the date of such resignation or removal, as the case may be.

(3)   Where the company fulfils the requirement of independent directors in its Board even without filling the vacancy created by such resignation or removal, as the case may be, the

requirement of replacement by a new independent director shall not apply.

VII. Separate meetings:

(1) The independent directors of the company shall hold at least one meeting in a financial year, **without the attendance of non-independent directors and members of management;**

(2) All the independent directors of the company shall strive to be present at such meeting;

(3) The meeting shall:

    (a) review the performance of non-independent directors and the Board as a whole;

    (b) review the performance of the Chairperson of the company, taking into account the views of executive directors and non-executive directors;

    (c) assess the quality, quantity and timeliness of flow of information between the company management and the Board that is necessary for the Board to effectively and reasonably perform their duties.

VIII. Evaluation mechanism:

(1) The performance evaluation of independent directors shall be done by the entire Board of Directors, excluding the director being evaluated.

(2)   On the basis of the report of performance evaluation, it shall be determined whether to extend or continue the term of appointment of the independent director.

Note:

The Provisions of sub-paragraph (2) and (7) of paragraph II, paragraph IV, paragraph V, clauses (a) and (b) of sub-paragraph (3) of paragraph VI and paragraph VIII shall not apply in the case of a Government company as defined under clause (45) of section 2 of the Companies Act, 2013 (18 of 2013), if the requirements in respect of matters specified in these paragraph are specified by the concerned Ministries or Departments of the Central Government or as the case may be, the State Governments and **such requirements are complied with by the Government companies.**

Sec 150. Manner of selection of independent directors and maintenance of databank of independent directors —

(1)   An independent director may be selected from a data bank containing names, addresses and qualifications of persons who are eligible and willing to act as independent directors, maintained by any body, institute or association, as may be notified by the Central Government, having expertise in creation and maintenance of such data bank and put on their website for the use by the company making the appointment of such directors:

Provided that responsibility of exercising due diligence before selecting a person from the data bank referred to above, as an independent director shall lie with the company making such appointment.

Under Rule 6(2) the data bank shall contain the required details in respect of each person included in the data bank to be eligible and willing to be appointed as independent director-

Under Rules 6 (3) A disclaimer shall be conspicuously displayed on the website hosting the databank that a company must carry out its own due diligence before appointment of any person as an independent director and "the agency" maintaining the databank or the Central Government shall not be held responsible for the accuracy of information or lack of suitability of the person whose particulars form part of the databank.

Under Rule 6 (4) Any person who desires to get his name included in the data bank of independent directors shall make an application to "the agency" in Form DIR-1.

Under Rule 6 (6) Any person who has applied for inclusion of his name in the data bank of independent directors or any person whose name appears in the data bank , shall intimate to the agency about any changes in his particulars within fifteen days of such change.

(2)   The appointment of independent director shall be approved by the company in general meeting and the explanatory statement annexed to the notice of the general meeting called to consider the said appointment **shall indicate the justification for choosing** the appointee for appointment as independent director.

Every individual who is already an Independent director and who intends to be appointed as independent director shall compulsorily pass Online Proficiency Self- Assessment Test conducted by the Indian Institute of Corporate Affairs **(IICA)** within one year from the date of registration.

Director's report shall include a statement regarding the opinion of the Board with regard to integrity, expertise and experience (including the proficiency ascertained in online test) of the independent directors appointed during the year.

C. Reg. 25 of SEBI, LODR, 2015 Obligations with respect to independent directors.

(1) **No person** shall be appointed or continue as an **alternate director for an independent director** of a listed entity with effect from October 1, 2018.

(2) The maximum tenure of independent directors shall be in accordance with the Companies Act, 2013 and rules made thereunder, in this regard, from time to time.

(2A) The **appointment, re-appointment or removal** of an independent director of a listed entity, shall be **subject to the approval of shareholders by way of a special resolution**.

Provided that where a special resolution for the appointment of an independent director fails to get the requisite majority of votes but the votes cast in favour of the resolution exceed the votes cast against the resolution **and the votes cast by the public shareholders in favour of the resolution exceed the votes cast against the resolution**, then the appointment of such an independent director **shall be deemed to have been made** under sub-regulation (2A):

Provided further that an independent director appointed under the first proviso shall be removed only if the votes cast in favour of the resolution proposing the removal exceed the votes cast against the resolution and the votes cast by the public shareholders in favour of the resolution exceed the votes cast against the resolution.

(3)   The independent directors of the listed entity shall hold at least one meeting in a financial year, without the presence of non-independent directors and members of the management and all the independent directors shall strive to be present at such meeting.

(4)   The independent directors in the meeting referred in sub-regulation (3) shall, inter alia –

   (a)   review the performance of non-independent directors and the board of directors as a whole;

   (b)   review the performance of the chairperson of the listed entity, taking into account the views of executive directors and non-executive directors;

   (c)   assess the quality, quantity and timeliness of flow of information between the management of the listed entity and the board of directors that is necessary for the board of directors to effectively and reasonably perform their duties.

(5)   An independent director shall be held liable, only in respect of such acts of omission or commission by the listed entity which had occurred with his/her knowledge, attributable **through processes of board of directors, and with his/her consent or connivance** or where he /she had not acted diligently with respect to the provisions contained in these regulations.

(6)   An independent director who resigns or is removed from the board of directors of the listed entity shall be replaced by a new independent director by listed entity at the earliest but not later than three months from the date of such vacancy

(7)   The listed entity shall familiarize the independent directors through various programme about the listed entity, including the following:

(a)   nature of the industry in which the listed entity operates;

(b)   business model of the listed entity;

(c)   roles, rights, responsibilities of independent directors; and

(d)   any other relevant information

(8)   Every independent director shall, at the first meeting of the board in which he participates as a director and thereafter at the first meeting of the board in every financial year or whenever there is any change in the circumstances which **may affect his status as an independent director, submit a declaration that he meets the criteria of independence** as provided in clause (b) of sub-regulation (1) of regulation 16 and that he is not aware of any circumstance or situation, which exist or may be reasonably anticipated, that could impair or impact his ability to discharge his duties with an objective independent judgment and without any external influence.

(9)   The board of directors of the listed entity shall take on record the declaration and confirmation submitted by

the independent director under sub-regulation (8) after undertaking due assessment of the veracity of the same.

(10)   With effect from January 1, 2022,the top 100 listed entities by market capitalization calculated as on March 31 of the preceding financial year, shall undertake **Directors and Officers insurance** ('D and O insurance') for all their independent directors of such quantum and for such risks as may be determined by its board of directors.

(11)   No independent director, who resigns from a listed entity, shall be appointed as an executive / whole time director on the board of the listed entity, its holding, subsidiary or associate company or on the board of a company belonging to its promoter group, unless a period of one year has elapsed from the date of resignation as an independent director.

(12)   A 'high value debt listed entity' *(NCD of Rs 500 cr and above}* shall undertake Directors and Officers insurance (D & O insurance) for all its independent directors for such sum assured and for such risks may be determined by its board of directors.

D. Reg 26: Obligations with respect to employees including senior management, key managerial personnel, directors and promoters.

(1)   A **director shall not be a member in more than ten committees or act as chairperson of more than five committees** across all listed entities in which he /she is a director which shall be determined as follows:

(a)   the limit of the committees on which a director may serve in all public limited companies, whether listed or not, shall be included and all other companies including private limited companies, foreign companies, high value debt listed entities and companies under Section 8 of the Companies Act, 2013 shall be excluded;

(b)   for the purpose of determination of limit, chairpersonship and membership of the audit committee and the Stakeholders' Relationship Committee **alone shall be considered.**

(2)   **Every director shall inform the listed entity about the committee positions he or she occupies in other listed entities and notify changes as and when they take place.**

(3)   All members of the board of **directors and senior management personnel shall affirm compliance with the code of conduct of board of directors and senior management on an annual basis.**

(5)   Senior management shall make **disclosures to the board of directors relating to all material, financial and commercial transactions, where they have personal interest that may have a potential conflict** with the interest of the listed entity at large.

Explanation — For the purpose of this sub-regulation, conflict of interest relates to dealing in the shares of listed entity, commercial dealings with bodies, which have shareholding of management and their relatives etc.

(6)	No employee including key managerial personnel or director or promoter of a listed entity shall enter into any agreement for himself /herself or on behalf of any other person, with any shareholder or any other third party **with regard to compensation or profit sharing in connection with dealings in the securities of such listed entity, unless prior approval for the same has been obtained from the Board of Directors as well as public shareholders by way of an ordinary resolution**:

Provided that such agreement, if any, whether subsisting or expired, entered during the preceding three years from the date of coming into force of this sub-regulation, **shall be disclosed to the stock exchanges** for public dissemination:

Provided further that subsisting agreement, if any, as on the date of coming into force of this sub-regulation shall be placed for approval before the Board of Directors in the forthcoming Board meeting:

Provided further that if the Board of Directors approve such agreement, the same shall be placed before the public shareholders for **approval by way of an ordinary resolution in the forthcoming general meeting**:

Provided further that **all interested persons involved in the transaction covered under the agreement shall abstain from voting in the general meeting.**

Explanation — For the purposes of this sub-regulation, 'interested person' shall mean any person holding voting rights in the listed entity and who is in any manner, whether directly or indirectly, interested in an agreement or proposed agreement, entered into or to be entered into by such a person or by any employee or key managerial personnel or director or promoter of such listed entity with any shareholder or any other third party **with respect to compensation or profit sharing in connection with the securities of such listed entity.**

E.   **Are the Independent Directors, non-promoters and non-KMP directors held liable for acts of omissions and commissions by the management of companies?**

A gist of clarification issued by the Ministry of Corporate Affairs to the Regional Directors, Registrar of Companies and Official Liquidators .The gist of the General Circular 1/2020 dated March 2, 2020 is noteworthy.

"Quote"

"It referred to the prosecutions filed or internal adjudication proceedings initiated against Independent Directors, non-promoters and non-KMP non-executive directors. The Ministry specifically laid emphasis that civil or criminal proceedings should not be unnecessarily initiated against the IDs or the NEDs, unless sufficient evidence exists to the contrary.

> ➤ **The Ministry contended that WTDs and KMPs would be liable for defaults committed by a company.**

> ➤ **In their absence, such director or directors who have expressly given their consent for incurring liability in terms of e-form GNL-3 filed with the Registrar would be liable.**

The records available in the office of the Registrar, including e-forms DIR-11 or DIR-12, along with copies of the annual returns or financial statements should also be examined so as to ascertain whether a particular director or the KMP was serving in the company as on the date of default.

In case of any doubts, with regard to the liability of any person, for any proceedings required to be initiated by the Registrar, guidance may be sought from the Ministry of Corporate Affairs through the office of Director General of Corporate Affairs. Consequently, any such proceedings must be initiated after receiving due sanction from the Ministry".

"Unquote"

Several provisions of the Companies Act, 2013 stipulates proceedings against 'officers in default' liable for non-compliances {*Chapter XII*}.

It is the intention of the Government is not to implicate the IDs and NEDs (non-promoter and non-KMP) in any criminal or and civil proceedings under the Act, unless they were a part of a default/non-compliance committed by the company, which had occurred with the knowledge of the IDs or NEDs attributable through Board processes with their consent or connivance or where they did not act diligently.

The presence of IDs and NEDs are an important cog in the wheel of corporate governance.

The circular has cast a responsibility/obligation on the registrar to examine relevant information to ascertain participation of the directors in deliberations of board meetings; records of appointment and resignation of directors and copies of the annual returns or financial statements before proceeding against the IDs and NEDs (non-promoter and non-KMP). **It is most important for the IDs and NEDs to guard on the manner their names** are represented by the company management while filing Returns with the Registrar especially that of Annual Returns.

F. Extra care that may be taken by the IDs, non-promoters and non-KMP directors

a.   Acquire knowledge on the board process. {*Chapter VI*}

b.   Insist for a copy of a Return filed with Registrar using the name of concerned ID/NED.

c.   Study thoroughly the agenda papers including back-up documents and satisfy that they give full information needed for active deliberation at the meetings of board/committee thereof.

d.   Wherever required, seek professional guidance company In-house or external at company's cost.

e.   Voice clearly without ambiguity dissent on the motions, wherever there is disagreement.

f.   When the draft minutes is received and if the dissent on the particular subject has not been recorded or improperly recorded, raise the alarm in writing by seeking alteration to the draft minutes to reflect the reality. Ensure that at the next board meeting final minutes signed by the Chairman carries the corrections.

g.   If the over-all in-house training program is not covering all aspects of the business, ask for additional sessions.

h. Allot adequate time to study board papers, financial statements, compliance certificate in entirety, internal audit reports related to fraud, if any and internal financial controls.

i. It is critical to insist that all statutory liabilities towards dues to Government authorities such as Income Taxes, all kinds of TDS, employees dues such as PF, ESI etc., GST Dues etc., are paid and action plans for clearance of arrears are obtained at each meeting and properly recorded in the minutes book and disowning responsibility of non-WTDs for lapses in payments. Otherwise, personal liability under section 179 of the Income Tax Axt, 1961 may be attracted.

j. Never consider the role as mere strategic advisor or watchdog.

k. It is most advisable for every director to ever remain alert and vigilant so that ay no point of time the director, especially the one, who is not involved with the day-to-day management of the company is not tagged under the definition of Officer in Default at a later date.

l. **Further Safeguards to be taken by Directors on some other Matters**

I. Civil Liability

(i) Debts/Contracts of the Company

Generally, a Director is not personally liable for any debt or contract of the company unless fraud on the part of such Director is proved.

(ii)   Refund of Share application Money

A Director is personally liable along with the company to repay the share application or excess share application money, as the case may be, if the same is not repaid within the stipulated time limit.

(iii)   Mis-statement in the Prospectus

Director may be held liable for civil liability for any untrue statement in the prospectus of a public company if he or she is a Director at the time of the issue of the prospectus, unless he or she proves that he or she withdrew consent before the issue of the prospectus or that it was issued without his or her authority or consent or without his or her knowledge or that, once he or she came to know of the untrue statement, he or she withdrew consent and gave reasonable public notice of the same, or proves that he or she believed the impugned statements to be true.

(iv)   Fraudulent Conduct of Business

Director may be personally responsible, for all or any of the debts or other liabilities of the company if he was knowingly party to the fraudulent business activity.

(v)   Persons may approach NCLT under section 244 of the Companies Act, 2013 **for prevention of oppression and mismanagement,** where the majority acts in a manner that oppresses the minority; or where the affairs of the company are being conducted in a manner prejudicial to public interests or oppressive to any member(s) or in a manner prejudicial to the interests of the company including an adverse material change in the management or control of the company.

(vi)   Actions can be brought against a Director for **failure to discharge his duties.**

(vii)   In the case of listed entities, **SEBI may act against the Directors** ail to make required disclosures under the SEBI (Acquisition of Shares & Takeovers) Regulations, 1997 and SEBI (Prohibition of Insider Trading) Regulations, 1992, in respect of their shareholdings in the company.

(viii)   For contraventions of **Foreign Exchange Management Act (FEMA), 1999,** the "person in-charge" who was responsible to the company for conduct of its business at the time when the contravention was committed, shall be held guilty and such director may face penal consequences and legal proceeding against them.

II. Criminal Liability

A.   **Signatory Director to a dishonoured Cheques Shall** be prosecuted for dishonour under the Negotiable Instruments Act, 1881.

B.   **Director who has signed a prospectus containing mis-statement in the Prospectus**

Liability for Offences of company under Labour Laws befall on the persons who were responsible for and had control over the affairs of the company.

Chapter V

Duties, Functions, Responsibilities and Powers of Directors

I. Duties, Functions, Responsibilities of Directors

1. **Under Companies Act, 2013**

Section 166.

(1) Subject to the provisions of this Act, a director of a company shall act in accordance with the **articles** of the company.

(2) A director of a company shall **act in good faith** in order to promote the objects of the company for the benefit of its members as a whole, and in the best interests of the company, its employees, the shareholders, the community and for the protection of environment.

(3) A director of a company shall exercise his duties with due and reasonable care, skill and diligence and **shall exercise independent judgment.**

(4) A director of a company **shall not involve** in a situation in which he may have a direct or indirect interest that **conflicts,** or possibly may conflict, with the interest of the company.

(5)   **A director of a company shall not achieve or attempt to achieve any undue gain or advantage either to himself or to his relatives, partners, or associates and if such director is found guilty of making any undue gain, he shall be liable to pay an amount equal to that gain to the company.**

(6)   A director of a company shall not assign his office and any assignment so made shall be void.

(7)   **If a director of the company contravenes the provisions of this section such director shall be punishable with fine which shall not be less than one lakh rupees but which may extend to five lakh rupees.**

Reg: 4. Principles governing disclosures and obligations.

(1)   The listed entity which has listed securities shall make disclosures and abide by its obligations under these regulations, in accordance with the following principles:

   (a)   Information shall be prepared and disclosed in **accordance with applicable standards of accounting and financial disclosure**.

   (b)   The listed entity shall implement the prescribed **accounting standards in letter and spirit in the preparation of financial statements** taking into consideration the interest of all stakeholders and shall also ensure that the annual audit is conducted **by an independent, competent and qualified auditor.**

(c)   The listed entity shall refrain from misrepresentation and ensure that the information provided to recognised stock exchange(s) and investors is not misleading.

(d)   The listed entity shall provide adequate and timely information to recognised stock exchange(s) and investors.

(e)   The listed entity shall ensure that disseminations made under provisions of these regulations and circulars made thereunder, are adequate, accurate, explicit, timely and presented in a simple language.

(f)   Channels for disseminating information shall provide for equal, timely and cost efficient access to relevant information by investors.

(g)   The listed entity shall abide by all the provisions of the applicable laws including the securities laws and also such other guidelines as may be issued from time to time by the Board and the recognised stock exchange(s) in this regard and as may be applicable.

(h)   The listed entity shall make the specified disclosures and follow its obligations in letter and spirit taking into consideration the interest of all stakeholders.

(i)   Filings, reports, statements, documents and information which are event based or are filed periodically shall contain relevant information.

(j)   Periodic filings, reports, statements, documents and information reports shall contain information that shall enable investors to track the performance of a listed entity over regular intervals of time and shall provide sufficient information to enable investors to assess the current status of a listed entity.

(2)   The listed entity which has listed its specified securities shall comply with the corporate governance provisions as specified in chapter IV which shall be implemented in a manner so as to achieve the objectives of the principles as mentioned below.

(a) The rights of shareholders:

The listed entity shall seek to **protect and facilitate** the exercise of the following rights of shareholders:

(i)   right to participate in, and to be sufficiently informed of, decisions concerning fundamental corporate changes.

(ii)   opportunity to participate effectively and vote in general shareholder meetings.

(iii)   being informed of the rules, including voting procedures that govern general shareholder meetings.

(iv)   opportunity to ask questions to the board of directors, to place items on the agenda of general meetings, and to propose resolutions, subject to reasonable limitations.

(v)   Effective shareholder participation in key corporate governance decisions, such as the nomination and election of members of board of directors.

(vi)   exercise of ownership rights by all shareholders, including institutional investors.

(vii)   adequate mechanism to address the grievances of the shareholders.

(viii)   protection of minority shareholders from abusive actions by, or in the interest of, controlling shareholders acting either directly or indirectly, and effective means of redress.

(b) Timely information:

The listed entity shall provide adequate and timely information to shareholders, including but not limited to the following:

(i)   sufficient and timely information concerning the date, location and agenda of general meetings, as well as full and timely information regarding the issues to be discussed at the meeting.

(ii)   Capital structures and arrangements that enable certain shareholders to obtain a degree of control disproportionate to their equity ownership.

(iii)   rights attached to all series and classes of shares, which shall be disclosed to investors before they acquire shares.

(c) Equitable treatment:

The listed entity shall ensure equitable treatment of all shareholders, including minority and foreign shareholders, in the following manner:

(i)   All shareholders of the same series of a class shall be treated equally.

(ii)   Effective shareholder participation in key corporate governance decisions, such as the nomination and election of members of board of directors, shall be facilitated.

(iii)   Exercise of voting rights by foreign shareholders shall be facilitated.

(iv)   The listed entity shall devise a framework to avoid insider trading and abusive self-dealing.

(v)   Processes and procedures for general shareholder meetings shall allow for equitable treatment of all shareholders.

(vi)   Procedures of listed entity shall not make it unduly difficult or expensive to cast votes.

(d) Role of stakeholders in corporate governance:

The listed entity shall recognise the rights of its stakeholders and encourage co-operation between listed entity and the stakeholders, in the following manner:

(i)   The listed entity shall respect the rights of stakeholders that are established by law or through mutual agreements.

(ii)   Stakeholders shall have the opportunity to obtain effective redress for violation of their rights.

(iii)   Stakeholders shall have access to relevant, sufficient and reliable information on a timely and regular basis to enable them to participate in corporate governance process.

(iv)   The listed entity shall devise an effective **vigil mechanism/ whistle blower policy** enabling stakeholders, including individual employees and their representative bodies, to freely communicate their concerns about illegal or unethical practices.

(e) Disclosure and transparency:

The listed entity shall ensure timely and accurate disclosure on all material matters including the financial situation, performance, ownership, and governance of the listed entity, in the following manner:

(i)   Information shall be prepared and disclosed in accordance with the prescribed standards of accounting, financial and non-financial disclosure.

(ii)   Channels for disseminating information shall provide for equal, timely and cost efficient access to relevant information by users.

(iii)   Minutes of the meeting shall be maintained explicitly recording dissenting opinions, if any.

(f) Responsibilities of the board of directors:

The board of directors of the listed entity shall have the following responsibilities:

(i)   **Disclosure** of information:

        (1)   Members of board of directors and key managerial personnel shall disclose to the board of directors whether they, directly, indirectly, or on behalf of third parties, have a **material interest** in any transaction or matter directly affecting the listed entity.

        (2)   The board of directors and senior management shall conduct themselves so as to meet the expectations of operational transparency to stakeholders while

at the same time maintaining **confidentiality of information** in order to foster a culture of good decision-making.

(ii)   **Key functions of the board of directors –**

(1)   **Reviewing and guiding** corporate strategy, major plans of action, risk policy, annual budgets and business plans, setting performance objectives, monitoring implementation and corporate performance, and overseeing major capital expenditures, acquisitions and divestments.

(2)   **Monitoring** the effectiveness of the listed entity's **governance practices** and making changes as needed.

(3)   Selecting, compensating, monitoring and, when necessary, replacing key managerial personnel and overseeing **succession planning**.

(4)   Aligning key managerial personnel and remuneration of board of directors with the **longer term interests** of the listed entity and its shareholders.

(5)   Ensuring a **transparent nomination process** to the board of directors with the diversity of thought, experience, knowledge, perspective and gender in the board of directors.

(6)   Monitoring and managing potential **conflicts of interest** of management, members of the board of directors and shareholders, including misuse of corporate assets and abuse in related party transactions

(7)   Ensuring the **integrity of the listed entity's accounting and financial reporting systems,** including the independent audit, and that appropriate systems of control are in place, in particular, systems for risk management, financial and operational control, and compliance with the law and relevant standards.

(8)   Overseeing the process of **disclosure and communications**.

(9)   Monitoring and reviewing **board of director's evaluation framework**.

(iii) Other responsibilities:

(1)   The board of directors shall provide **strategic guidance** to the listed entity, ensure effective monitoring of the management **and shall be accountable** to the listed entity and the shareholders.

(2)   The board of directors shall **set a corporate culture** and the values by which executives throughout a group shall behave.

(3)   Members of the board of directors shall **act on a fully informed basis,** in good faith, with due diligence and care, **and in the best interest of the listed entity** and the shareholders.

(4)   The board of directors shall encourage continuing **directors training** to ensure that the members of board of directors are kept up to date.

(5)   Where decisions of the board of directors may affect different shareholder groups differently, the board of directors shall **treat all shareholders fairly.**

(6)   The board of directors shall **maintain high ethical standards** and shall take into account the interests of stakeholders.

(7)   The board of directors shall **exercise objective independent judgement** on corporate affairs.

(8)   The board of directors shall consider **assigning a sufficient number of non-executive members** of the board of directors capable of exercising independent judgement to tasks where there is a potential for conflict of interest.

(9)   The board of directors shall ensure that, while rightly encouraging positive thinking, these **do not result in over-optimism** that either leads to significant risks not being recognised or exposes the listed entity to excessive risk.

(10)   The board of directors shall have ability to 'step back' to assist executive management by **challenging the assumptions** underlying: strategy, strategic initiatives (such as acquisitions), risk appetite, exposures and the key areas of the listed entity's focus.

(11)   When **committees** of the board of directors are established, their mandate, composition and working procedures shall be **well defined and disclosed** by the board of directors.

(12)   Members of the board of directors shall be able to **commit** themselves effectively **to their responsibilities**.

(13)   In order to fulfil their responsibilities, members of the board of directors shall have **access to accurate, relevant and timely information**.

(14) The board of directors and senior management shall **facilitate the independent directors** to perform their role effectively as a member of the board of directors and also a member of a committee of board of directors.

Reg. 17 of SEBI LODR, 2015

(3) The board of directors shall periodically **review compliance reports** pertaining to all laws applicable to the listed entity, prepared by the listed entity as well as steps taken by the listed entity to rectify instances of non-compliances.

(4) The board of directors of the listed entity shall satisfy itself that plans are in place for orderly **succession for appointment to the board of directors and senior management.**

(5) (a) The board of directors shall **lay down a code of conduct** for all members of board of directors and senior management of the listed entity.

(d) The code of conduct shall suitably incorporate the **duties of independent Directors** as laid down in the Companies Act, 2013.

(6) (a) The board of directors shall **recommend all fees or compensation**, if any, paid to non-executive directors, including independent directors and shall require approval of shareholders in general meeting.

(b) The requirement of obtaining approval of shareholders in general meeting shall not apply to payment of sitting fees to non-executive directors, if made within the limits of one lakh rupees presently prescribed under the Companies Act, 2013 for payment of sitting fees without approval of the Central Government.

(c) The approval of shareholders mentioned in clause (a), shall specify the limits for the maximum number of stock options that may be granted to non-executive directors, in any financial year and in aggregate.

(ca) The **approval of shareholders by special resolution shall be obtained every year,** in which the annual remuneration payable to a single non-executive director exceeds fifty per cent of the total annual remuneration payable to all non-executive directors, giving details of the remuneration thereof.

(d) Independent directors shall not be entitled to any stock option.

(e) The fees or compensation **payable to executive directors who are promoters or members of the promoter group,** shall be subject to the approval of the **shareholders by special resolution in general meeting, if –**

(i) the annual remuneration payable to such executive director exceeds rupees Five crore or 2.5 per cent of the net profits of the listed entity, whichever is higher; or

(ii) where there is more than one such director, the aggregate annual remuneration to such directors exceeds 5 per cent of the net profits of the listed entity:

Provided that the approval of the shareholders under this provision shall be valid only till the expiry of the term of such director.

(7) The minimum information to be placed before the board of directors is specified in Part A of Schedule II.

(8) The chief executive officer and the chief financial officer shall provide the compliance certificate to the board of directors as specified in Part B of Schedule II.

(9) (a) The listed entity shall lay down procedures to inform members of board of directors about risk assessment and minimization procedures.

> (b) The board of directors shall be responsible for framing, implementing and monitoring the risk management plan for the listed entity.

(10) The evaluation of independent directors shall be done by the entire board of directors which shall include -

> (a) performance of the directors; and

> (b) fulfillment of the independence criteria as specified in these regulations and their independence from the management:

Provided that in the above evaluation, the directors who are subject to evaluation shall not participate.

(11) The statement to be annexed to the notice as referred to in sub-section (1) of section 102 of the Companies Act, 2013 for each item of special business to be transacted at a general meeting shall also set forth clearly the recommendation of the board to the shareholders on each of the specific items.

II. POWERS OF THE BOARD

1, Sec 179 of Companies Act, 2013 —

(1)   The Board of Directors of a company shall be entitled to exercise all such powers, and to do all such acts and things, as the company is authorised to exercise and do:

Provided that in exercising such power or doing such act or thing, the Board shall be subject to the **provisions contained in that behalf in this Act, or in the memorandum or articles, or in any regulations not inconsistent therewith and duly made thereunder, including regulations made by the company in general meeting:**

Provided further that the Board **shall not exercise any power or do any act or thing** which is directed or required, whether under this Act or by the memorandum or articles of the company or otherwise, **to be exercised or done by the company in general meeting**.

(2)   No regulation made by the company in general meeting shall invalidate any prior act of the Board which would have been valid if that regulation had not been made.

(3)   The Board of Directors of a company shall exercise the following powers on behalf of the company **by means of resolutions passed at meetings of the Board,** namely:—

    (a)   to make calls on shareholders in respect of money unpaid on their shares;

    (b)   to authorise buy-back of securities under section 68;

    (c)   to issue securities, including debentures, whether in or outside India;

    (d)   to borrow monies;

    (e)   to invest the funds of the company;

    (f)   to grant loans or give guarantee or provide security in respect of loans;

    (g)   to approve financial statement and the Board's report;

(h)   to diversify the business of the company;

(i)   to approve amalgamation, merger or reconstruction;

(j)   to take over a company or acquire a controlling or substantial stake in another company;

(k)   **Rule 8:**

(1)   to make political contributions;

(2)   to appoint or remove key managerial personnel (KMP);

(3)   to take note of appointment(s) or removal(s) of one level below the Key Management Personnel;

(4)   to appoint internal auditors and secretarial auditor;

(5)   to take note of the disclosure of director's interest and shareholding;

(6)   to buy, sell investments held by the company (other than trade investments), constituting five percent or more of the paid up share capital and free reserves of the investee company;

(7)   to invite or accept or renew public deposits and related matters;

(8)   to review or change the terms and conditions of public deposit;

(9)   to approve quarterly, half yearly and annual financial statements or financial results as the case may be.

(l) any other matter which may be prescribed:

Provided that the Board may, by a **resolution passed at a meeting, delegate** to any committee of directors, the managing director, the manager or any other principal officer of the company or in the case of a branch office of the company, the principal officer of the branch office, **the powers specified in clauses (d) to (f)** on such conditions as it may specify:

(4) Nothing in this section shall be deemed to affect the right of the company in general meeting to impose restrictions and conditions on the exercise by the Board of any of the powers specified in this section.

Sec 180. Restriction on powers of Board —

(1) The Board of Directors of a company shall exercise the following powers only with the consent of the company by a special resolution, namely:—

(a) to sell, lease or otherwise dispose of the whole or substantially the whole of the undertaking of the company or where the company owns more than one undertaking, of the whole or substantially the whole of any of such undertakings.

Explanation — For the purposes of this clause,—

(i)   "undertaking" shall mean an undertaking in which the investment of the company exceeds twenty per cent. of its net worth as per the audited balance sheet of the preceding financial year or an undertaking which generates twenty per cent. of the total income of the company during the previous financial year;

(ii)   the expression "substantially the whole of the undertaking "in any financial year shall mean twenty per cent. or more of the value of the undertaking as per the audited balance sheet of the preceding financial year:

(b)   to invest otherwise in trust securities the amount of compensation received by it as a result of any merger or amalgamation;

(c)   to borrow money, where the money to be borrowed, together with the money already borrowed by the company will exceed aggregate of its paid-up share capital and free reserves, apart from temporary loans obtained from the company's bankers in the ordinary course of business:

Provided that the acceptance by a banking company, in the ordinary course of its business, of deposits of money from the public, repayable on demand or otherwise, and withdrawable by cheque, draft, order or otherwise, shall not be deemed to be a borrowing of monies by the banking company within the meaning of this clause.

Explanation — For the purposes of this clause, the expression "temporary loans" means loans repayable on demand or within six months from the date of the loan such as short-term, cash credit arrangements, the discounting of bills and the issue of other short-term loans of a seasonal character, but does not include loans raised for the purpose of financial expenditure of a capital nature;

(d) to remit, or give time for the repayment of, any debt due from a director.

(2) Every special resolution passed by the company in general meeting in relation to the exercise of the powers referred to in clause (c) of sub-section (1) **shall specify the total amount up to which monies may be borrowed by the Board of Directors.**

(3) Nothing contained in clause (a) of sub-section (1) shall affect—

(a)   the title of a buyer or other person who buys or takes on lease any property, investment or undertaking as is referred to in that clause, in good faith; or

(b)   the sale or lease of any property of the company where the ordinary business of the company consists of, or comprises, such selling or leasing.

(4) Any special resolution passed by the company consenting to the transaction as is referred to in clause (a) of sub-section (1) may stipulate such conditions as may be specified in such resolution, including conditions regarding the use, disposal or investment of the sale proceeds which may result from the transactions:

Provided that this sub-section shall not be deemed to authorise the company to effect any reduction in its capital except in accordance with the provisions contained in this Act.

(5) No debt incurred by the company in excess of the limit imposed by clause (c) of sub-section (1) shall be valid or effectual, unless the lender proves that he advanced the loan in good faith and without knowledge that the limit imposed by that clause had been exceeded.

SEBI LODR, 2015 Reg 24:

The management of the **unlisted subsidiary shall periodically** bring to the notice of the board of directors of the listed entity, a statement of **all significant transactions and arrangements entered into by the unlisted subsidiary**.

Explanation — For the purpose of this regulation, the term "significant transaction or arrangement" shall mean any individual transaction or arrangement that exceeds or is likely to exceed ten percent of the total revenues or total expenses or total assets or total liabilities, as the case may be, of the unlisted subsidiary for the immediately preceding accounting year.

(2)   The audit committee of the listed entity shall also review the financial statements, in particular, the investments made by the unlisted subsidiary.

(3)   The minutes of the meetings of the board of directors of the unlisted subsidiary shall be placed at the meeting of the board of directors of the listed entity.

(4)   The management of the unlisted subsidiary shall periodically bring to the notice of the board of directors of the listed entity, a statement of all significant transactions and arrangements entered into by the unlisted subsidiary.

Explanation — For the purpose of this regulation, the term "significant transaction or arrangement" shall mean any individual transaction or arrangement that exceeds or is likely to exceed ten percent of the total revenues or total expenses or total assets or total liabilities, as the case may be, of the unlisted subsidiary for the immediately preceding accounting year.

(5)   **A listed entity shall not dispose of shares in its material subsidiary** resulting in reduction of its shareholding (either on its own or together with other subsidiaries) **to less than or equal to fifty percent or cease the exercise of control over the subsidiary without passing a special resolution** in its General Meeting except in cases where such divestment is made under a scheme of arrangement duly approved by a Court/Tribunal[, or under a resolution plan duly approved under section 31 of the Insolvency Code and

such an event is disclosed to the recognized stock exchanges within one day of the resolution plan being approved]

(6)   Selling, disposing and leasing of assets amounting to more than twenty percent of the assets of the material subsidiary on an aggregate basis during a financial year shall require prior approval of shareholders by way of special resolution, unless the sale/disposal/lease is made under a scheme of arrangement duly approved by a Court/Tribunal, or under a resolution plan duly approved under section 31 of the Insolvency Code and such an event 36is disclosed to the recognized stock exchanges within one day of the resolution plan being approved.

(7)   Where a listed entity has a listed subsidiary, which is itself a holding company, the provisions of this regulation shall apply to the listed subsidiary in so far as its subsidiaries are concerned.

Sec 181. Directors may contribute to bona fide and charitable funds, etc — in any financial year, amounts not exceeding five per cent. of its average net profits for the three immediately preceding financial years.

Sec 182. Prohibitions and restrictions regarding political contributions —

(1)   A company, other than a Government company and a company which has been in existence for less than three financial years, may contribute amount directly or indirectly to any political party: the aggregate of the which in any financial year shall not exceed seven and a half per cent. of its

average net profits during the three immediately preceding financial years:

(2)   Provided further that no such contribution shall be made by a company unless a resolution authorising the making of such contribution is passed at a meeting of the Board of Directors and **such resolution shall**, subject to the other provisions of this section, **be deemed to be justification in law** for the making and the acceptance of the contribution authorised by it.

(3)   Every company shall disclose in its profit and loss account any amount or amounts contributed by it to any political party during the financial year to which that account relates, giving particulars of the total amount contributed and the name of the party to which such amount has been contributed.

(4)   If a company makes any contribution in contravention of the provisions of this section, the company shall be punishable with fine which may extend to five times the amount so contributed and **every officer** of the company **who is in default** shall be punishable with imprisonment for a term which may extend to six months and with fine which may extend to five times the amount so contributed.

Sec 183. Power of Board and other persons to make contributions to national defense fund, etc — such amount as it thinks fit,

(2)   Every company shall disclose in its profits and loss account the total amount or amounts contributed by it to the Fund during the financial year to which the amount relates.

184. Disclosure of interest by director —

(1)   Every director shall at the first meeting of the Board in which he participates as a director and thereafter at the first meeting of the Board in every financial year or whenever there is any change in the disclosures already made, then at the first Board meeting held after such change, disclose his concern or interest in any company or companies or bodies corporate, firms, or other association of individuals which shall include the shareholding, in Form MBP-1. *{Rule 9}*. It shall be the duty of the director giving notice of interest to cause it to be disclosed at the meeting held immediately after the date of the notice.

(2)   Every director of a company who is in any way, whether directly or indirectly, concerned or interested in a contract or arrangement or proposed contract or arrangement entered into or to be entered into—

   (a)   with a body corporate in which such director or such director in association with any other director, holds more than two per cent. shareholding of that body corporate, or is a promoter, manager, Chief Executive Officer of that body corporate; or

   (b)   with a firm or other entity in which, such director is a partner, owner or member, as the case may be, shall disclose the nature of his concern or interest at the meeting of the Board in which the contract or arrangement is discussed and shall not participate in such meeting:

Provided that where any director who is not so concerned or interested at the time of entering into such contract or arrangement, he shall, if he becomes concerned or interested after the contract or arrangement is entered into, disclose his concern or interest forthwith when he becomes concerned or interested or at the first meeting of the Board held after he becomes so concerned or interested.

(4)   **If a director of the company contravenes the provisions of sub-section (1) or subsection (2), such director shall be** liable to a penalty of one lakh rupees".

(5)   Nothing in this section—

    (b)   shall apply to any contract or arrangement entered into or to be entered into between two companies where any of the directors of the one company or two or more of them together holds or hold **not more than two per cent.** of the paid-up share capital in the other company.

185. Loan to directors, etc —

(1)   No company shall, directly or indirectly, advance any loan, including any loan represented by a book debt, to any of its directors or to any other person in whom the director is interested or give any guarantee or provide any security in connection with any loan taken by him or such other person:

Provided that nothing contained in this sub-section shall apply to—

    (a)   the giving of any loan to a managing or whole-time director—

(i)   as a part of the conditions of service extended by the company to all its employees; or

(ii)   pursuant to any scheme approved by the members by a special resolution; or

(b)   a company which in the ordinary course of its business provides loans or gives guarantees or securities for the due repayment of any loan and in respect of such loans an interest is charged at a rate not less than the bank rate declared by the Reserve Bank of India;

(c)   any loan made by a holding company to its wholly owned subsidiary company or any guarantee given or security provided by a holding company in respect of any loan made to its wholly owned subsidiary company; or

(d)   any guarantee given or security provided by a holding company in respect of loan made by any bank or financial institution to its subsidiary company: Provided that the loans made under clauses (c) and (d) are utilised by the subsidiary company for its principal business activities.

Explanation — For the purposes of this section, the expression "to any other person in whom director is interested" means—

(a)   any director of the lending company, or of a company which is its holding company or any partner or relative of any such director;

(b)   any firm in which any such director or relative is a partner;

(c)   any private company of which any such director is a director or member;

(d)   anybody corporate at a general meeting of which not less than twenty-five per cent. of the total voting power may be exercised or controlled by any such director, or by two or more such directors, together; or

(e)   anybody corporate, the Board of directors, managing director or manager, whereof is accustomed to act in accordance with the directions or instructions of the Board, or of any director or directors, of the lending company.

(2)   If any loan is advanced or a guarantee or security is given or provided in contravention of the provisions of sub-section (1), the company shall be punishable with fine which shall not be less than five lakh rupees but which may extend to twenty-five lakh rupees, **and the director or the other person to whom any loan is advanced or guarantee or security is given or provided in connection with any loan taken by him or the other person, shall be punishable** with imprisonment which may extend to six months or with fine which shall not be less than five lakh rupees but which may extend to twenty-five lakh rupees, or with both.

186. Loan and investment by company —

(1)   A company shall unless otherwise prescribed, make investment through not more than two layers of investment companies:

Provided that the provisions of this sub-section shall not affect,—

(i)   a company from acquiring any other company incorporated in a country outside India if such other company has investment subsidiaries beyond two layers as per the laws of such country;

(ii) a subsidiary company from having any investment subsidiary for the purposes of meeting the requirements under any law or under any rule or regulation framed under any law for the time being in force.

(2)   No company shall directly or indirectly —

(a)   give any loan to any person or other body corporate;

(b)   give any guarantee or provide security in connection with a loan to any other body corporate or person; and

(c)   acquire by way of subscription, purchase or otherwise, the securities of any other body corporate, **exceeding sixty per cent. of its paid-up share capital, free reserves and securities premium account or one hundred per cent. of its free reserves and securities premium account, whichever is more.**

(3)   Where the giving of any loan or guarantee or providing any security or the acquisition under subsection (2) exceeds the limits specified in that sub-section, **prior approval by**

means of a special resolution passed at a general meeting shall be necessary.

(4) **The company shall disclose to the members in the financial statement** the full particulars of the loans given, investment made or guarantee given or security provided and the purpose for which the loan or guarantee or security is proposed to be utilised by the recipient of the loan or guarantee or security.

(5) **No investment shall be made or loan or guarantee or security given** by the company **unless the resolution sanctioning it is passed at a meeting of the Board with the consent of all the directors present** at the meeting and the prior approval of the public financial institution concerned where any term loan is subsisting, is obtained:

Provided that prior approval of a public financial institution shall not be required where the aggregate of the loans and investments so far made, the amount for which guarantee or security so far provided to or in all other bodies corporate, along with the investments, loans, guarantee or security proposed to be made or given does not exceed the limit as specified in sub-section (2), and **there is no default in repayment of** loan instalments or payment of interest thereon as per the terms and conditions of such loan to the public financial institution.

(6) No company, which is registered under section 12 of the Securities and Exchange Board of India Act, 1992 (15 of 1992) and covered under such class or classes of companies as may be prescribed, shall take inter-corporate loan or

deposits exceeding the prescribed limit and such company shall furnish in its financial statement the details of the loan or deposits.

(7)   No loan shall be given under this section at a rate of interest lower than the prevailing yield of one year, three year, five year or ten year Government Security closest to the tenor of the loan.

(8)   No company which is in default in the repayment of any deposits accepted before or after the commencement of this Act or in payment of interest thereon, shall give any loan or give any guarantee or provide any security or make an acquisition till such default is subsisting.

(9)   Every company giving loan or giving a guarantee or providing security or making an acquisition under this section shall keep a register in form MBP-2.

(13)   If a company contravenes the provisions of this section, the company shall be punishable with fine which shall not be less than twenty-five thousand rupees but which may extend to five lakh rupees **and every officer of the company who is in default shall be punishable** with imprisonment for a term which may extend to two years and with fine which shall not be less than twenty-five thousand rupees but which may extend to one lakh rupees.

187. Investments of company to be held in Company's its own name —

(2) Nothing in this section shall be deemed to prevent a company—

(a)   from depositing with a bank, being the bankers of the company, any shares or securities for the collection of any dividend or interest payable thereon; or

(b)   from depositing with, or transferring to, or holding in the name of, the State Bank of India or a scheduled bank, being the bankers of the company, shares or securities, in order to facilitate the transfer thereof within six months.

(d)   from holding investments in the name of a depository when such investments are in the form of securities held by the company as a beneficial owner.

(3) & Rule 14:

(1) Every company shall, from the date of its registration, maintain a register in Form MBP 3 and enter therein, chronologically, the particulars of investments in shares or other securities beneficially held by the company but which are not held in its own name and the company shall also record the reasons for not holding the investments in its own name and the relationship or contract under which the investment is held in the name of any other person. (2) The company shall also record whether such investments are held in a third party's name for the time being or otherwise.

"(4) If a company is in default in complying with the provisions of this section, the company shall be liable to a penalty of five lakh rupees **and every officer of the company who is in default shall be liable to a penalty of fifty thousand rupees.**

188. Related party transactions —

(1) Except with the consent of the Board of Directors given by a resolution at a meeting of the Board and subject to such conditions as may be prescribed, no company shall enter into any contract or arrangement with a related party with respect to—

(a)   sale, purchase or supply of any goods or materials;

(b)   selling or otherwise disposing of, or buying, property of any kind;

(c)   leasing of property of any kind;

(d)   availing or rendering of any services;

(e)   appointment of any agent for purchase or sale of goods, materials, services or property;

(f)   such related party's appointment to any office or place of profit in the company, its subsidiary company or associate company; and

(g)   underwriting the subscription of any securities or derivatives thereof, of the company:

Provided that no contract or arrangement, in the case of a company having a paid-up share capital of not less than such amount, or transactions exceeding such sums, as may be prescribed, shall be entered into except with the prior approval of the company by resolution:

Provided further that no member of the company shall vote on such resolution, to approve any contract or arrangement which may be entered into by the company, if such member is a related party:

Provided also that nothing in this sub-section shall apply to any transactions entered into by the company in its ordinary course of business other than transactions which are not on an arm's length basis:

Provided also that the requirement of passing the resolution under first proviso shall not be applicable for transactions entered into between a holding company and its wholly owned subsidiary whose accounts are consolidated with such holding company and placed before the shareholders at the general meeting for approval.

Explanation — In this sub-section,—

(a)   the expression "office or place of profit" means any office or place—

    (i)   where such office or place is held by a director, if the director holding it receives from the company anything by way of remuneration over and above the remuneration to which he is entitled as director, by way of salary, fee, commission, perquisites, any rent-free accommodation, or otherwise;

    (ii)   where such office or place is held by an individual other than a director or by any firm, private company or other body corporate, if the individual, firm, private company or body corporate holding it receives from the company anything by way of remuneration, salary, fee, commission, perquisites, any rent-free accommodation, or otherwise;

(b)   the expression "arm's length transaction" means a transaction between two related parties that is conducted as if they were unrelated, so that there is no conflict of interest.

(2)   Every contract or arrangement entered into under sub-section (1) shall be referred to in the Board's report to the shareholders along with the justification for entering into such contract or arrangement.

(3)   Where any contract or arrangement is entered into by a director or any other employee, without obtaining the consent of the Board or approval by a resolution in the general meeting under sub-section (1) and if it is not ratified by the Board or, as the case may be, by the shareholders at a meeting within three months from the date on which such contract or arrangement was entered into, such contract or arrangement shall be voidable at the option of the Board and if the contract or arrangement is with a related party to any director, or is authorised by any other director, the directors concerned shall indemnify the company against any loss incurred by it.

(4)   Without prejudice to anything contained in sub-section (3), it shall be open to the company to proceed against a director or any other employee who had entered into such contract or arrangement in contravention of the provisions of this section for recovery of any loss sustained by it as a result of such contract or arrangement.

(5)   **Any director or any other employee of a company, who had entered into or authorised the contract or arrangement in violation of the provisions of this section shall,—**

    (i)   **in case of listed company, be** liable to a penalty of twenty-five lakh rupees" **and**

    (ii)   **in case of any other company,** be liable to a penalty of five lakh rupees"

Rule 15. Contract or arrangement with a related party.–

A company shall enter into any contract or arrangement with a related party subject to the following conditions, namely:-

(1)   The agenda of the Board meeting at which the resolution is proposed to be moved shall disclose- (a) the name of the related party and nature of relationship;

    (b)   the nature, duration of the contract and particulars of the contract or arrangement;

    (c)   the material terms of the contract or arrangement including the value, if any;

    (d)   any advance paid or received for the contract or arrangement, if any;

    (e)   the manner of determining the pricing and other commercial terms, both included as part of contract and not considered as part of the contract;

    (f)   whether all factors relevant to the contract have been considered, if not, the details of factors not considered with the rationale for not considering those factors; and

    (g)   any other information relevant or important for the Board to take a decision on the proposed transaction.

(2)   Where any director is interested in any contract or arrangement with a related party, such director **shall not**

be present at the meeting during discussions on the subject matter of the resolution relating to such contract or arrangement –

(3)   For the purposes of first proviso to sub-section (1) of section 188, except with the prior approval of **the company by a special resolution** –

(i)   a company having a **paid-up share capital of ten crore rupees or more** shall not enter into a contract or arrangement with any related party; or

(ii)   a company shall not enter into a transaction or transactions, where the transaction or transactions to be entered into –

(a)   as contracts or arrangements **with respect to clauses (a) to (e)** of sub-section (1) of section 188 with criteria, as mentioned below –

(i)   sale, purchase or supply of any goods or materials directly or through appointment of agents **exceeding twenty five percent. of the annual turnover as mentioned in clause (a) and clause (e)** respectively of sub-section (1) of section 188;

(ii)   selling or otherwise disposing of, or buying, property of any kind directly or through appointment of agents **exceeding ten percent. of net worth as mentioned in clause (b) and clause (e)** respectively of sub-section (1) of section 188;

(iii)   **leasing of property** of any kind **exceeding ten percent. of the net worth or exceeding ten**

percent. of turnover as mentioned in clause (c) of sub-section (1) of section 188;

(iv) **availing or rendering of any services directly or through appointment of agents exceeding ten percent. of the net worth** as mentioned in **clause (d) and clause (e)** of sub-section (1) of section 188;

(b) **appointment to any office or place of profit in the company, its subsidiary company or associate company at a monthly remuneration exceeding two and half lakh rupees** as mentioned in clause (f) of sub-section (1) of section 188; or

(c) **remuneration for underwriting the subscription of any securities or derivatives** thereof of the company **exceeding one percent. of the net worth** as mentioned in clause (g) of sub-section (1) of section 188.

Explanation — (1) The Turnover or Net Worth referred in the above sub-rules shall be on the basis of the Audited Financial Statement of the preceding Financial year.

(2) In case of wholly owned subsidiary, the special resolution passed by the holding company shall be sufficient for the purpose of entering into the transactions between wholly owned subsidiary and holding company.

(3) **The explanatory statement** to be annexed to the notice of a general meeting convened pursuant to section 101 shall contain the following particulars namely: –

(a) name of the related party ;

(b)   name of the director or key managerial personnel who is related, if any;

(c)   nature of relationship;

(d)   nature, material terms, monetary value and particulars of the contract or arrangement;

(e)   any other information relevant or important for the members to take a decision on the proposed resolution.

Reg. 23. Related Party Transactions

(1)   The listed entity shall formulate a policy on materiality of related party transactions and on dealing with related party transactions including clear threshold limits duly approved by the board of directors and such policy **shall be reviewed by the board of directors at least once every three years** and updated accordingly:

Provided that a transaction with a related party shall be **considered material,** if the transaction(s) to be entered into individually or taken together with previous transactions during a financial year, **exceeds rupees one thousand crore or ten per cent of the annual consolidated turnover of the listed entity** as per the last audited financial statements of the listed entity, whichever is lower.

(1A) Notwithstanding the above, with effect from July 01, 2019 a transaction involving payments made to a **related party with respect to brand usage or royalty shall be considered material** if the transaction(s) to be entered into individually or taken together with previous transactions during a financial year,

exceed five percent of the annual consolidated turnover of the listed entity as per the last audited financial statements of the listed entity.

(2)   **All related party transactions and subsequent material modifications] shall require prior approval of the audit committee of the listed entity**:

Provided that **only those members of the audit committee, who are independent directors, shall approve** related party transactions.

Provided further that:

(a)   the audit committee of a listed entity shall define "material modifications" and disclose it as part of the policy on materiality of related party transactions and on dealing with related party transactions;

(b)   a related party transaction to which **the subsidiary of a listed entity is a party but the listed entity is not a party, shall require prior approval of the audit committee of the listed entity if the value of such transaction whether entered into individually or taken together with previous transactions during a financial year exceeds ten per cent of the annual consolidated turnover,** as per the last audited financial statements **of the listed entity;**

(c)   with effect from April 1, 2023, a related party transaction to which the subsidiary of a listed entity is a party but the listed entity is not a party, shall require prior approval of the audit committee of the listed entity if the value of such transaction whether entered into individually or taken together with previous transactions during a financial year, **exceeds ten per cent of the annual standalone turnover,** as per the last audited financial statements **of the subsidiary;**

(d)   prior approval of the audit committee of the listed entity shall not be required for a related party transaction to which the listed subsidiary is a party but the listed entity is not a party, if regulation 23 and sub-regulation (2) of regulation 15 of these regulations are applicable to such listed subsidiary. **Explanation:** For **related party transactions of unlisted subsidiaries of a listed subsidiary** as referred to in (d) above, the prior approval of the audit committee of the listed subsidiary shall suffice.

(3)   **Audit committee may grant omnibus approval** for related party transactions proposed to be entered into by the listed entity subject to the following conditions, namely –

(a)   the audit committee shall lay down the **criteria for granting the omnibus approval** in line with the policy on related party transactions of the listed entity and such approval shall be applicable in respect of transactions which are repetitive in nature;

(b)   the audit committee shall **satisfy itself regarding the need for such omnibus approval** and that such approval is in the interest of the listed entity;

(c)   **the omnibus approval shall specify:**

(i)   the name(s) of the related party, nature of transaction, period of transaction, maximum amount of transactions that shall be entered into,

(ii)   the indicative base price / current contracted price and the formula for variation in the price if any; and

(iii)   such other conditions as the audit committee may deem fit: Provided that where the need for related party transaction cannot be foreseen and aforesaid details are not available, audit committee may grant omnibus approval for such transactions subject to their value not exceeding rupees one crore per transaction.

(d)   the audit committee shall review, at least on a quarterly basis, the details of related party transactions entered into by the listed entity pursuant to each of the omnibus approvals given.

(e)   **Such omnibus approvals shall be valid for a period not exceeding one year and shall require fresh approvals after the expiry of one year:**

(4)   All material related party transactions and subsequent material modifications as defined by the audit committee under sub-regulation (2) shall require **prior approval of the shareholders through resolution and no related party shall vote to approve such resolutions whether the entity is a related party to the particular transaction or not:**

Provided that prior approval of the shareholders of a listed entity shall not be required for a related party transaction to which the listed subsidiary is a party but the listed entity is not a party, if regulation 23 and sub-regulation (2) of regulation 15 of these regulations are applicable to such listed subsidiary.

Explanation: For related party transactions of unlisted subsidiaries of a listed subsidiary as referred above, the prior approval of the shareholders of the listed subsidiary shall suffice.

Provided further that the requirements specified under this sub-regulation shall not apply in respect of a resolution plan approved under section 31 of the Insolvency Code, subject to the event being disclosed to the recognized stock exchanges within one day of the resolution plan being approved;

(5)   The provisions of sub-regulations (2), (3) and (4) shall not be applicable in the following cases: (a) transactions entered into between two government companies;

   (b)   transactions entered into between a holding company and its wholly owned subsidiary whose accounts are consolidated with such holding company and placed before the shareholders at the general meeting for approval.

   (c)   transactions entered into between two wholly-owned subsidiaries of the listed holding company, whose accounts are consolidated with such holding company and placed before the shareholders at the general meeting for approval.

(6)   The provisions of this regulation shall be applicable to all prospective transactions.

(8)   All existing material related party contracts or arrangements entered into prior to the date of notification of these regulations and which may continue beyond such date shall be placed for approval of the shareholders in the first General Meeting subsequent to notification of these regulations.

(9)   The listed entity shall submit to the stock exchanges disclosures of related party transactions in the format as specified by the Board from time to time, and publish the same on its website:

Provided that a 'high value debt listed entity' shall submit such disclosures along with its standalone financial results for the half year:

Provided further that the listed entity shall make such disclosures every six months within fifteen days from the date of publication of its standalone and consolidated financial results:

Provided further that the listed entity shall make such disclosures every six months on the date of publication of its standalone and consolidated financial results with effect from April 1, 2023.

189 and Rule 16: Register of contracts or arrangements in which directors are interested in Form MBP-4.

(4) The register to be kept under this section shall also be produced at the commencement of every annual general meeting of the company and shall remain open and accessible during the continuance of the meeting to any person having the right to attend the meeting.

(6) Every director who fails to comply with the provisions of this section and the rules made thereunder shall be liable to a penalty of twenty-five thousand rupees.

190. Contract of employment with managing or whole-time directions —

(1)   Every company shall keep at its registered office,—

    (a)   where a contract of service with a managing or whole-time director is in writing, a copy of the contract; or

    (b)   where such a contract is not in writing, a written memorandum setting out its terms.

(2)   The copies of the contract or the memorandum kept under sub-section (1) shall be open to inspection by any member of the company without payment of fee.

(3)   **If any default is made** in complying with the provisions of sub-section (1) or sub-section (2), the company shall be liable to a penalty of twenty-five thousand rupees **and every officer of the company who is in default shall be liable to a penalty of five thousand rupees for each default.**

(4)   The provisions of this section **shall not apply to a private company.**

191 and Rule 17: Payment to director for loss of office, etc., in connection with transfer of undertaking, property or shares —

192. Restriction on non-cash transactions involving directors —

193. Contract by One Person Company —

194. Prohibition on forward dealings in securities of company by director or key managerial personnel —

(1)   No director of a company or any of its key managerial personnel shall buy in the company, or in its holding, subsidiary or associate company—

(a)   a right to call for delivery or a right to make delivery at a specified price and within a specified time, of a specified number of relevant shares or a specified amount of relevant debentures; or

(b)   a right, as he may elect, to call for delivery or to make delivery at a specified price and within a specified time, of a specified number of relevant shares or a specified amount of relevant debentures.

(2)   **If a director or any key managerial personnel of the company contravenes** the provisions of subsection (1), such director or key managerial personnel **shall be punishable with imprisonment** for a term which may extend to two years or with fine which shall not be less than one lakh rupees but which may extend to five lakh rupees, or with both.

(3)   Where a director or other key managerial personnel acquires any securities in contravention of sub-section (1), he shall, subject to the provisions contained in sub-section (2), be **liable to surrender** the same to the company **and the company shall not register the securities** so acquired in his name in the register, and if they are in

dematerialised form, it shall inform the depository not to record such acquisition and such securities, in both the cases, shall continue to remain in the names of the transferors.

195. Prohibition on insider trading of securities —

(1) No person including any director or key managerial personnel of a company shall enter into insider trading:

Provided that nothing contained in this sub-section shall apply to any communication required in the ordinary course of business or profession or employment or under any law. Explanation — For the purposes of this section,—

(a)   —insider trading means—

    (i)   an act of subscribing, buying, selling, dealing or agreeing to subscribe, buy, sell or deal in any securities by any director or key managerial personnel or any other officer of a company either as principal or agent if such director or key managerial personnel or any other officer of the company is reasonably expected to have access to any non-public price sensitive information in respect of securities of company; or

    (ii)   an act of counselling about procuring or communicating directly or indirectly any nonpublic price-sensitive information to any person;

(b)   "price-sensitive information" means any information which relates, directly or indirectly, to a company and which if published is likely to materially affect the price of securities of the company.

(2) If any person contravenes the provisions of this section, he shall be punishable with imprisonment for a term which may extend to five years or with fine which shall not be less than five lakh rupees but which may extend to twenty-five crore rupees or three times the amounts of profits made out of insider trading, whichever is higher, or with both.

Chapter VI

Meetings of the Board; Committees of the Board & their Role; Board Process {Mandatory Secretarial Standards-SS-1} and Recommendatory Secretarial Standard on Report of the Board of Directors {SS-4}

A. Meetings of Board—

Sec. 173

(1) Every company shall hold the **first meeting of the Board** of Directors within thirty days of the date of its incorporation **and thereafter hold a minimum number of four meetings** of its Board of Directors every year in such a manner that not more than one hundred and twenty days shall intervene between two consecutive meetings of the Board:

Reg 17 (2): The board of directors shall meet at least four times a year, with a maximum time gap of one hundred and twenty days between any two meetings

(2) The participation of directors in a meeting of the Board may be either in person or through video conferencing or other audio visual means, as prescribed under Rule 3 of the Companies (Meetings of Board and its Powers) Rules ,2014, which are capable of recording and recognizing the participation of the directors and of recording and storing the proceedings of such meetings along with date and time:

Rule 4. Matters not to be dealt with in a meeting through video conferencing or other audio visual means.-

(i)   the approval of the annual financial statements;

(ii)   the approval of the Board's report;

(iii)   the approval of the prospectus;

(iv)   the Audit Committee Meetings for consideration of accounts; and

(v)   the approval of the matter relating to amalgamation, merger, demerger, acquisition and takeover.

(3) A meeting of the Board shall be called by giving not less than seven days' notice in writing to every director at his address registered with the company and such notice shall be sent by hand delivery or by post or by electronic means:

Provided that a meeting of the Board may be called **at shorter notice to transact urgent business subject to the condition** that at least one independent director, if any, shall be present at the meeting:

Provided further that in case of absence of independent directors from such a meeting of the Board, decisions taken at such a meeting shall be circulated to all the directors and shall be final only on ratification thereof by at least one independent director, if any.

(4) Every officer of the company **whose duty is to give notice** under this section and who fails to do so shall be liable to a penalty of twenty-five thousand rupees.

(5) A One Person Company, small company and dormant company shall be deemed to have complied with the provisions of this section if at least one meeting of the Board of Directors has been conducted in each half of a calendar year and the gap between the two meetings is not less than ninety days:

Reg 24 (3): The minutes of the meetings of the board of directors of the unlisted subsidiary shall be placed at the meeting of the board of directors of the listed entity.

Sec. 174. Quorum for meetings of Board —

(1)   The quorum for a meeting of the Board of Directors of a company hall be **one-third of its total strength or two directors,** whichever is higher, and the participation of the directors by video conferencing or by other audio visual means shall also be counted for the purposes of quorum under this sub-section.

(2)   The continuing directors may act notwithstanding any vacancy in the Board; but, if and so long as their number is reduced below the quorum fixed by the Act for a meeting of the Board, the continuing directors or director may act for the purpose of increasing the number of directors to that fixed for the quorum, or of summoning a general meeting of the company and for no other purpose.

(3)   Where at any time the number of interested directors exceeds or is equal to two-thirds of the total strength of the Board of Directors, the number of directors who are not interested directors and present at the meeting, being not less than two, shall be the quorum during such time.

Explanation — For the purposes of this sub-section, —interested director— means a director within the meaning of sub-section (2) of section 184.

(4) Where a meeting of the Board could not be held for want of quorum, then, unless the articles of the company otherwise provide, the meeting shall automatically stand adjourned to the same day at the same time and place in the next week or if that day is a national holiday, till the next succeeding day, which is not a national holiday, at the same time and place.

Reg 17 (2A) The quorum for every meeting of the board of directors of the top 2000 listed entities with effect from April 1, 2020 shall be **one-third of its total strength or three directors,** whichever is higher, including at least one independent director.

Sec 175. Passing of resolution by circulation —

(1) No resolution shall be deemed to have been duly passed by the Board or by a committee thereof by circulation, **unless** the resolution has been circulated in draft, together with the necessary papers, if any, to all the directors, or members of the committee, as the case may be, at their addresses registered with the company in India by hand delivery or by post or by courier, or through such electronic means as may be prescribed and has been approved by a majority of the directors or members, who are entitled to vote on the resolution:

Provided that, where not less than **one-third of the total number of directors** of the company for the time being require that any resolution under circulation must be decided at a meeting, the chairperson **shall put the resolution to be decided** at a meeting of the Board.

(1)   A resolution passed by circulation shall be noted at a subsequent meeting of the Board or the committee thereof, as the case may be, and made part of the minutes of such meeting.

Rule 5. A resolution in draft form may be circulated to the directors together with the necessary papers for seeking their approval, by electronic means which may include E-mail or fax.

> **Minimum Information to be placed before the Board of Directors for Listed Entities:**

Reg. 17 (7): Part A of Schedule II is as under:

A.   Annual operating plans and budgets and any updates.

B.   Capital budgets and any updates.

C.   Quarterly results for the listed entity and its operating divisions or business segments.

D.   Minutes of meetings of audit committee and other committees of the board of directors.

E.   The information on recruitment and remuneration of senior officers just below the level of board of directors, including appointment or removal of Chief Financial Officer and the Company Secretary.

F.   Show cause, demand, prosecution notices and penalty notices, which are materially important.

G.   Fatal or serious accidents, dangerous occurrences, any material effluent or pollution problems.

H.   Any material default in financial obligations to and by the listed entity, or substantial non-payment for goods sold by the listed entity.

I.   Any issue, which involves possible public or product liability claims of substantial nature, including any judgement or order which, may have passed strictures on the conduct of the listed entity or taken an adverse view regarding another enterprise that may have negative implications on the listed entity.

J.   Details of any joint venture or collaboration agreement.

K.   Transactions that involve substantial payment towards goodwill, brand equity, or intellectual property.

L.   Significant labour problems and their proposed solutions. Any significant development in Human Resources/ Industrial Relations front like signing of wage agreement, implementation of Voluntary Retirement Scheme etc.

M.   Sale of investments, subsidiaries, assets which are material in nature and not in normal course of business.

N.   Quarterly details of foreign exchange exposures and the steps taken by management to limit the risks of adverse exchange rate movement, if material.

O.   Non-compliance of any regulatory, statutory or listing requirements and shareholders service such as non-payment of dividend, delay in share transfer etc.

Reg. 17 (8) : Compliance Certificates to be Placed

The chief executive officer and the chief financial officer shall provide the compliance certificate to the board of directors as specified in **Part B of Schedule II given hereunder:**

A.   They have reviewed financial statements and the cash flow statement for the year and that to the best of their knowledge and belief:

    (1)   these statements do not contain any materially untrue statement or omit any material fact or contain statements that might be misleading;

    (2)   these statements together present a true and fair view of the listed entity's affairs and are in compliance with existing accounting standards, applicable laws and regulations.

B.   There are, to the best of their knowledge and belief, no transactions entered into by the listed entity during the year which are fraudulent, illegal or violative of the listed entity's code of conduct.

C.   They accept responsibility for establishing and maintaining internal controls for financial reporting and that they have evaluated the effectiveness of internal control systems of the listed entity pertaining to financial reporting and they have disclosed to the auditors and the audit committee, deficiencies in the design or operation of such internal controls, if any, of which they are aware and the steps they have taken or propose to take to rectify these deficiencies.

D.   They have indicated to the auditors and the Audit committee

(1)   significant changes in internal control over financial reporting during the year;

(2)   significant changes in accounting policies during the year and that the same have been disclosed in the notes to the financial statements; and

(3)   instances of significant fraud of which they have become aware and the involvement therein, if any, of the management or an employee having a significant role in the listed entity's internal control system over financial reporting.

Reg. (9)(a) The listed entity shall lay down procedures to inform members of board of directors about risk assessment and minimization procedures.

(b) The board of directors shall be responsible for framing, implementing and monitoring the risk management plan for the listed entity.

Reg. (10) The evaluation of independent directors shall be done by the entire board of directors which shall include

(a)   performance of the directors; and

(b)   fulfillment of the independence criteria as specified in these regulations and their independence from the management:

Provided that in the above evaluation, the directors who are subject to evaluation shall not participate.

Reg (11). The statement to be annexed to the notice as referred to in sub-section (1) of section 102 of the Companies Act, 2013 for each item of special business to be transacted at a general meeting shall also set forth clearly the recommendation of the board to the shareholders on each of the specific items.

B. Committees of the Board of Directors—

Sec 177. Audit Committee —

Rule 6. Committees of the Board.-

The Board of directors of every listed company and the following classes of companies shall constitute an **Audit Committee and a Nomination and Remuneration Committee of the Board-**

(i)   all public companies with a paid up capital of ten crore rupees or more;

(ii)   all public companies having turnover of one hundred crore rupees or more;

(iii)   all public companies, having in aggregate, outstanding loans or borrowings or debentures or deposits exceeding fifty crore rupees or more.

(2) The Audit Committee shall consist of a **minimum of three directors** with independent directors forming a majority:

Provided that **majority of members** of Audit Committee including its Chairperson shall be persons **with ability to read and understand, the financial statement.**

(4) Every Audit Committee shall act in accordance with the terms of reference specified in writing by the Board which shall, inter alia, include,—

(i)   the recommendation for appointment, remuneration and terms of appointment of auditors of the company;

(ii)   review and monitor the auditor's independence and performance, and effectiveness of audit process;

(iii)   examination of the financial statement and the auditors' report thereon;

(iv)   approval or any subsequent modification of transactions of the company with related parties:

Provided that the Audit Committee may make omnibus approval for related party transactions proposed to be entered into by the company subject to such conditions as may be prescribed;

(v)   scrutiny of inter-corporate loans and investments;

(vi)   valuation of undertakings or assets of the company, wherever it is necessary;

(vii)   evaluation of internal financial controls and risk management systems;

(viii)   monitoring the end use of funds raised through public offers and related matters.

(5) The Audit Committee **may call for the comments of the auditors about internal control systems,** the scope of audit, including the observations of the auditors and review of financial statement before their submission to the Board and may also discuss any related issues with the internal and statutory auditors and the management of the company.

(6) The Audit Committee shall have authority to investigate into any matter in relation to the items specified in sub-section (4) or referred to it by the Board and for this purpose shall have power

to obtain professional advice from external sources and have full access to information contained in the records of the company.

(7) The auditors of a company and the key managerial personnel shall have a right to be heard in the meetings of the Audit Committee when it considers the auditor's report but shall not have the right to vote.

(8) The Board's report under sub-section (3) of section 134 shall disclose the composition of an Audit Committee and where the Board had not accepted any recommendation of the Audit Committee, the same shall be disclosed in such report along with the reasons therefor.

(9) Every listed company or such class or classes of companies, as may be prescribed, shall establish a vigil mechanism for directors and employees to report genuine concerns in such manner as may be prescribed.

(10) **Rule 7. Establishment of vigil mechanism.**

(1)   Every listed company and the companies belonging to the following class or classes shall establish a vigil mechanism for their directors and employees to report their genuine concerns or grievances- (a) the Companies which accept deposits from the public;

(b)   the Companies which have borrowed money from banks and public financial institutions in excess of fifty crore rupees.

(2)   The companies which are required to constitute an audit committee shall oversee the vigil mechanism through the committee and if any of the members of the committee

have a conflict of interest in a given case, they should recuse themselves and the others on the committee would deal with the matter on hand.

(3)   In case of other companies, the Board of directors shall nominate a director to play the role of audit committee for the purpose of vigil mechanism to whom other directors and employees may report their concerns.

(4)   The vigil mechanism shall provide for adequate safeguards against victimisation of employees and directors who avail of the vigil mechanism and also provide for direct access to the Chairperson of the Audit Committee or the director nominated to play the role of Audit Committee, as the case may be, in exceptional cases.

(5)   In case of repeated frivolous complaints being filed by a director or an employee, the audit committee or the director nominated to play the role of audit committee may take suitable action against the concerned director or employee including reprimand.

Reg 18 of SEBI LODR, 2015: Audit Committee.

(1)   Every listed entity shall constitute a qualified and independent audit committee in accordance with the terms of reference, subject to the following:

    (a)   The audit committee shall have minimum three directors as members.

    (b)   **At least two-thirds of the members** of audit committee shall be **independent directors** and in case of a listed entity having outstanding **SR equity shares,** the audit committee **shall only comprise of independent directors**.

(c) All members of audit committee shall be financially literate and at least one member shall have accounting or related financial management expertise.

Explanation (1)

For the purpose of this regulation, "financially literate" shall mean the ability to read and understand basic financial statements i.e. balance sheet, profit and loss account, and statement of cash flows.

Explanation (2)

For the purpose of this regulation , a member shall be considered to have accounting or related financial management expertise if he or she possesses experience in finance or accounting, or requisite professional certification in accounting, or any other comparable experience or background which results in the individual's financial sophistication, including being or having been a chief executive officer, chief financial officer or other senior officer with financial oversight responsibilities.

(d) **The chairperson of the audit committee shall be an independent director** and he/she] shall be present at Annual general meeting to answer shareholder queries.

(e) The Company Secretary shall act as the secretary to the audit committee.

(f) The audit committee at its discretion shall invite the finance director or head of the finance function, head of internal audit and a representative of the statutory auditor and any other such executives to be present at the meetings of the committee:

Provided that occasionally the audit committee may meet without the presence of any executives of the listed entity.

(2)   The listed entity shall conduct the meetings of the audit committee in the following manner:

  (a)   The **audit committee shall meet at least four times in a year** and not more than one hundred and twenty days shall elapse between two meetings.

  (b)   The **quorum** for audit committee meeting shall either be **two members or one third of the members of the audit committee**, whichever is greater, **with at least two independent directors.**

  (c)   The audit committee shall have powers to investigate any activity within its terms of reference, seek information from any employee, obtain outside legal or other professional advice and secure attendance of outsiders with relevant expertise, if it considers necessary.

(3)   The role of the audit committee and the information to be reviewed by the audit committee shall be as **specified in Part C of Schedule II.**

PART C: Role of the Audit Committee and Review of information by Audit Committee

[See Regulation 18(3)]

A. The role of the audit committee shall include the following:

(1)   **oversight of the listed entity's financial reporting process** and the disclosure of its financial information to ensure that the financial statement is correct, sufficient and credible;

(2)   **recommendation for appointment, remuneration and terms of appointment** of auditors of the listed entity;

(3)   **approval of payment to statutory auditors for any other services** rendered by the statutory auditors;

(4)   reviewing, with the management, the annual financial statements and auditor's report thereon before submission to the board for approval, with particular reference to:

    (a)   matters required to be included in the **director's responsibility statement** to be included in the board's report in terms of clause (c) of sub-section (3) of Section 134 of the Companies Act, 2013;

    (b)   **changes, if any, in accounting policies and practices and reasons** for the same;

    (c)   **major accounting entries involving estimates** based on the exercise of judgment by management;

    (d)   significant **adjustments made in the financial statements** arising out of audit findings;

(e) **compliance with listing and other legal requirements** relating to financial statements;

(f) **disclosure of any related party transactions;**

(g) **modified opinion(s)** in the draft audit report;

(5) **reviewing,** with the management, **the quarterly financial statements** before submission to the board for approval;

(6) **reviewing,** with the management, the **statement of uses / application of funds** raised through an issue (public issue, rights issue, preferential issue, etc.), the statement of funds utilized for purposes other than those stated in the offer document / prospectus / notice and the **report submitted by the monitoring agency** monitoring the utilization of proceeds of a public issue or rights issue or preferential issue or qualified institutions placement, and making appropriate recommendations to the board to take up steps in this matter;

(7) **reviewing and monitoring the auditor's independence and performance,** and effectiveness of audit process;

(8) **approval or any subsequent modification of transactions** of the listed entity **with related parties;**

(9) **scrutiny of inter-corporate loans** and investments;

(10) **valuation of undertakings or assets** of the listed entity, wherever it is necessary;

(11) **evaluation of internal financial controls and risk management systems;**

(12) reviewing, with the management, **performance of statutory and internal auditors, adequacy of the internal control systems;**

(13) **reviewing the adequacy of internal audit function,** if any, including the structure of the internal audit department, staffing and seniority of the official heading the department, reporting structure coverage and frequency of internal audit;

(14) **discussion with internal auditors of any significant findings** and follow up there on;

(15) reviewing the findings of any **internal investigations by the internal auditors** into matters where there is **suspected fraud or irregularity or a failure of internal control systems** of a material nature and reporting the matter to the board;

(16) **discussion with statutory auditors** before the audit commences, about the nature and scope of audit as well as post-audit discussion **to ascertain any area of concern;**

(17) to look into the **reasons for substantial defaults in the payment to the depositors, debenture holders, shareholders** (in case of non-payment of declared dividends) and creditors;

(18) to review the **functioning of the whistle blower mechanism**

(19) **approval of appointment of chief financial officer** after assessing the qualifications, experience and background, etc. of the candidate;

(20) Carrying out **any other function** as is mentioned in the terms of reference of the audit committee.

(21) **reviewing the utilization of loans and/ or advances** from/investment by the holding company in the subsidiary exceeding rupees 100 crore or 10% of the asset size of the subsidiary, whichever is lower including existing loans / advances / investments existing as on the date of coming into force of this provision.

(22) **consider and comment on rationale, cost-benefits and impact of schemes** involving merger, demerger, amalgamation etc., on the listed entity and its shareholders.

A. The audit committee shall **mandatorily review** the following information:

(1) **management discussion and analysis of financial condition and results of** operations;

(3) management letters / letters of internal control weaknesses issued by the statutory auditors;

(4) internal audit reports **relating to internal control weaknesses; and**

(5) **the appointment, removal** and terms of remuneration of **the chief internal auditor** shall be subject to review by the audit committee.

(6) **statement of deviations:**

(a) quarterly statement of deviation(s) including report of monitoring agency, if applicable, submitted to stock exchange(s) in terms of Regulation 32(1).

(b)   annual statement of funds utilized for purposes other than those stated in the offer document/prospectus/notice in terms of Regulation 32(7).

Reg. 24(2): The audit committee of the listed entity shall also review the financial statements, in particular, the investments made by the unlisted subsidiary

Reg. 22 Vigil mechanism.

(1)   The listed entity shall formulate a vigil mechanism whistle blower policy for directors and employees to report genuine concerns.

(2)   The vigil mechanism shall provide for adequate safeguards against victimization of director(s) or employee(s) or any other person who avail the mechanism and also provide for direct access to the chairperson of the audit committee in appropriate or exceptional cases.

Sec 178. Nomination and Remuneration Committee and Stakeholders Relationship Committee —

(1)   The Board of Directors covered under Rule 7 shall constitute the Nomination and Remuneration Committee consisting of **three or more non-executive directors out of which not less than one-half shall be independent directors:**

Provided that the chairperson of the company (whether executive or non-executive) may be appointed as a member of the Nomination and Remuneration Committee but **shall not chair** such Committee.

(2)   The Nomination and Remuneration Committee shall identify persons who are qualified to become directors and who

may be appointed in senior management in accordance with the criteria laid down, recommend to the Board their appointment and removal and shall carry out evaluation of every director's performance.

(3)   The Nomination and Remuneration Committee shall formulate the criteria for determining qualifications, positive attributes and independence of a director and recommend to the Board a policy, relating to the remuneration for the directors, key managerial personnel and other employees.

(4)   The Nomination and Remuneration Committee shall, while formulating the policy ensure that—

   (a)   the level and composition of remuneration is reasonable and sufficient to attract, retain and motivate directors of the quality required to run the company successfully;

   (b)   relationship of remuneration to performance is clear and meets appropriate performance benchmarks; and

   (c)   remuneration to directors, key managerial personnel and senior management involves a balance between fixed and incentive pay reflecting short and long-term performance objectives appropriate to the working of the company and its goals: Provided that such policy shall be disclosed in the Board's report.

(5)   **The Board of Directors of a company which consists of more than one thousand shareholders, debenture-holders, deposit-holders and any other security holders at any time during a financial**

year shall constitute a Stakeholders Relationship Committee consisting of a chairperson who shall be a nonexecutive director and such other members as may be decided by the Board.

(6)   The Stakeholders Relationship Committee shall consider and resolve the grievances of security holders of the company.

(7)   The chairperson of each of the committees constituted under this section or, in his absence, any other member of the committee authorised by him in this behalf shall attend the general meetings of the company.

(8)   **In case of any contravention of the provisions of section 177 and this section, the company shall be** liable to a penalty of five lakh rupees and every officer in default shall be liable to a penalty of one lakh rupees"

Provided that non-consideration of resolution of any grievance by the Stakeholders Relationship Committee in good faith shall not constitute a contravention of this section.

Explanation —The expression —senior management— means personnel of the company who are members of its core management team excluding Board of Directors comprising all members of management one level below the executive directors, including the functional heads.

Reg 19. Nomination and remuneration committee in case of Listed Entities:

(1)   The board of directors shall constitute the nomination and remuneration committee as follows:

(a)   the committee shall **comprise of at least three directors**;

(b)   **all directors of the committee shall be non-executive directors;** and

(c)   at least **two-thirds of the directors shall be independent directors**

(2)   The **Chairperson** of the nomination and remuneration committee **shall be an independent director:**

Provided that the chairperson of the listed entity, whether executive or non-executive, may be appointed as a member of the Nomination and Remuneration Committee **and shall not chair such Committee.**

(2A)   The **quorum** for a meeting of the nomination and remuneration committee shall be **either two members or one third of the members** of the committee, whichever is greater, including **at least one independent director in attendance.**

(3)   The Chairperson of the nomination and remuneration committee may be present at the annual general meeting, to answer the shareholders' queries; however, it shall be up to the chairperson to decide who shall answer the queries.

(3A)   The nomination and remuneration committee shall meet at least once in a year.

(4)   The role of the nomination and remuneration committee shall be as specified as in Part D of the Schedule II.

PART D: Role of Committee

[See Regulation 19(4), 20(4) and 21(4)]

A. Role of Nomination and Remuneration Committee-Shall inter-alia include:

(1)   formulation of the **criteria for determining qualifications, positive attributes and independence of a director** and recommend to the board of directors a policy relating to, the remuneration of the directors, key managerial personnel and other employees;

(1A)   For every appointment of an independent director, the Nomination and Remuneration Committee shall **evaluate the balance of skills, knowledge and experience on the Board** and on the basis of such evaluation, prepare a description of the role and capabilities required of an independent director. The person recommended to the Board for appointment as an independent director shall have the capabilities identified in such description. For the purpose of identifying suitable candidates, the Committee may:

   a.   **use** the services of an **external agencies,** if required;

   b.   consider candidates from a wide range of backgrounds, having due regard to diversity; and

   c.   consider the time commitments of the candidates.

(2)   formulation of **criteria for evaluation of performance of independent directors and the board of directors;**

(3)   devising a **policy on diversity of board of directors;**

(4)   **identifying persons who are qualified to become directors** and who may be appointed in senior management in accordance with the criteria laid down, and recommend to the board of directors their appointment and removal.

(5)   **whether to extend or continue the term of appointment of the independent director,** on the basis of the report of performance evaluation of independent directors.

(6)   recommend to the board, all remuneration, in whatever form, payable to senior management.

Reg 20. Stakeholders Relationship Committee.

(1)   The listed entity shall constitute a Stakeholders Relationship Committee to specifically look into various aspects of interest of shareholders, debenture holders and other security holders.

(2)   The chairperson of this committee shall be a non-executive director.

(2A)   At least three directors, with at least one being an independent director, shall be members of the Committee and in case of a listed entity having outstanding SR equity share, at least two thirds of the Stakeholders Relationship Committee shall comprise of independent directors.

(3)   The Chairperson of the Stakeholders Relationship Committee shall be present at the annual general meetings to answer queries of the security holders.

(3A)   The stakeholders relationship committee shall meet at least once in a year.

(4)   The role of the Stakeholders Relationship Committee shall be as specified as in **Part D of the Schedule II**

B. Stakeholders Relationship Committee

The role of the committee shall inter-alia include the following:

(1)   Resolving the grievances of the security holders of the listed entity including complaints related to transfer/transmission of shares, non-receipt of annual report, non-receipt of declared dividends, issue of new/duplicate certificates, general meetings etc.

(2)   Review of measures taken for effective exercise of voting rights by shareholders.

(3)   Review of adherence to the service standards adopted by the listed entity in respect of various services being rendered by the Registrar & Share Transfer Agent.

(4)   Review of the various measures and initiatives taken by the listed entity for reducing the quantum of unclaimed dividends and ensuring timely receipt of dividend warrants/ annual reports/statutory notices by the shareholders of the company.

Reg 21. Risk Management Committee.

(1)   The board of directors **shall constitute a Risk Management Committee.**

(2)   The Risk Management Committee shall have **minimum three members with majority of them being members of the board of directors, including at least**

one independent director and in case of a listed entity having outstanding SR equity shares, at least two thirds of the Risk Management Committee shall comprise independent directors.

(3)   The **Chairperson** of the Risk management committee **shall be a member of the board of directors** and senior executives of the listed entity may be members of the committee.

(3A)   The risk management committee shall meet at least twice in a year.

(3B)   The quorum for a meeting of the Risk Management Committee shall be either two members or one third of the members of the committee, whichever is higher, including at least one member of the board of directors in attendance.

(3C)   The meetings of the risk management committee shall be conducted in such a manner that on a continuous basis not more than one hundred and eighty days shall elapse between any two consecutive meetings.

(4)   The board of directors shall define the role and responsibility of the Risk Management Committee and may delegate monitoring and reviewing of the risk management plan to the committee and such other functions as it may deem fit such function shall specifically cover cyber security.

PART D: Role of Committee {Other than Audit Committee)

[See Regulation 19(4), 20(4) and 21(4)]

C. Risk Management Committee

The role of the committee shall, Inter alia, include the following:

(1)   To formulate a detailed risk management policy which shall include:

   (a)   A framework for identification of internal and external risks specifically faced by the listed entity, in particular including financial, operational, sectoral, sustainability (particularly, ESG related risks), information, cyber security risks or any other risk as may be determined by the Committee.

   (b)   Measures for risk mitigation including systems and processes for internal control of identified risks.

   (c)   Business continuity plan.

(2)   To ensure that appropriate methodology, processes and systems are in place to monitor and evaluate risks associated with the business of the Company;

(3)   To monitor and oversee implementation of the risk management policy, including evaluating the adequacy of risk management systems;

(4)   To periodically review the risk management policy, at least once in two years, including by considering the changing industry dynamics and evolving complexity;

(5)   To keep the board of directors informed about the nature and content of its discussions, recommendations and actions to be taken;

(6)   The appointment, removal and terms of remuneration of the Chief Risk Officer (if any) shall be subject to review by the Risk Management Committee.

The Risk Management Committee shall coordinate its activities with other committees, in instances where there is any overlap with activities of such committees, as per the framework laid down by the board of directors

C. Secretarial Standard on Meetings of The Board of Directors {SS-1} {Effective April 1, 2024} {By ICSI}

1. Convening a Meeting

1.1 Authority

1.1.1   Any Director of a company may, at any time, summon a Meeting of the Board, and the Company Secretary or where there is no Company Secretary, any person authorised by the Board in this behalf, on the requisition of a Director, shall convene a Meeting of the Board, in consultation with the Chairman or in his absence, the Managing Director or in his absence, the Whole-time Director, where there is any, unless otherwise provided in the Articles.

1.1.2   The Chairman may, unless dissented to or objected by the majority of Directors present at a Meeting at which a Quorum is present, adjourn the Meeting for any reason, at any stage of the Meeting.

1.2 Day, Time, Place, Mode and Serial Number of Meeting

1.2.1   Every Meeting shall have a serial number.

1.2.2   A Meeting may be convened at any time and place, on any day.

Notice of the Meeting shall clearly mention a venue, whether registered office or otherwise, to be the venue of the Meeting and all the recordings of the proceedings of the Meeting, if conducted through Electronic Mode, shall be deemed to be made at such place.

1.2.3   Any Director may participate through Electronic Mode in a Meeting unless the Act or any other law specifically prohibits such participation through Electronic Mode in respect of any item of business. **Directors shall not participate through Electronic Mode in the discussion on restricted items unless there is a Quorum in a Meeting through physical presence of Directors.**

1.3 Notice

1.3.1 Notice in writing of every Meeting shall be given to every Director by hand or by speed post or by registered post or by facsimile or by e-mail or by any other electronic means.

The Notice shall be sent to the postal address or e-mail address, registered by the Director with the company or in the absence of such details or any change thereto, any of such addresses appearing in the Director Identification Number (DIN) registration of the Director. Where a Director specifies a particular means of delivery of Notice, the Notice shall be given to him by such means.

However, in case of a Meeting conducted at a shorter Notice, the company may choose an expedient mode of sending Notice.

Proof of sending Notice and its delivery shall be maintained by the company for such period as decided by the Board, which shall not be less than three years from the date of the Meeting.

1.3.2   Notice shall be issued by the Company Secretary or where there is no Company Secretary, any Director or any other person authorised by the Board for the purpose.

1.3.3   The Notice shall specify the serial number, day, date, time and full address of the venue of the Meeting.

1.3.4   The Notice shall inform the Directors about the option available to them to participate through Electronic Mode and provide them all the necessary information.

If a Director intends to participate through Electronic Mode, he shall give sufficient prior intimation to the Chairman or the Company Secretary to enable them to make suitable arrangements in this behalf.

The Director may intimate his intention of participation through Electronic Mode at the beginning of the Calendar Year also, which shall be valid for such Calendar Year. Such intimation shall not debar him from participation in the Meeting in person provided he gives such intimation sufficiently in advance to the company.

The Notice shall also contain the contact number or e-mail address(es) of the Chairman or the Company Secretary or any other person authorised by the Board, to whom the Director shall confirm in this regard.

In the absence of an advance communication or confirmation from the Director as above, it shall be assumed that he will attend the Meeting physically.

1.3.5   The Notice of a Meeting shall be given even if Meetings are held on pre-determined dates or at pre-determined intervals.

1.3.6   Notice convening a Meeting shall be **given at least seven days before the date of the Meeting,** unless the Articles prescribe a longer period. In case the company sends the Notice by speed post or by registered post, an additional two days shall be added for the service of Notice.

Notice of an adjourned Meeting shall be given to all Directors including those who did not attend the Meeting on the originally convened date and unless the date of adjourned Meeting is decided at the Meeting, Notice thereof shall also be given not less than seven days before the Meeting.

1.3.7   The **Agenda,** setting out the business to be transacted at the Meeting, and Notes on Agenda shall be given to the Directors **at least seven days before the date of the Meeting,** unless the Articles prescribe a longer period. Agenda and Notes on Agenda shall be sent to all Directors by hand or by speed post or by registered post or by e-mail or by any other electronic means.

These shall be sent to the postal address or e-mail address or any other electronic address registered by the Director with the company or in the absence of such details or any change thereto, to any of such addresses appearing in the Director Identification Number (DIN) registration of the Directors.

In case the company sends the Agenda and Notes on Agenda by speed post or by registered post, an additional two days shall be added for the service of Agenda and Notes on Agenda.

Where a Director specifies a particular means of delivery of Agenda and Notes on Agenda, these papers shall be sent to him by such means.

However, in case of a Meeting **conducted at a shorter Notice**, the company may choose an expedient mode of sending Agenda and Notes on Agenda.

Proof of sending Agenda and Notes on Agenda and their delivery shall be maintained by the company for such period as decided by the Board, which shall **not be less than three years** from the date of the Meeting.

The Notice, Agenda and Notes on Agenda shall be sent to the Original Director also at the address registered with the company, even if these have been sent to the Alternate Director.

However, the mode of sending Notice, Agenda and Notes on Agenda to the Original Director shall be decided by the company.

Notes on items of business which are in the nature of Unpublished Price Sensitive Information may be given at a shorter period of time than stated above, with the consent of a majority of the Directors, which shall include at least one Independent Director, if any.

For this purpose, "Unpublished Price Sensitive Information" means any information, relating to a company or its securities, directly or indirectly, that is not generally available, which upon becoming generally available, is likely to materially affect the price of the securities and shall, ordinarily including but not restricted to, information relating to the following: –

(i)   financial results;

(ii)   dividends;

(iii)   change in capital structure;

(iv)   mergers, de-mergers, acquisitions, de-listing, disposals and expansion of business and such other transactions; and

(v)   changes in key managerial personnel*.

General consent for giving Notes on items of Agenda which are in the nature of Unpublished Price Sensitive Information at a shorter Notice **may be taken in the first Meeting** of the Board held in each financial year and also whenever there is any change in Directors.

Where general consent as above has not been taken, the requisite consent shall be taken before the concerned items are taken up for consideration at the Meeting.

The fact of consent having been taken shall be recorded in the Minutes.

Supplementary Notes on any of the Agenda Items may be circulated at or prior to the Meeting but shall be taken up with the permission of the Chairman and with the consent of a majority of the Directors present in the Meeting, which shall include at least one Independent Director, if any.

1.3.8 **Each item of business requiring approval at the Meeting shall be supported by a note** setting out the details of the proposal, relevant material facts that enable the Directors to understand the meaning, scope and implications of the proposal and the nature of concern or interest, if any, of any Director in the proposal, which the Director had earlier disclosed.

Where approval by means of a Resolution is required, the draft of such Resolution shall be either set out in the note or placed at the Meeting.

However, any other decision taken at the Meeting may also be recorded in the Minutes in the form of Resolution.

The items of business that are required by the Act or any other applicable law to be considered at a Meeting of the Board shall be placed before the Board at its Meeting.

An illustrative list of such items is given at Annexure 'A'. There are certain items which shall be placed before the Board at its first Meeting. An illustrative list thereof is given at Annexure 'B'.

Annexure 'A' (Paragraph 1.3.8)

Illustrative list of items of business which shall not be passed by circulation and shall be placed before the Board at its Meeting.

General Business Items

- Noting Minutes of Meetings of Audit Committee and other Committees.

- Approving financial statements and the Board's Report.

- Considering the Compliance Certificate to ensure compliance with the provisions of all the laws applicable to the company.

- Specifying list of laws applicable specifically to the company.

- Appointment of Secretarial Auditors and Internal Auditors.

Specific Items

- Borrowing money otherwise than by issue of debentures.

- Investing the funds of the company.

- Granting loans or giving guarantee or providing security in respect of loans.

- Making political contributions.

- Making calls on shareholders in respect of money unpaid on their shares.

- Approving Remuneration of Managing Director, Whole-time Director and Manager.

- Appointment or Removal of Key Managerial Personnel.

- Appointment of a person as a Managing Director / Manager in more than one company.

- Appointment of Director(s) in casual vacancy subject to the provisions in the Articles of the company. To be subsequently approved in the immediate next general meeting.

- According sanction for related party transactions which are not in the ordinary course of business or which are not on arm's length basis.

- Sale of subsidiaries.

- Purchase and Sale of material tangible/intangible assets not in the ordinary course of business.

- Approve Payment to Director for loss of office.

- Items arising out of separate Meeting of the Independent Directors if so decided by the Independent Directors.

Corporate Actions

- Authorise Buy Back of Securities.

- Issue of securities, including debentures, whether in or outside India.

- Approving amalgamation, merger or reconstruction.

- Diversify the business.

- Takeover another company or acquiring controlling or substantial stake in another company.

Additional List of Items in case of Listed Companies

- Approving Annual operating plans and budgets.

- Capital budgets and any updates.

- Information on remuneration of Key Managerial Personnel.

- Show cause, demand, prosecution notices and penalty notices which are materially important.

- Fatal or serious accidents, dangerous occurrences, any material effluent or pollution problems.

- Any material default in financial obligations to and by the company, or substantial non-payment for goods sold by the company.

- Any issue, which involves possible public or product liability claims of substantial nature, including any judgement or order which, may have passed strictures on the conduct of the company or taken an adverse view regarding another enterprise that can have negative implications on the company.

- Details of any joint venture or collaboration agreement.

- Transactions that involve substantial payment towards goodwill, brand equity, or intellectual property.

- Significant labour problems and their proposed solutions. Any significant development in Human Resources/ Industrial Relations front like signing of wage agreement, implementation of Voluntary Retirement Scheme etc.

- Quarterly details of foreign exchange exposures and the steps taken by management to limit the risks of adverse exchange rate movement, if material.

- Non-compliance of any regulatory, statutory or listing requirements and shareholder services such as non-payment of dividend, delay in share transfer etc.

Annexure 'B' (Paragraph 1.3.8)

Illustrative list of items of business for the Agenda for the First Meeting of the Board of the company

1. To appoint the Chairman of the Meeting.

2. To note the Certificate of Incorporation of the company, issued by the Registrar of Companies.

3. To take note of the Memorandum and Articles of Association of the company, as registered.

4.   To note the situation of the Registered Office of the company and ratify the registered document of the title of the premises of the registered office in the name of the company or a Notarised copy of lease / rent agreement in the name of the company.

5.   To note the first Directors of the company.

6.   To read and record the Notices of disclosure of interest given by the Directors.

7.   To consider appointment of Additional Directors.

8.   To consider appointment of the Chairman of the Board.

9.   To consider appointment of the first Auditors.

10.   To adopt the Common Seal of the company, if any.

11.   To appoint Bankers and to open bank accounts of the company.

12.   To authorise printing of share certificates and correspondence with the depositories, if any.

13.   To authorise the issue of share certificates to the subscribers to the Memorandum and Articles of Association of the company.

14.   To approve and ratify preliminary expenses and preliminary agreements.

15.   To approve the appointment of the Key Managerial Personnel, if applicable and other senior officers.

1.3.9 Each item of business to be taken up at the Meeting shall be serially numbered. Numbering shall be in a manner which would enable ease of reference or cross-reference.

1.3.10 Any item not included in the Agenda may be taken up for consideration with the permission of the Chairman and with the consent of a majority of the Directors present in the Meeting.

The decision taken in respect of any other item shall be final only on its ratification by a majority of the Directors of the company, unless such item was approved at the Meeting itself by a majority of Directors of the company.

1.3.11 To transact urgent business, the Notice, Agenda and Notes on Agenda may be given at **shorter period of** time than stated above, if **at least one Independent Director, if any, shall be present** at such Meeting.

If no Independent Director is present, decisions taken at such a Meeting shall be circulated to all the Directors and shall be final only on ratification thereof by at least one Independent Director, if any. In case the company does not have an Independent Director, the decisions shall be final only on ratification thereof by a majority of the Directors of the company, unless such decisions were approved at the Meeting itself by a majority of Directors of the company.

The fact that the Meeting is being held at a shorter Notice shall be stated in the Notice.

2. Frequency of Meetings

2.1 Meetings of the Board

The company shall hold **at least four Meetings of its Board in each Calendar Year** with a maximum **interval of one hundred and twenty days** between any two consecutive Meetings.

The company shall hold **first Meeting of its Board within thirty days of the date of incorporation**. It shall be sufficient if subsequent Meetings are held with a maximum interval of one hundred and twenty days between any two consecutive Meetings.

Further, it shall be sufficient if a **One Person Company, Small Company, Dormant Company or private company** which is recognised as start-up holds **one Meeting of the Board in each half of a Calendar Year** and the gap between the two Meetings of the Board is **not less than ninety days**.

An adjourned Meeting being a continuation of the original Meeting, the interval period in such a case, shall be counted from the date of the original Meeting.

For the purposes of this Standard, the term "start-up" means a private company incorporated under the Act and recognised as start-up in accordance with the notification issued by the Department for Promotion of Industry and Internal Trade, Ministry of Commerce and Industry, Government of India.

2.2 Meetings of Committees

Committees shall meet as often as necessary subject to the minimum number and frequency prescribed by any law or any authority or as stipulated by the Board.

2.3 Meeting of Independent Directors

Where a company is required to appoint Independent Directors under the Act, such Independent Directors shall hold **at least one Meeting in a financial year without attendance of Non-Independent Directors and members of management.**

The Meeting shall be held to review the performance of Non-Independent Directors and the Board as a whole; to review the performance of the Chairman and to assess the quality, quantity and timeliness of flow of information between the company management and the Board and its members that is necessary for the Board to effectively and reasonably perform their duties.

The Company Secretary, wherever appointed, shall facilitate convening and holding of such Meeting, if so desired by the Independent Directors.

3. Quorum

3.1   **Quorum shall be present throughout the Meeting.** Quorum shall be present not only at the time of commencement of the Meeting but also while transacting business.

3.2   **A Director shall neither be reckoned for Quorum nor shall be entitled to participate in respect of an item of business in which he is interested.**

However, in case of a private company, a Director shall be reckoned for Quorum and entitled to participate in respect of such item after disclosure of his interest.

For this purpose, a Director shall be treated as interested in a contract or arrangement entered into or proposed to be entered into by the company:

(a)   with any, body corporate, if **such Director, along with other Directors holds more than two**

> percent of the paid-up share capital of that body corporate, or he is a promoter, or manager or chief executive officer of that body corporate; or

(b) **with a firm or other entity, if such Director is a partner, owner or Member,** as the case may be, of that firm or other entity.

If the item of business is a related party transaction, then he shall not be present at the Meeting, whether physically or through Electronic Mode, during discussions and voting on such item.

3.3 Directors participating through Electronic Mode in a Meeting shall be counted for the purpose of Quorum, except for restricted items in which Quorum shall be ascertained on the basis of physical presence of Directors.

3.4 Meetings of the Board

3.4.1 **The Quorum for a Meeting of the Board shall be one-third of the total strength** of the Board, or two Directors, whichever is higher. Any fraction contained in the above one-third shall be rounded off to the next one.

Where the Quorum requirement provided in the Articles is higher than one-third of the total strength, the company shall conform to such higher requirement. **Total strength for this purpose, shall not include Directors whose places are vacant.**

If the number of Interested Directors exceeds or is equal to two-thirds of the total strength, the remaining Directors

present at the Meeting, being not less than two, shall be the Quorum during such item.

If a Meeting of the Board could not be held for want of Quorum, then, unless otherwise provided in the Articles, **the Meeting shall automatically stand adjourned to the same day in the next week, at the same time and place** or, if that day is a National Holiday, to the next succeeding day which is not a National Holiday, at the same time and place.

If there is no Quorum at the adjourned Meeting also, the Meeting shall stand cancelled.

3.4.2   Where the number of Directors is reduced below the minimum fixed by the Articles, no business shall be transacted unless the number is first made up by the remaining Director(s) or through a General Meeting. If the number of Directors is reduced below the Quorum fixed by the Act for a Meeting of the Board, the continuing Directors may act for the purpose of increasing the number of Directors to that fixed for the Quorum or of summoning a general meeting of the company, **and for no other purpose.**

3.5 Meetings of Committees

Unless otherwise stipulated in the Act or the Articles or under any other law, the Quorum for Meetings of any Committee constituted by the Board shall be as specified by the Board.

If no such Quorum is specified, the presence of all the members of any such Committee is necessary to form the Quorum.

Regulations framed under any other law may contain provisions for the Quorum of a Committee and such stipulations shall be followed.

4. Attendance at Meetings

4.1 Attendance register

4.1.1 **Every company shall maintain attendance register for the Meetings of the Board and Meetings of the Committee. The pages of the attendance register shall be serially numbered. If an attendance register is maintained in loose-leaf form, it shall be bound periodically, at least once in every three years.**

4.1.2 The attendance register shall contain the following particulars: **serial number and date of the Meeting; in case of a Committee Meeting name of the Committee; place of the Meeting; time of the Meeting; names and signatures of the Directors, the Company Secretary and also of persons attending the Meeting by invitation and their mode of presence, if participating through Electronic Mode.**

4.1.3 **The attendance register shall be deemed to have been signed by the Directors participating through Electronic Mode, if their attendance is recorded in the attendance register and authenticated by the Company Secretary or where there is no Company Secretary, by the Chairman or by any other Director present at the Meeting,** if so authorised by the Chairman and the fact of such participation is also recorded in the Minutes.

In case of Directors participating through Electronic Mode, the Chairman shall confirm the attendance of such Directors. For this purpose, at the commencement of the Meeting, the Chairman shall take a roll call. The Chairman or Company Secretary shall request the Director participating through Electronic Mode to state his full name and location from where he is participating and shall record the same in the Minutes.

The proceedings of such Meetings shall be recorded through any electronic recording mechanism and the details of the venue, date and time shall be mentioned.

4.1.4   The attendance register shall be maintained at the Registered Office of the company or such other place as may be approved by the Board. The attendance register may be taken to any place where a Meeting of the Board or Committee is held.

4.1.5   The attendance register is open for inspection by the Directors. Even after a person ceases to be a Director, he shall be entitled to inspect the attendance register of the Meetings held during the period of his Directorship.

The Company Secretary in Practice appointed by the company or the Secretarial Auditor or the Statutory Auditor of the company can also inspect the attendance register as he may consider necessary for the performance of his duties. **A Member of the company is not entitled to inspect the attendance register.**

4.1.6   **The attendance register shall be preserved for a period of at least eight financial years from the date of last entry made therein and may be destroyed thereafter with the approval of the Board.**

4.1.7   The attendance register shall be in the custody of the Company Secretary. Where there is no Company Secretary, the attendance register shall be in the custody of any other person authorised by the Board for this purpose.

4.2 Leave of absence shall be granted to a Director only when a request for such leave has been communicated to the Company Secretary or to the Chairman or to any other person authorised by the Board to issue Notice of the Meeting.

> **The office of a Director shall become vacant in case the Director absents himself from all the Meetings of the Board held during a period of twelve months with or without seeking leave of absence of the Board.**

5. Chairman

5.1 Meetings of the Board

5.1.1   The Chairman of the company shall be the Chairman of the Board.

If the company does not have a Chairman, the Directors may elect one of themselves to be the Chairman of the Board.

5.1.2   **The Chairman of the Board shall conduct the Meetings of the Board.**

If no such Chairman is elected or if the Chairman is unable to attend the, the Directors present at the Meeting shall elect one of themselves to chair and conduct the Meeting, unless otherwise provided in the Articles.

> **It would be the duty of the Chairman to check, with the assistance of Company Secretary, that the Meeting**

is duly convened and constituted in accordance with the Act or any other applicable guidelines, Rules and Regulations before proceeding to transact business.

The Chairman shall then conduct the Meeting.

The Chairman shall encourage deliberations and debate and assess the sense of the Meeting. If the Chairman is interested in an item of business, he shall entrust the conduct of the proceedings in respect of such item to any NonInterested Director, with the consent of the majority of Directors present, and resume the chair after that item of business has been transacted.

However, in case of a private company, the Chairman may continue to chair, be reckoned for quorum and entitled to participate in respect of such item after disclosure of his interest.

If the item of business is a related party transaction, the Chairman shall not be present at the Meeting, whether physically or through Electronic Mode, during discussions and voting on such item.

In case some of the Directors participate through Electronic Mode, the Chairman and the Company Secretary shall take due and reasonable care to safeguard the integrity of the Meeting by ensuring sufficient security and identification procedures to record proceedings and safe keeping of the recordings.

No person other than the Director concerned shall be allowed access to the proceedings of the Meeting where Director(s) participate through Electronic Mode, except a Director who is differently abled, provided such Director requests the Board to allow a person to accompany him and ensures that such person maintains confidentiality of the matters discussed at the Meeting.

The Chairman shall ensure that the required Quorum is present throughout the Meeting and at the end of discussion on each agenda item the Chairman shall announce the summary of the decision taken thereon.

Unless otherwise provided in the Articles, in case of an equality of votes, the Chairman shall have a second or casting vote.

5.2 Meetings of Committees

A member of the Committee appointed by the Board or elected by the Committee as Chairman of the Committee, in accordance with the Act or any other law or the Articles, shall conduct the Meetings of the Committee.

If no Chairman has been so elected or if the elected Chairman is unable to attend the Meeting, the Committee shall elect one of its members present to chair and conduct the Meeting of the Committee, unless otherwise provided in the Articles.

6. Passing of Resolution by Circulation

The Act requires certain business to be approved only at Meetings of the Board.

However, other business that requires urgent decisions can be approved by means of Resolutions passed by circulation.

Resolutions passed by circulation are deemed to be passed at a duly convened Meeting of the Board and have equal authority.

6.1 Authority

6.1.1 The Chairman of the Board or in his absence, the Managing Director or in their absence, any Director other than an Interested Director, shall decide, before the draft Resolution is circulated to all the Directors, whether the approval of the Board for a particular business shall be obtained by means of a Resolution by circulation.

An illustrative list of items which shall be placed before the Board at its Meeting and shall not be passed by circulation is given at Annexure 'A'.

6.1.2 Where not less than one-third of the total number of Directors for the time being require the Resolution under circulation to be decided at a Meeting, the Chairman shall put the Resolution for consideration at a Meeting of the Board. Interested Directors shall not be excluded for the purpose of determining the above one-third of the total number of Directors.

6.2 Procedure

6.2.1 A Resolution proposed to be passed by circulation shall be sent in draft, together with the necessary papers, to all the Directors **including Interested Directors on the same day.**

6.2.2   The draft of the Resolution to be passed and the necessary papers shall be circulated amongst the Directors by hand, or by speed post or by registered post or by courier, or by e-mail or by any other recognised electronic means.

The draft of the Resolution and the necessary papers shall be sent to the postal address or e-mail address registered by the Director with the company or in the absence of such details or any change thereto, any of the addresses appearing in the Director Identification Number (DIN) registration of the Director.

Proof of sending and delivery of the draft of the Resolution and the necessary papers shall be maintained by the company for such period as decided by the Board, which shall not be less than three years from the date of circulation of such Resolution.

6.2.3   Each business proposed to be passed by way of Resolution by circulation shall be explained by a note setting out the details of the proposal, relevant material facts that enable the Directors to understand the meaning, scope and implications of the proposal, the nature of concern or interest, if any, of any Director in the proposal, which the Director had earlier disclosed and the draft of the Resolution proposed. The note shall also indicate how a Director shall signify assent or dissent to the Resolution proposed and the date by which the Director shall respond. Each Resolution shall be separately explained. The decision of the Directors shall be sought for each Resolution separately.

Not more than seven days from the date of circulation of the draft of the Resolution shall be given to the Directors

to respond and the last date shall be computed accordingly. An additional two days shall be added for the service of the draft Resolution, in case the same has been sent by the company by speed post or by registered post or by courier.

6.3 Approval

6.3.1 The Resolution is passed when it is approved by a majority of the Directors entitled to vote on the Resolution, unless not less than one-third of the total number of Directors for the time being require the Resolution under circulation to be decided at a Meeting.

Every such Resolution shall carry a serial number.

If any special majority or the affirmative vote of any particular Director or Directors is specified in the Articles, the Resolution shall be passed only with the assent of such special majority or such affirmative vote.

An Interested Director shall not be entitled to vote.

For this purpose, a Director shall be treated as interested in a contract or arrangement entered or proposed to be entered into by the company:

(a)   with any, body corporate, if such Director, along with other Directors holds more than two percent of the paid-up share capital of that body corporate, or he is a promoter, or manager or chief executive officer of that body corporate; or

(b)   with a firm or other entity, if such Director is a partner, owner or Member, as the case may be, of that firm or other entity.

6.3.2 The Resolution, if passed, shall be deemed to have been passed on the earlier of:

(a)   the last date specified for signifying assent or dissent by the Directors, or

(b)   the date on which assent has been received from the required majority, provided that on that date the number of Directors, who have not yet responded on the resolution under circulation, along with the Directors who have expressed their desire that the resolution under circulation be decided at a Meeting of the Board, shall not be one third or more of the total number of Directors; and shall be effective from that date, if no other effective date is specified in such Resolution.

Directors shall signify their assent or dissent by signing the Resolution to be passed by circulation or by e-mail or any other electronic means.

Directors shall append the date on which they have signed the Resolution.

In case a Director does not append a date, the date of receipt by the company of the signed Resolution shall be taken as the date of signing.

In cases where the interest of a Director is yet to be communicated to the company, the concerned Director shall disclose his interest before the last date specified for the response and abstain from voting.

In case not less than one-third of the Directors wish the matter to be discussed and decided at a Meeting, each of the concerned Directors shall communicate the same before the last date specified for the response.

In case the Director does not respond on or before the last date specified for signifying assent or dissent, it shall be presumed that the Director has abstained from voting.

If the approval of the majority of Directors entitled to vote is not received by the last date specified for receipt of such approval, the Resolution shall be considered as not passed.

6.4 Recording Resolutions passed by circulation shall be noted at a subsequent Meeting of the Board and the text thereof with dissent or abstention, if any, shall be recorded in the Minutes of such Meeting.

6.5 Validity

Passing of Resolution by circulation shall be considered valid as if it had been passed at a duly convened Meeting of the Board.

This shall not dispense with the requirement for the Board to meet at the specified frequency.

7. Minutes

Every company shall keep Minutes of all Board and Committee Meetings in a Minutes Book.

Minutes kept in accordance with the provisions of the Act evidence the proceedings recorded therein.

Minutes help in understanding the deliberations and decisions taken at the Meeting.

7.1 Maintenance of Minutes

7.1.1   Minutes shall be recorded in books maintained for that purpose.

7.1.2 A distinct Minutes Book shall be maintained for Meetings of the Board and each of its Committees.

7.1.3 A company may maintain its Minutes in physical or in electronic form.

Minutes may be maintained in electronic form in such manner as prescribed under the Act and as may be decided by the Board.

Minutes in electronic form shall be maintained with Timestamp.

A company shall however follow a uniform and consistent form of maintaining the Minutes.

Any deviation in such form of maintenance shall be authorised by the Board.

7.1.4 The pages of the Minutes Books shall be consecutively numbered. This shall be followed irrespective of a break in the Book arising out of periodical binding in case the Minutes are maintained in physical form. This shall be equally applicable for maintenance of Minutes Book in electronic form with Timestamp.

In the event any page or part thereof in the Minutes Book is left blank, it shall be scored out and initialed by the Chairman who signs the Minutes.

7.1.5 Minutes shall not be pasted or attached to the Minutes Book, or tampered with in any manner.

7.1.6 Minutes Books, if maintained in loose-leaf form, shall be bound periodically depending on the size and volume and coinciding with one or more financial years of the company. There shall be a proper locking device to ensure security and proper control to prevent removal or manipulation of the loose leaves.

7.1.7 Minutes Books shall be kept at the Registered Office of the company or at such other place as may be approved by the Board.

7.2 Contents of Minutes

7.2.1 General Contents

7.2.1.1 Minutes shall state, at the beginning the serial number and type of the Meeting, name of the company, day, date, venue and time of commencement of the Meeting.

In respect of a Meeting adjourned for want of Quorum, a statement to that effect by the Chairman or in his absence, by any other Director present at the Meeting shall be recorded in the Minutes.

7.2.1.2 Minutes shall record the names of the Directors present physically or through Electronic Mode, the

Company Secretary who is in attendance at the Meeting and Invitees, if any, including Invitees for specific items. The names of the Directors shall be listed in alphabetical order or in any other logical manner, but in either case starting with the name of the person in the Chair.

The capacity in which an Invitee attends the Meeting and where applicable, the name of the entity such Invitee represents and the relation, if any, of that entity to the company shall also be recorded.

7.2.1.3 Minutes shall contain a record of all appointments made at the Meeting. Where the Minutes have been kept in accordance with the Act and all appointments have been recorded, then until the contrary is proved, all appointments of Directors, First Auditors, Key Managerial Personnel, Secretarial Auditors, Internal Auditors and Cost Auditors, shall be deemed to have been duly approved by the Board.

7.2.2 Specific Contents

7.2.2.1 Minutes shall inter-alia contain:

(a)   The name(s) of Directors present and their mode of attendance, if through Electronic Mode.

(b)   In case of a Director participating through Electronic Mode, his particulars, the location from where he participated and wherever required, his consent to sign the statutory registers placed at the Meeting.

(c)   The name of Company Secretary who is in attendance and Invitees, if any, for specific items and mode of their attendance if through Electronic Mode.

(d)   Record of election, if any, of the Chairman of the Meeting.

(e)   Record of presence of Quorum.

(f)   The names of Directors who sought and were granted leave of absence.

(g)   Noting of the Minutes of the preceding Meeting.

(h)   Noting the Minutes of the Meetings of the Committees.

(i)   The text of the Resolution(s) passed by circulation since the last Meeting, including dissent or abstention, if any.

(j)   The fact that an Interested Director did not participate in the discussions and did not vote on item of business in which he was interested and in case of a related party transaction such director was not present in the meeting during discussions and voting on such item.

(k)   The views of the Directors particularly the Independent Director, if specifically insisted upon by such Directors, provided these, in the opinion of the Chairman, are not defamatory of any person, not irrelevant or immaterial to the proceedings or not detrimental to the interests of the company.

(l)   If any Director has participated only for a part of the Meeting, the Agenda items in which he did not participate.

(m)   The fact of the dissent and the name of the Director who dissented from the Resolution or abstained from voting thereon.

(n)   Ratification by Independent Director or majority of Directors, as the case may be, in case of Meetings held at a shorter Notice.

(o)   Consideration of any item other than those included in the Agenda with the consent of majority of the Directors present at the Meeting and ratification of the decision taken in respect of such item by a majority of Directors of the company.

(p)   The time of commencement and conclusion of the Meeting.

7.2.2.2 Apart from the Resolution or the decision, Minutes shall mention the brief background of all proposals and summarise the deliberations thereof.

In case of major decisions, the rationale thereof shall also be mentioned. The decisions shall be recorded in the form of Resolutions, where it is statutorily or otherwise required.

In other cases, the decisions can be recorded in a narrative form.

Where a Resolution was passed pursuant to the Chairman of the Meeting exercising his second or casting vote, the Minutes shall record such fact.

7.3 Recording of Minutes

7.3.1 Minutes shall contain a fair and correct summary of the proceedings of the Meeting. The Company Secretary shall record the proceedings of the Meetings.

Where there is no Company Secretary, any other person duly authorised by the Board or by the Chairman in this behalf shall record the proceedings.

The Chairman shall ensure that the proceedings of the Meeting are correctly recorded.

The Chairman has absolute discretion to exclude from the Minutes, matters which in his opinion are or could reasonably be regarded as defamatory of any person, irrelevant or immaterial to the proceedings or which are detrimental to the interests of the company.

7.3.2 Minutes shall be written in clear, concise and plain language. Minutes shall be written in third person and past tense. Resolutions shall however be written in present tense.

Minutes need not be an exact transcript of the proceedings at the Meeting.

In case any Director requires his views or opinion on a particular item to be recorded verbatim in the Minutes, the decision of the Chairman whether or not to do so shall be final.

7.3.3 Wherever the decision of the Board is based on any unsigned documents including reports or notes or presentations tabled or presented at the Meeting, which were not part of the Notes on Agenda and are referred to in the Minutes, shall be identified by initialing of such documents by the Company Secretary or the Chairman.

7.3.4 Where any earlier Resolution(s) or decision is superseded or modified, Minutes shall contain a specific reference to such earlier Resolution(s) or decision or state that the Resolution is in supersession of all earlier Resolutions passed in that regard.

7.3.5 Minutes of the preceding Meeting shall be noted at a Meeting of the Board held immediately following the date of entry of such Minutes in the Minutes Book.

Minutes of the Meetings of any Committee shall be noted at a Meeting of the Board held immediately following the date of entry of such Minutes in the Minutes Book.

7.4   Finalisation of Minutes

Within fifteen days from the date of the conclusion of the Meeting of the Board or the Committee, the draft Minutes thereof shall be circulated by hand or by speed post or by registered post or by courier or by e-mail or by any other recognised electronic means to all the members of the Board or the Committee, as on the date of the Meeting, for their comments.

Where a Director specifies a particular means of delivery of draft Minutes, these shall be sent to him by such means.

Proof of sending draft Minutes and its delivery shall be maintained by the company for such period as decided by the Board, which shall not be less than three years from the date of the Meeting.

The Directors, whether present at the Meeting or not, shall communicate their comments, if any, in writing on the draft Minutes within seven days from the date of

circulation thereof, so that the Minutes are finalised and entered in the Minutes Book within the specified time limit of thirty days.

If any Director communicates his comments after the expiry of the said period of seven days, the Chairman, if so authorised by the Board, shall have the discretion to consider such comments.

In the event a Director does not comment on the draft Minutes, the draft Minutes shall be deemed to have been approved by such Director.

A Director, who ceases to be a Director after a Meeting of the Board is entitled to receive the draft Minutes of that particular Meeting and to offer comments thereon, irrespective of whether he attended such Meeting or not.

7.5 Entry in the Minutes Book

7.5.1 Minutes shall be entered in the Minutes Book within thirty days from the date of conclusion of the Meeting.

In case a Meeting is adjourned, the Minutes in respect of the original Meeting as well as the adjourned Meeting shall be entered in the Minutes Book within thirty days from the date of the respective Meetings.

7.5.2 The date of entry of the Minutes in the Minutes Book shall be recorded by the Company Secretary. Where there is no Company Secretary, it shall be entered by any other person duly authorised by the Board or by the Chairman.

7.5.3 Minutes, once entered in the Minutes Book, shall not be altered. Any alteration in the Minutes as entered shall be made only by way of express approval of the Board at its subsequent Meeting at which the Minutes are noted by the Board and the fact of such alteration shall be recorded in the Minutes of such subsequent Meeting.

7.6 Signing and Dating of Minutes

7.6.1 Minutes of the Meeting of the Board shall be signed and dated by the Chairman of the Meeting or by the Chairman of the next Meeting. Minutes of the previous Meeting may be signed either by the Chairman of such Meeting at any time before the next Meeting is held or by the Chairman of the next Meeting at the next Meeting.

7.6.2 The Chairman shall initial each page of the Minutes, sign the last page and append to such signature the date on which and the place where he has signed the Minutes. Any blank space in a page between the conclusion of the Minutes and signature of the Chairman shall be scored out. If the Minutes are maintained in electronic form, the Chairman shall sign the Minutes digitally.

7.6.3 Minutes, once signed by the Chairman, shall not be altered, save as mentioned in this Standard.

7.6.4 Within fifteen days of signing of the Minutes, a copy of the said signed Minutes, certified by the Company Secretary or where there is no Company Secretary

by any Director authorised by the Board, shall be circulated to all the Directors, as on the date of the Meeting and appointed thereafter, except to those Directors who have waived their right to receive the same either in writing or such waiver is recorded in the Minutes. Proof of sending signed Minutes and its delivery shall be maintained by the company for such period as decided by the Board, which shall not be less than three years from the date of the Meeting.

7.7 Inspection and Extracts of Minutes

7.7.1 The Minutes of Meetings of the Board and any Committee thereof can be inspected by the Directors. **A Director is entitled to inspect the Minutes of a Meeting held before the period of his Directorship. A Director is entitled to inspect the Minutes of the Meetings held during the period of his Directorship, even after he ceases to be a Director.**

The Company Secretary in Practice appointed by the company, the Secretarial Auditor, the Statutory Auditor, the Cost Auditor or the Internal Auditor of the company can inspect the Minutes as he may consider necessary for the performance of his duties. Inspection of Minutes Book may be provided in physical or in electronic form.

While providing inspection of Minutes Book, the Company Secretary or the official of the company authorised by the Company Secretary to facilitate inspection shall take all precautions to ensure that the Minutes Book is not mutilated or in any way tampered with by the person inspecting.

A Member of the company is not entitled to inspect the Minutes of Meetings of the Board.

7.7.2 Extracts of the Minutes shall be given only after the Minutes have been duly entered in the Minutes Book.

However, certified copies of any Resolution passed at a Meeting may be issued even earlier, if the text of that Resolution had been placed at the Meeting.

- A Director is entitled to receive, a copy of the Minutes of a Meeting held before the period of his Directorship.

- A Director is entitled to receive a copy of the signed Minutes of a Meeting held during the period of his Directorship, even if he ceases to be a Director.

- Extracts of the duly signed Minutes may be provided in physical or electronic form.

8. Preservation of Minutes and other Records

8.1   Minutes of all Meetings shall be preserved permanently in physical or in electronic form with Timestamp.

Where, under a scheme of arrangement, a company has been merged or amalgamated with another company, Minutes of all Meetings of the transferor company, as handed over to the transferee company, shall be preserved permanently by the transferee company, notwithstanding that the transferor company might have been dissolved.

8.2   Office copies of Notices, Agenda, Notes on Agenda and other related papers shall be preserved in good

order in physical or in electronic form for as long as they remain current or for eight financial years, whichever is later and may be destroyed thereafter with the approval of the Board.

Office copies of Notices, Agenda, Notes on Agenda and other related papers of the transferor company, as handed over to the transferee company, shall be preserved in good order in physical or electronic form for as long as they remain current or for eight financial years, whichever is later and may be destroyed thereafter with the approval of the Board and permission of the Central Government, where applicable.

8.3 **Minutes Books shall be in the custody** of the Company Secretary. Where there is no Company Secretary, Minutes Books shall be in the custody of any Director duly authorised for the purpose by the Board.

9. Disclosure The Report of the Board of Directors shall include a statement on compliances of applicable Secretarial Standards.

D. {Recommendatory} SECRETARIAL STANDARD ON REPORT OF THE BOARD OF DIRECTORS {SS-4} BY ICSI

Introduction

The Companies Act, 2013, requires the Board of Directors of **every company** to attach its report to the financial statements to be laid before the members at the annual general meeting.

The Board's Report is an important means of communication by the Board of Directors of a company with its stakeholders.

The Board's Report provides the stakeholders with both financial and non-financial information, including the performance and prospects of the company, relevant changes in the management and capital structure, recommendations as to the distribution of profits, future and on-going programmes of expansion, modernisation and diversification, capitalisation of reserves, further issue of capital and other relevant information.

The Companies Act, 2013, mandates certain disclosures to be made in the Board's Report.

A listed company is also required to comply with certain additional requirements as stated under the Securities and Exchange Board of India (Listing Obligations and Disclosure Requirements) Regulations, 2015. Similarly, a company, whose securities are listed on an overseas stock exchange, is required to comply with additional requirements as may be specified by such stock exchange. Further, a company which is regulated under other laws, may also be required to make additional disclosures in its Board's Report as stated in the respective applicable laws.

The Board's Report should be based on **the company's standalone financial statement and not on the consolidated financial statement and should relate to the financial year** for which such financial statement is prepared.

The Board's Report should avoid repetition of information. If any information is mentioned elsewhere in the financial statement, a reference thereof should be given in Board's Report instead of repeating the same.

Scope

This Standard prescribes a set of principles for making disclosures in the Report of the Board of Directors of a company and matters related thereto.

In case, a particular disclosure which is required to be made as per this Standard is not applicable to a particular company, the company need not disclose the same in the Board's Report except where the Standard requires specific disclosure in this respect.

The Board's Report of a One Person Company (OPC) and Small Company shall be prepared in the abridged form as prescribed by the Central Government.

This Standard is in conformity with the provisions of the Act. However, if due to subsequent changes in the Act, any part of this Standard becomes inconsistent with the Act, the provisions of the Act shall prevail.

Adherence to this Standard is recommendatory.

Definitions

- ➢ **"Act"** means the Companies Act, 2013 (Act No. 18 of 2013) or any previous enactment thereof, or any statutory modification thereto or reenactment thereof and includes any Rules and Regulations framed thereunder.

- ➢ **"Committee"** means a Committee of Directors mandatorily required to be constituted by the Board under the Act.

- ➢ **"Listing Regulations"** means SEBI (Listing Obligations and Disclosure Requirements) Regulations, 2015, including any amendment thereto.

> **"Report"** means Board's Report or the Report of the Board of Directors.

> **"Specified Securities"** means the specified securities as defined in the Listing Regulations.

> **"Year"** means the financial year to which the Board's Report relates.

Disclosures

The Report shall, inter alia, include the following:

1. Company Specific Information

1.1 Financial summary and highlights

1.2   Amount, if any, which the Board proposes to carry to **any reserves** The amount proposed to be transferred to any reserves of the company. If no amount is proposed to be transferred to reserves, **a statement to that effect shall be included.**

1.3 Dividend

a.   The amount of dividend per share and the percentage thereof which the Board recommends for the year and the dividend distribution tax thereon.

   In case no dividend has been recommended by the Board, a statement to that effect shall be made.

b.   The amount and the percentage of **interim dividend declared,** if any, during the year and the dividend distribution tax thereon.

c. The **total amount of dividend for the year**.

d. A statement on **compliance with the Dividend Distribution Policy,** if applicable, and the reasons for deviation and the rationale for additional parameters considered, if any.

e. **Payment of dividend from reserves**.

1.4 Major events occurred during the year

a) **State of the company's affairs**

The state of affairs of the company shall, inter alia, include the following information-

    i.   segment-wise position of business and its operations;

    ii.   change in status of the company;

    iii.   key business developments;

    iv.   change in the financial year;

    v.   capital expenditure programmes;

    vi.   details and status of acquisition, merger, expansion, modernization and diversification;

    vii. developments, acquisition and assignment of material Intellectual Property Rights;

    viii. any other material event having an impact on the affairs of the company.

b) **Change in the nature of business** In case the company has commenced any new business or discontinued/sold or disposed of any of its existing businesses or hived off any segment or division during the year, the Report shall disclose the details of the same highlighting the key focus areas.

c)   **Material changes and commitments,** if any, affecting the financial position of the company, having occurred since the end of the Year and till the date of the Report

The effect of such changes and commitments and an estimate of their financial impact shall also be disclosed in the Report.

If evaluation of such an estimate cannot be made, a statement to that effect be made.

The causes for such material changes and commitments and the remedial measures taken shall also be disclosed.

The Report shall also disclose the information with respect to changes in external and internal environment including technical, legal and financial, strikes, lockouts and breakdowns affecting the business of the company.

1.5 Details of revision of financial statement or the Report
In case the company has revised its financial statement or the Report in respect of any of the three preceding financial years either voluntarily or pursuant to the order of a judicial authority, the detailed reasons for such revision shall be disclosed in the Report of the year as well as in the Report of the relevant financial year in which such revision is made.

2. General Information

2.1   Overview of the industry and important changes in the industry during the last year;

2.2   External environment and economic outlook;

2.3   Induction of strategic and financial partners during the year; and

2.4   In case of a company, which has delisted its equity shares, during the year or till the date of the Report, the particulars of delisting activity giving details like price offered pursuant to delisting offer, offer period of delisting, number of shares tendered and accepted, total consideration paid and the holding of the Promoters in the company post delisting.

3. Capital and Debt Structure

Any changes in the capital structure of the company during the year, including the following:

(a)   change in the authorised, issued, subscribed and paid-up share capital;

(b)   reclassification or sub-division of the authorised share capital;

(c)   reduction of share capital or buy back of shares;

(d)   change in the capital structure resulting from restructuring; and

(e)   change in voting rights.

3.1 Issue of shares or other convertible securities

During the year, if the company has issued any equity shares or preference shares or any securities which carry a right or option to convert such securities into shares, the disclosure shall include the following:

(a)   date of issue and allotment;

(b)   method of allotment (QIP, FPO, ADRs, GDRs, rights issue, bonus issue, preferential issue, private placement, conversion of securities, etc.);

(c)   issue price;

(d)   conversion price;

(e)   number of shares allotted or to be allotted in case the right or option is exercised by all the holders of such securities;

(f)   number of shares or securities allotted to the promoter group (including shares represented by depository receipts);

(g)   in case, shares or securities are issued for consideration other than cash, a confirmation that price was determined on the basis of a valuation report of a registered valuer.

3.2 Issue of equity shares with differential rights

The disclosure shall include the following:

(a)   total number of shares allotted with differential rights;

(b)   details of the differential rights relating to voting rights and dividend;

(c)   percentage of the shares with differential rights to the total post issue equity share capital with differential rights issued at any point of time and percentage of voting rights which the equity share capital with differential voting rights shall carry to the total voting rights of the aggregate equity share capital;

(d)   price at which shares with differential rights have been issued;

(e)   particulars of Promoters, Directors or Key Managerial Personnel to whom shares with differential rights have been issued;

(f)   change in control, if any, in the company consequent to the issue of equity shares with differential voting rights;

(g)   diluted earnings per share pursuant to the issue of each class of shares, calculated in accordance with the applicable accounting standards;

(h)   pre and post issue shareholding pattern along with voting rights in the prescribed format.

3.3 Issue of Sweat Equity Shares The disclosure shall include the following:

(a)   class of Directors or employees to whom sweat equity shares were issued;

(b)   class of shares issued as sweat equity shares;

(c)   number of sweat equity shares issued to the Directors, Key Managerial Personnel or other employees showing separately the number of such shares issued to them, if any, for consideration other than cash and the names of allottees holding one percent or more of the issued share capital;

(d)   reasons or justification for the issue; (e) principal terms and conditions for the issue, including pricing formula;

(f)   total number of shares arising as a result of the issue ;

(g)   percentage of the sweat equity shares to the total post issued and paid up share capital;

(h)   consideration, including consideration other than cash, received or benefit accrued to the company from the issue ;

(i)   diluted earnings per share pursuant to the issue.

3.4 Details of Employee Stock Options

The disclosure shall include the following details of all the Employee Stock Options Scheme(s) implemented from time to time:

(a)   options granted;

(b)   options vested;

(c)   options exercised;

(d)   the total number of shares arising as a result of exercise of options;

(e)   options lapsed;

(f)   the exercise price;

(g)   variation in terms of options;

(h)   money realised by exercise of options;

(i)   total number of options in force;

(j)   employee wise details of options granted to:

     (i)   Key Managerial Personnel;

     (ii)   any other employee who receives a grant of options in any one year of options amounting to five percent or more of total options granted during that year;

     (iii)   identified employees who were granted options, during any one year, equal to or exceeding one percent of the issued capital, excluding outstanding warrants and conversions, of the company at the time of grant.

(k)   in case of a company whose shares are listed:

(i)   any material change to the scheme and whether such scheme is in compliance with the SEBI (Share Based Employee Benefits) Regulations, 2014;

(ii)   web-link of disclosures made on the website of the company, as required under SEBI (Share Based Employee Benefits) Regulations, 2014.

3.5 Shares held in trust for the benefit of employees where the voting rights are not exercised directly by the employees. The disclosure shall include the following:

(a)   names of the employees who have not exercised the voting rights directly;

(b)   reasons for not voting directly;

(c)   name of the person who is exercising such voting rights;

(d)   number of shares held by or in favour of such employees and the percentage of such shares to the total paid up share capital of the company;

(e)   date of the general meeting in which such voting power was exercised;

(f)   resolutions on which votes have been cast by persons holding such voting power;

(g)   percentage of such voting power to the total voting power on each resolution;

(h)   whether the votes were cast in favour of or against the resolution.

3.6 Issue of debentures, bonds or any non-convertible securities The disclosure shall include the following:

(a)   date of issue and allotment of the securities;

(b)   number of securities;

(c)   whether the issue of the securities was by way of preferential allotment, private placement or public issue;

(d)   brief details of the debt restructuring pursuant to which the securities are issued;

(e)   issue price;

(f)   coupon rate;

(g)   maturity date;

(h)   amount raised.

3.7 Issue of warrants The disclosure shall include the following:

(a)   date of issue and allotment of warrants;

(b)   number of warrants;

(c)   whether the issue of warrants was by way of preferential allotment, private placement, public issue;

(d)   issue price;

(e)   maturity date;

(f)   amount raised, specifically stating as to whether twenty five percent of the consideration has been collected upfront from the holders of the warrants;

(g)   terms and conditions of warrants including conversion terms.

4. Credit Rating of Securities

The disclosure shall include the following:

(a)   credit rating obtained in respect of various securities;

(b)   name of the credit rating agency;

(c)   date on which the credit rating was obtained;

(d)   revision in the credit rating;

(e)   reasons provided by the rating agency for a downward revision, if any.

5. Investor Education and Protection Fund (IEPF)

The disclosure shall include the following:

(a)   details of the transfer/s to the IEPF made during the year as mentioned below:

   (i)   amount of unclaimed/unpaid dividend and the corresponding shares;

   (ii)   redemption amount of preference shares;

   (iii)   amount of matured deposits, for companies other than banking companies, along with interest accrued thereon;

   (iv)   amount of matured debentures along with interest accrued thereon;

   (v)   application money received for allotment of any securities and due for refund along with interest accrued;

(vi)   sale proceeds of fractional shares arising out of issuance of bonus shares, merger and amalgamation;

(b)   details of the resultant benefits arising out of shares already transferred to the IEPF;

(c)   year wise amount of unpaid/unclaimed dividend lying in the unpaid account up to the Year and the corresponding shares, which are liable to be transferred to the IEPF, and the due dates for such transfer;

(d)   the amount of donation, if any, given by the company to the IEPF;

(e)   such other amounts transferred to the IEPF, if any, during the year.

6. Management

6.1 **Directors and Key Managerial Personnel** The disclosure shall include the following:

(a)   names of the persons who have been appointed / ceased to be Directors and/or Key Managerial Personnel of the company:

(i)   during the year;

(ii)   after the end of the year and up to the date of the Report;

(b)   mode of such appointment/cessation;

(c)   names of the Directors retiring by rotation at the ensuing annual general meeting and whether or not they offer themselves for re-appointment. In case the company operates in a specific sector where approval of any regulatory authority is required before the appointment of a Director/ Key Managerial Personnel, the Report shall also state whether the company has obtained the approval of such regulatory authority.

6.2 Independent Directors

The disclosure shall include the following:

(a)   in case of appointment of Independent Directors, the justification for choosing the proposed appointees for appointment as Independent Directors; and

(b)   in case of re-appointment after completion of the first term, the rationale for such re-appointment.

6.3 Declaration by Independent Directors and statement on compliance of code of conduct

The Report shall include a statement:

(a)   that necessary declaration with respect to independence has been received from all the Independent Directors of the company;

(b)   that the Independent Directors have complied with the Code for Independent Directors prescribed in Schedule IV to the Act, If the company has formulated a Code of Conduct, for Directors and senior management personnel.

The Report shall also include a statement on compliance of such Code.

6.4 Board Meetings

The number and dates of meetings of the Board held during the year shall be disclosed in the Report.

6.5 Committees

The Report shall disclose:

(a)   Composition of Committees constituted by the Board under the Act and the Listing Regulations as well as changes in their composition, if any, during the year;

(b)   The number and dates of meetings of such committees held during the year.

6.6 Recommendations of Audit Committee

Where the Board has not accepted any recommendation of the Audit Committee, a statement to that effect shall be disclosed in the Report along with the reasons for such non-acceptance.

6.7 Company's Policy on Directors' appointment and remuneration

The Report of every listed public company and other prescribed class of companies shall disclose company's policy on directors' appointment and remuneration and the criteria for determining qualifications, positive attributes and independence of a Director.

Where the said policy is available on the website of the company, it would be sufficient to disclose salient features of such policy, any change therein and the web-link at which the complete policy is available.

6.8 Board Evaluation

The Report of every listed company and other prescribed class of public companies shall include a statement indicating the manner in which formal annual evaluation of the performance of the Board, its Committees and of individual Directors has been made.

6.9 Remuneration of Directors and Employees of Listed Companies

The following disclosures, shall be made, either in the Report or by way of an annexure thereto:

(a)   the number of permanent employees on the rolls of the company;

(b)   the ratio of remuneration of each Director to the median remuneration of the employees of the company for the year;

[The expression "median" means the numerical value separating the higher half of a population from the lower half and the median of a finite list of numbers may be found by arranging all the observations from lowest value to highest value and picking the middle one; (ii) if there is an even number of observations, the median shall be the average of the two middle values.]

(c)   the percentage increase in remuneration of each Director, Chief Financial Officer, Chief Executive Officer, Company Secretary or Manager, if any, in the year;

(d)   the percentage increase in the median remuneration of employees in the year;

[The expression "Remuneration" means any money or its equivalent given or passed to an employee for services rendered by him and includes perquisites under the Income tax Act.]

(e)   average percentile increase already made in the salaries of employees other than managerial personnel in the last year and its comparison with the percentile increase in the managerial remuneration and justification thereof and whether there are any exceptional circumstances for increase in the managerial remuneration;

(f)   affirmation that the remuneration is as per the remuneration policy of the company.

In addition to the above, the Report shall include a statement indicating:

(a)   names of top ten employees of the company in terms of remuneration drawn.

Employees who have resigned / retired during the year shall also be considered for this purpose.

In case of companies having less than ten employees, such statement shall include details of all employees.

(b)   name of every employee who:

(i)   if employed throughout the year, was in receipt of remuneration not less than one crore and two lakh rupees in the aggregate;

(ii)   if employed for a part of the year, was in receipt of remuneration not less than eight lakh and fifty thousand rupees per month in the aggregate;

(iii)   if employed throughout the year or part thereof, was in receipt of remuneration which is in excess of that drawn by the Managing Director or Whole-time

Director or Manager and who holds by himself or along with his spouse and dependent children, not less than two percent of the equity shares of the company.

The aforesaid statement shall also indicate the following:

(a)   designation of the employee;

(b)   remuneration received;

(c)   nature of employment, whether contractual or otherwise;

(d)   qualifications and experience of the employee;

(e)   date of commencement of employment;

(f)   the age of such employee;

(g)   the last employment held by such employee before joining the company;

(h)   the percentage of equity shares held by the employee along with his spouse and dependent children, if such shareholding is not less than two percent of the total equity shares;

(i)   whether any such employee is a relative of any Director or Manager of the company and if so, the name of such Director or Manager.

Particulars of employees posted and working in a country outside India, not being Directors or their relatives, drawing more than sixty lakh rupees per year or five lakh rupees per month, as the case may be, as may be decided by the Board, need not be circulated to the members in the Report, but such particulars shall be filed with the Registrar of Companies while filing the financial statement and the Report.

6.10 Remuneration received by Managing/Whole time Director from holding or subsidiary company

In case the Managing/Whole time Director of the company is in receipt of any commission from the company, and also receives any remuneration or commission from its holding company or subsidiary company, details of such remuneration or commission shall be disclosed in the Report.

6.11 Directors' Responsibility Statement

The Report shall include a Directors' Responsibility Statement stating the following:

(a)   in the preparation of the annual accounts, the applicable accounting standards had been followed along with proper explanation relating to material departures;

(b)   the Directors had selected such accounting policies and applied them consistently and made judgments and estimates that are reasonable and prudent so as to give a true and fair view of the state of affairs of the company at the end of the year and of the profit and loss of the company for that period;

(c)   the Directors had taken proper and sufficient care for the maintenance of adequate accounting records in accordance with the provisions of the Act for safeguarding the assets of the company and for preventing and detecting fraud and other irregularities;

(d)   the Directors had prepared the annual accounts on a going concern basis;

(e)   the Directors had devised proper systems to ensure compliance with the provisions of all applicable laws and that such systems are adequate and operating effectively;

(f)   the Directors, in case of a listed company, had laid down internal financial controls to be followed by the company and that such internal financial controls are adequate and operating effectively.

6.12 Internal Financial Controls

Details in respect of adequacy of internal financial controls with reference to the financial statement.

6.13 Frauds reported by the Auditor

The following details of frauds reported by the Auditor (Statutory Auditor, Secretarial Auditor or Cost Auditor) to the Audit Committee/ Board, as the case may be, and the frauds reported to the Central Government shall be disclosed in the Report:

(a)   nature of fraud with description;

(b)   approximate amount involved;

(c)   parties involved, if remedial action not taken;

(d)   remedial action taken to prevent occurrence of such frauds in future.

If no fraud is reported by the Auditor, a statement to this effect shall be given in the Report.

7. Disclosures Relating to Subsidiaries, Associates and Joint Ventures.

7.1 Report on performance and financial position of the subsidiaries, associates and joint ventures

In case of companies having subsidiaries, associates and joint ventures, the Report shall include a separate section highlighting the performance of each of the subsidiaries, associates and joint venture companies and their contribution to the overall performance of the company.

7.2 Companies which have become or ceased to be subsidiaries, associates and joint ventures

During the year or at any time after the closure of the year and till the date of the Report, if the company has acquired or formed any new subsidiary, associate or joint venture, details of such companies shall be disclosed.

Where any of the subsidiaries, associates or joint ventures of the company has ceased to be a subsidiary, associate or joint venture on account of sale of shares, amalgamation, or by any other manner, then, the names of such companies along with the manner of such cessation shall also be disclosed in the Report.

Companies which have listed their specified securities shall also state in the Report the name of its material subsidiary as per the Listing Regulations. If such material subsidiary has sold, disposed of and leased assets of more than twenty percent of the assets of the material subsidiary on an aggregate basis during a year then details of such sale shall be disclosed.

8. Details of Deposits.

The disclosure shall include the following:

(a)   details of deposits accepted during the year;

(b)   deposits remaining unpaid or unclaimed as at the end of the year;

(c)   whether there has been any default in repayment of deposits or payment of interest thereon during the year and if so, the number of such cases and the total amount involved:

   (i)   at the beginning of the year;

   (ii)   maximum during the year (i.e. highest number of cases pending repayment of deposits or interest during the year and maximum amount that was due);

   (iii)   at the end of the year;

(d)   details of deposits which are not in compliance with the requirements of the Act;

(e)   details of National Company Law Tribunal (NCLT)/National Company Law Appellate Tribunal (NCLAT) orders with respect to depositors for extension of time for repayment, penalty imposed, if any;

(f)   in case of a private company, details of amount received from a person who at the time of the receipt of the amount was a Director of the company or relative of the Director of the company.

9. Particulars of Loans, Guarantees and Investments.

Particulars of the loans given, investments made, guarantees given or securities provided during the year and the purpose for which the loans / guarantees / securities are proposed to be utilised by the recipient of such loan / guarantee / security.

A company shall disclose the aforesaid particulars in the notes to the financial statement and give reference thereof in the Report.

10. Particulars of Contracts or Arrangements with related Parties.

The disclosure shall include the following:

(a)   contracts / arrangements / transactions with related parties which are not at arm's length basis;

(b)   material contracts / arrangements / transactions with related parties which are at arm's length basis;

(c)   contracts / arrangements with related parties which are not in the ordinary course of business and justification for entering into such contract.

Such disclosure in the prescribed form shall be annexed to the Report.

11. Corporate Social Responsibility (CSR)

The Report shall disclose about the CSR policy of the company and the CSR initiatives taken during the year.

Where the said policy is available on the website of the company, it would be sufficient to disclose salient features of such policy, any change therein and the web-link at which the complete policy is available.

The Report shall include an Annual Report on the CSR activities and shall comprise the following:

(a)   a brief outline of the CSR Policy, including overview of projects or programs proposed to be undertaken and a reference to the web link to the CSR Policy and projects or programs;

(b)   composition of the CSR Committee, number of meetings held during the year;

(c)   average net profits for the three immediately preceding years;

(d)   prescribed CSR expenditure i.e. two percent of clause (c) above;

(e)   details of amount spent on CSR during the year including total amount to be spent, amount unspent and manner in which the amount has been spent;

(f)   in case the prescribed CSR amount has not been spent, reasons for not spending the same;

(g)   a responsibility statement from the CSR Committee that the implementation and monitoring of the CSR Policy is in compliance with the CSR objectives and policy of the company.

12. Conservation of Energy, Technology Absorption, Foreign Exchange Earnings and Outgo.

The disclosure shall include the following:

(a) Conservation of energy –

(i)   the steps taken or impact on conservation of energy;

(ii)   the steps taken by the company for utilising alternate sources of energy;

(iii)   the capital investment on energy conservation equipment.

(b) Technology absorption –

(i)   the efforts made towards technology absorption;

(ii)   the benefits derived like product improvement, cost reduction, product development or import substitution;

(iii)   in case of imported technology (imported during the last three years reckoned from the beginning of the year under reference) –

   a)   details of the technology imported;

   b)   the year of import;

   c)   whether the technology has been fully absorbed and if not, areas where absorption has not taken place, and the reasons thereof;

(iv)   the expenditure incurred on Research and Development.

(c) Foreign exchange earnings and Outgo –

The Foreign Exchange earned in terms of actual inflows during the year and the Foreign Exchange outgo during the year in terms of actual outflows.

In cases where such disclosures are not applicable, the Report shall include a statement to that effect.

13. Risk Management.

A statement indicating the development and implementation of a risk management policy for the company. Such statement shall, inter alia, disclose:

(a)   various elements of risk which, in the opinion of the Board, may threaten the existence of the company and

(b)   strategy to mitigate such risks.

14. Details of Establishment of Vigil Mechanism.

Every listed company and other prescribed class of companies shall disclose in its Board's Report, details of establishment of a vigil mechanism.

The disclosure shall, inter alia, include the mechanism for:

a) the Directors and employees to report their genuine concerns about unethical behaviour, actual or suspected fraud or violation of the company's code of conduct;

b) providing adequate safeguards against victimisation;

c) providing direct access to the higher levels of supervisors and/ or to the Chairman of the Audit Committee, in appropriate or exceptional cases. Web-link of the aforesaid mechanism shall also be disclosed in the Report.

15. Material Orders of Judicial Bodies/ Regulators.

Details of significant and material orders passed by any Regulator, Court, Tribunal, Statutory and quasi-judicial body, impacting the going concern status of the company and its future operations shall be disclosed.

16. Auditors.

Names of the Statutory Auditor, Cost Auditor and Secretarial Auditor and details of any change in such Auditors, during the year and up to the date of the Report due to resignation / casual vacancy / removal / completion of term shall be disclosed in the Report.

17. Secretarial Audit Report.

The Secretarial Audit Report shall be annexed to the Report.

18. Explanations in Response to Auditors' Qualifications.

The Report shall include explanations or comments on every qualification, reservation or adverse remark or disclaimer made in the Auditor's Report and the Secretarial Auditor's Report.

If there are no qualifications, reservations or adverse remarks made by the Statutory Auditors / Secretarial Auditors in their respective Report, a statement to this effect shall be given in the Report.

Further, if such qualification, reservation, adverse remark or disclaimer has a material adverse effect on

the financial statement or on the functioning of the company, its likely impact and the corrective measures that are proposed to be taken shall also be disclosed in the Report.

19. Compliance with Secretarial Standards.

The Report shall include a statement on compliance of applicable Secretarial Standards and other **Secretarial Standards voluntarily adopted by the company.**

20. Corporate Insolvency Resolution Process Initiated under the Insolvency and Bankruptcy Code, 2016 (IBC).

The disclosure shall include the following:

(a)   details of any application filed for corporate insolvency resolution process, by a financial or operational creditor or by the company itself under the IBC before the NCLT;

(b)   status of such application; and

(c)   status of corporate insolvency resolution process, if any, initiated under the IBC.

21. Failure to Implement any Corporate Action.

In case the company has failed to complete or implement any corporate action within the specified time limit, the Report shall disclose the same and the reasons for such failure.

For the purpose of this clause, the term "corporate action" includes buy back of securities, payment of dividend declared, mergers and de-mergers, delisting, split and issue of any securities.

22. Annual Return.

A copy of the annual return shall be placed on the website of the company, if any, and the web-link of such annual return shall be disclosed in the Report.

23. Other Disclosures.

Other disclosures shall include the following:

(a)   a statement, wherever applicable, that the consolidated financial statement is also being presented in addition to the standalone financial statement of the company.

(b)   key initiatives with respect to Stakeholder relationship, Customer relationship, Environment, Sustainability, Health and Safety.

(c)   reasons for delay, if any, in holding the annual general meeting;

(d)   a statement as to whether cost records is required to be maintained by the company pursuant to an order of the Central Government and accordingly such records and accounts are maintained.

24. Additional Disclosures under Listing Regulations.

24.1 Statement of deviation or variation Companies which have listed their specified securities shall furnish in the Report an explanation for any deviation or variation in connection with certain terms of a public issue, rights issue, preferential issue etc. as under:

(a)   Statement indicating deviations, if any, in the use of proceeds from the objects stated in the offer document or explanatory statement to the notice for the general meeting, as applicable;

(b)   Statement indicating category wise variation (capital expenditure, sales and marketing, working capital etc.) between the projected utilisation of funds made by the company in its offer document or explanatory statement to the notice for the general meeting, as applicable, and the actual utilisation of funds.

24.2 Management Discussion and Analysis Report (MDAR)

In case of companies which have listed their specified securities, the Report shall include an MDAR, either as a part of the Report or as an annexure to the Report.

The MDAR shall include the following details in relation to the company:

(a)   industry structure and developments;

(b)   opportunities and threats;

(c)   segment wise and product wise performance;

(d)   outlook;

(e)   risks and concerns;

(f)   internal control systems and their adequacy;

(g)   discussion on financial performance with respect to operational performance;

(h)   material developments in human resources / industrial relations, including number of people employed;

(i)   details of significant changes (i.e. change of 25% or more as compared to the immediately previous financial year) in key financial ratios, along with detailed explanations therefor, including:

>   (i)   Debtors Turnover

>   (ii)   Inventory Turnover

>   (iii)   Interest Coverage Ratio

>   (iv)   Current Ratio

>   (v)   Debt Equity Ratio

>   (vi)   Operating Profit Margin (%) (vii) Net Profit Margin (%) or sector-specific equivalent ratios, as applicable.

(j)   details of any change in Return on Net Worth as compared to the immediately previous financial year along with a detailed explanation thereof.

24.3 Certificate on Compliance of conditions of Corporate Governance.

Companies which have listed their specified securities, shall annex with the Report a certificate obtained from either the Statutory Auditor or a practicing Company Secretary regarding compliance of the conditions of corporate governance.

24.4 Suspension of Trading

In case the securities of the company are suspended from trading, the Report shall explain the reasons thereof.

25. Disclosures Pertaining to Sexual Harassment pfWomen at the Work Place (Prevention, Prohibition and Redressal) Act, 2013

The disclosure shall include the following:

(a) a statement that the company has complied with the provision relating to the constitution of Internal Complaints Committee under the Sexual Harassment of Women at the Workplace (Prevention, Prohibition and Redressal) Act, 2013.

(b) the details of number of cases filed and disposed as required under the Sexual Harassment of Women at the Workplace (Prevention, Prohibition and Redressal) Act, 2013.

PART II:

Other Requirements.

26. Approval of the Report.

The Report shall be considered and approved by means of a resolution passed at a duly convened meeting of the Board.

27. Signing of the Report.

The Report shall be signed by the Chairman of the company, if authorised in that behalf by the Board or by two Directors one of whom shall be the Managing Director or in the case of a One Person Company, by one Director.

The financial statement, including consolidated financial statement, if any, shall be approved by the Board before they are signed on behalf of the Board.

The statements so approved are required to be signed on behalf of the Board by the Chairman of the company if authorised in that behalf by the Board or by two Directors one of whom shall be the Managing Director and the Chief Executive Officer, the Chief Financial Officer and the Company Secretary of the company, wherever they are appointed or in the case of a One Person Company, by one Director.

The financial statement so approved and signed on behalf of the Board are required to be submitted to the auditor(s) for their report thereon.

The financial statement is thus signed by the auditor(s) and the audit report thereon is submitted to the Board after such approval.

The annexures to the Report shall be signed in the similar manner as the Report, except the Report on CSR activities of the company, which is required to be signed by the Chief Executive Officer or the Managing Director or any other Director of the company and by the Chairman of the CSR Committee of the company.

28. Dissemination

28.1 Right of Members to have Copies of the Report

A copy of the Report along with the financial statement and the Auditor's Report shall be sent, either physically or in electronic form, to every member at least twenty-one clear days in advance of the annual general meeting.

The copies of the above documents can be sent less than twenty-one clear days in advance of the annual general meeting, if it is so agreed by members:

(a)   holding, if the company has a share capital, majority in number of members entitled to vote and who **represent not less than ninety-five per cent** of such part of the paid-up share capital of the company as gives a right to vote at the meeting; or

(b)   having, if the company has no share capital, not less than ninety-five per cent of the total voting power exercisable at the meeting. In case of section 8 companies, the said documents shall be sent to the members not less than fourteen clear days before the date of the annual general meeting.

28.2 Placing of the Report on the Website

The Report shall be placed on the website of the company, if any.

29. Filing and Submission of the Report.

29.1 The Report along with the audited financial statement of the company shall be filed with the Registrar of Companies.

The resolution passed by the Board approving such Report shall also be filed with the Registrar of Companies.

However private companies are not required to file such resolution with the Registrar of Companies.

29.2 **Every listed company shall submit to the stock exchanges** on which its securities are listed, its financial statement together with a copy of the Report within twenty one working days of it being approved and adopted in the annual general meeting.

Annexures to the Report

The following matters, wherever applicable, will be annexed to the Report:

- Particulars of prescribed contracts / arrangements with related parties in Form AOC-2

- Prescribed particulars of remuneration of Directors and employees.

- Secretarial Audit Report for the relevant year in Form MR-3.

- Annual Report on CSR activities.

- Prescribed details of conservation of energy, research and development, technology absorption, foreign exchange earnings and outgo.

- Auditors' certificate on Corporate Governance in case of companies which have listed their specified securities.

- Dividend Distribution Policy in case of companies which have listed their specified securities.

- Company's policy on directors' appointment and remuneration including criteria for determining qualifications, positive attributes, independence of a director and other matters.

Chapter VII

Management and Administration; Companies {Management & Administration} Rules, 2014 & Mandatory Secretarial Standard on General Meetings {SS-2}

88.& Rule 5 Every company to maintain Register of members, register of debenture-holders; register of any other security holders etc.

(5) If a company does not maintain a register of members or debenture-holders or other security holders in {Forms MGT-1, MGT-2} or fails to maintain them within seven days of approval by the board or committee, the company shall be liable to a penalty of three lakh rupees and **every officer of the company who is in default** shall be liable to a penalty of fifty thousand rupees.".

89. & Rule 9. Declaration in respect of beneficial interest in any share —

(1) Where the name of a person is entered in the register of members of a company as the holder of shares in that company but who does not hold the beneficial interest in such shares, such

person shall make a declaration within thirty days in Form MGT-4 to the company specifying the name and other particulars of the person who holds the beneficial interest in such shares.

(5) If **any person fails to make a declaration,** he shall be liable to a penalty of fifty thousand rupees and in case of continuing failure, with a further penalty of two hundred rupees for each day after the first during which such failure continues, subject to a maximum of five lakh rupees.";

(6) The company shall make a note of such declaration in the register concerned and shall file, within thirty days from the date of receipt of declaration by it, a return in the form MGT-6 with the Registrar in respect of such declaration with such fees or additional fees within thirty days.

"(7) If a company, required to file a return, fails to do so before the expiry of the time specified therein, the company and **every officer of the company who is in default** shall be liable to a penalty of one thousand rupees for each day during which such failure continues, subject to a maximum of five lakh rupees in the case of a company and two lakh rupees in case of an officer who is in default."

90. Investigation of beneficial ownership of shares in certain cases —

(4) Every company shall file a return of significant beneficial owners of the company and changes therein with the Registrar containing names, addresses and other details as prescribed within such thirty days.

(4A) Every company shall take necessary steps to identify an individual who is a significant beneficial owner in relation to the company and require him to comply with the provisions of this section.

(11) If a company, required to maintain register and file the information or required to take necessary steps under sub-section (4A), fails to do so or denies inspection as provided therein, the company shall be liable to a penalty of one lakh rupees and in case of continuing failure, with a further penalty of five hundred rupees for each day, after the first during which such failure continues, subject to a maximum of five lakh rupees and **every officer of the company who is in default** shall be liable to a penalty of twenty-five thousand rupees and in case of continuing failure, with a further penalty of two hundred rupees for each day, after the first during which such failure continues, subject to a maximum of one lakh rupees.

(12) If any person willfully furnishes any false or incorrect information or suppresses any material information of which he is aware in the declaration made under this section, he shall be liable to action under section 447.]

91. & Rule 10. Power to close register of members or debenture-holders or other security holders — for any period or periods not exceeding in the aggregate forty-five days in each year, but not exceeding thirty days at any one time, subject to giving of previous notice of at least seven days or such lesser period as may be specified by Securities and Exchange Board for listed companies.

(2) For contravention, the company **and every officer of the company who is in default** shall be liable to a penalty of five thousand rupees for every day subject to a maximum of one lakh rupees during which the register is kept closed.

92. & Rule 11. Annual return —

(1)   Every company shall prepare a return (hereinafter referred to as the annual return) in the prescribed form containing the particulars as they stood on the close of the financial year regarding *inter alia* —

(e)   its promoters, directors, key managerial personnel along with changes therein since the close of the previous financial year;

(f)   meetings of members or a class thereof, Board and its various committees along with attendance details;

(g)   remuneration of directors and key managerial personnel;

(h)   penalty or punishment imposed on the company, its directors or officers and details of compounding of offences and appeals made against such penalty or punishment;

(i)   matters relating to certification of compliances, disclosures as may be prescribed;

(k)   such other matters as may be prescribed, **and signed by a director and the company secretary, or where there is no company secretary, by a company secretary in practice:**

(2)   The annual return, filed by a listed company or, by a company having such paid-up capital of ten crore or more and turnover of fifty crore or more, shall be certified by a company secretary in practice in Form MGT-8, stating that the annual return discloses the facts correctly and adequately and that the company has complied with all the provisions of this Act.

(3)   An extract of the annual return in form MGT-9 shall form part of the Board's report.

(4)   Every company shall file with the Registrar a copy of the annual return, within sixty days from the date on which the annual general meeting is held or where no annual general meeting is held in any year within sixty days from the date on which the annual general meeting should have been held together with the statement specifying the reasons for not holding the annual general meeting, with such fees or additional fees as may be prescribed, within the time as specified, under section 403.

(5)   If any company fails to file its annual return, before the expiry of sixty days of AGM, , such company and **its every officer who is in default** shall be liable to a penalty of ten thousand rupees and in case of continuing failure, with a further penalty of one hundred rupees for each day after the first during which such failure continues, subject to a maximum of two lakh rupees in case of a company and fifty thousand rupees in case of an officer who is in default.

93. Return to be filed with Registrar in case promoters' stake changes —

Every listed company shall file a return in the prescribed form with the Registrar with respect to change in the number of shares held by promoters and top ten shareholders of such company, within fifteen days of such change.

94. & Rule 15 Place of keeping and inspection of registers, returns, etc —

(1) The registers required to be kept and maintained by a company and copies of the annual return filed under section 92 shall be kept at the registered office of the company:

> Provided that such registers or copies of return may also be kept at any other place in India **in which more than one-tenth of the total number of members** entered in the register of members reside, if approved by a special resolution passed at a general meeting of the company and the Registrar has been given a copy of the proposed special resolution in advance:

(4) If any inspection or the making of any extract or copy required under this section is refused, the company and **every officer of the company who is in default** shall be liable, for each such default, to a penalty of one thousand rupees for every day subject to a maximum of one lakh rupees during which the refusal or default continues.

Requirements related to the annual General Meeting has been covered in later in this Chapter under the Mandatory Secretarial Standards SS-2 prescribed by the Institute of Company Secretaries of India and approved by the Central Government.

96. Annual general meeting —

97. Power of Tribunal to call annual general meeting —

98. Power of Tribunal to call meetings of members, etc —

99. Punishment for default in complying with provisions of sections 96 to 98 —

If any default is made in holding a meeting of the company in accordance with section 96 or section 97 or section 98 or in complying with any directions of the Tribunal, the company **and every officer of the company who is in default** shall be punishable with fine which may extend to one lakh rupees and in the case of a continuing default, with a further fine which may extend to five thousand rupees for every day during which such default continues.

100. & Rule 17 Calling of extraordinary general meeting —

101. & Rule 18 Notice of meeting —

102. Statement to be annexed to notice —

(1)   A statement setting out the following material facts concerning each item of special business to be transacted at a general meeting, shall be annexed to the notice calling such meeting, namely:—

    (a)   **the nature of concern or interest, financial or otherwise, if any, in respect of each item of—**

    (i)   **every director and the manager, if any;**

    (ii)   **every other key managerial personnel; and**

    (iii)   **relatives of the persons mentioned in sub-clauses (i) and (ii);**

(2)   For the purposes of sub-section (1),—

(a)   in the case of an annual general meeting, all business to be transacted thereat shall be deemed special, other than—

(i)   the consideration of financial statements and the reports of
         the Board of Directors and auditors;

(ii)   the declaration of any dividend;

(iii)   the appointment of directors in place of those retiring;

(iv)   the appointment of, and the fixing of the remuneration of,
         the auditors; and

(b)   in the case of any other meeting, all business shall be deemed
         to be special:

Provided that where any item of special business to be transacted at
a meeting of the company relates to or affects any other company,
the extent of shareholding interest in that other company of every
promoter, director, manager, if any, and of every other key managerial
personnel of the first mentioned company shall, if the extent of such
shareholding is not less than two per cent. of the paid-up share
capital of that company, also be set out in the statement.

(3)   Where any item of business refers to any document, which
         is to be considered at the meeting, the time and place where
         such document can be inspected shall be specified in the
         statement under subsection (1).

(4)   **Where as a result of the non-disclosure or insufficient
         disclosure** in any statement referred to in sub-section
         (1), **being made by a promoter, director, manager,** if
         any, or other key managerial personnel, any benefit which
         accrues to **such promoter, director, manager or other
         key managerial personnel or their relatives, either
         directly or indirectly, the promoter, director, manager
         or other key managerial personnel, as the case may**

be, shall hold such benefit in trust for the company, and shall, without prejudice to any other action being taken against him under this Act or under any other law for the time being in force, be liable to compensate the company to the extent of the benefit received by him.

"(5)   Without prejudice to the provisions of sub-section (4), if any default is made in complying with the provisions of this section, **every promoter, director, manager or other key managerial personnel of the company who is in default** shall be liable to a penalty of fifty thousand rupees or five times the amount of benefit accruing to the promoter, director, manager or other key managerial personnel or any of his relatives, whichever is higher.".

103. Quorum for meetings —

104. Chairman of meetings —

105. & Rule 19. Proxies —

(2) In every notice calling a meeting of a company which has a share capital, or the articles of which provide for voting by proxy at the meeting, there shall appear with reasonable prominence a statement that a member entitled to attend and vote is entitled to appoint a proxy, or, where that is allowed, one or more proxies, to attend and vote instead of himself, and that a proxy need not be a member.

(3) If default is made in complying with sub-section (2), **every officer of the company who is in default** shall be to a penalty of five thousand rupees.

(5) If for the purpose of any meeting of a company, invitations to appoint as proxy a person or one of a number of persons specified in the invitations are issued at the company's expense to any member entitled to have a notice of the meeting sent to him and to vote threat by proxy, **every officer of the company** who issues the invitation as aforesaid or authorises or permits their issue, shall be liable to a penalty of fifty thousand rupees.

106. Restriction on voting rights —

(1) Notwithstanding anything contained in this Act, the articles of a company may provide that no member shall exercise any voting right in respect of any shares registered in his name on which any calls or other sums presently payable by him have not been paid, or in regard to which the company has exercised any right of lien.

107. Voting by show of hands —

108. & Rule 20 Voting through electronic means —

109. Demand for poll —

110. & Rule 22 Postal ballot —

111. Circulation of members' resolution —

—(1) A company shall, on requisition in writing of such number of members, as required in section 100,—

(a)   give notice to members of any resolution which may properly be moved and is intended to be moved at a meeting; and

(b)   circulate to members any statement with respect to the matters referred to in proposed resolution or business to be dealt with at that meeting.

(3) The company shall not be bound to circulate any statement as required by clause (b) of subsection (1), if on the application either of the company or of any other person who claims to be aggrieved, the Central Government, by order, declares that the rights conferred by this section are being abused to secure needless publicity for defamatory matter.

(5) If any default is made in complying with the provisions of this section, **the company and every officer of the company who is in default** shall be liable to a penalty of twenty-five thousand rupees.

114. Ordinary and special resolutions —

117. Resolutions and agreements to be filed with Registrar in form MGT-14 —

(1) A copy of every resolution or any agreement, in respect of matters specified in sub-section (3) together with the explanatory statement under section 102, if any, annexed to the notice calling the meeting in which the resolution is proposed, shall be filed with the Registrar within thirty days of the passing or making thereof in within the time specified under section 403:

Provided that the copy of every resolution which has the effect of altering the articles and the copy of every agreement Cont referred to in sub-section (3) shall be embodied in or annexed to every copy of the articles issued after passing of the resolution or making of the agreement.

"(2) If any company fails to file the resolution or the agreement before the expiry of the period specified therein, such company shall be liable to a penalty of ten thousand rupees and in case of continuing failure, with a further penalty of one hundred rupees for each day after the first during which such failure continues, subject to a maximum of two lakh rupees **and every officer of the company who is in default** including liquidator of the company, if any, shall be liable to a penalty of ten thousand rupees and in case of continuing failure, with a further penalty of one hundred rupees for each day after the first during which such failure continues, subject to a maximum of fifty thousand rupees.";

(3) The provisions of this section shall apply to—

(a)   special resolutions;

(b)   resolutions which have been agreed to by all the members of a company, but which, if not so agreed to, would not have been effective for their purpose unless they had been passed as special resolutions;

(c)   any resolution of the Board of Directors of a company or agreement executed by a company, relating to the appointment, re-appointment or renewal of the appointment, or variation of the terms of appointment, of a managing director;

(d)   resolutions or agreements which have been agreed to by any class of members but which, if not so agreed to, would not have been effective for their purpose unless they had been passed by a specified majority or otherwise in some particular manner; and all resolutions or agreements which effectively bind such class of members though not agreed to by all those members;

(e)   resolutions passed by a company according consent to the exercise by its Board of Directors of any of the powers under clause (a) and clause (c) of sub-section (1) of section 180;

(f)   resolutions requiring a company to be wound up voluntarily passed in pursuance of section 304;

(g)   resolutions passed in pursuance of sub-section (3) of section 179:

Provided that no person shall be entitled under section 399 to inspect or obtain copies of such resolutions;

"Provided further that nothing contained in this clause shall apply in respect of a resolution passed to grant loans, or give guarantee or provide security in respect of loans under clause (f) of sub-section (3) of section 179 in the ordinary course of its business by,—

(a)   a banking company;

(b)   any class of non-banking financial company registered under Chapter IIIB of the Reserve Bank of India Act, 1934, as may be prescribed in consultation with the Reserve Bank of India;

(c)   any class of housing finance company registered under the National Housing Bank Act, 1987, as may be prescribed in consultation with the National Housing Bank; and".

(h) any other resolution or agreement as may be prescribed and placed in the public domain.

Reg 10. Filing of Information

(1)   The listed entity shall file the reports, statements, documents, filings and any other information with the recognised stock exchange(s) on the electronic platform as specified by the Board or the recognised stock exchange(s).

(2)   The listed entity shall put in place infrastructure as required for compliance with sub-regulation (1).

118. & Rule 25, 26 Minutes of proceedings of general meeting, meeting of Board of Directors and other meeting and resolutions passed by postal ballot —

(11) If any default is made in complying with the provisions of this section in respect of any meeting, the company shall be liable to a penalty of twenty-five thousand rupees **and every officer of the company who is in default** shall be liable to a penalty of five thousand rupees.

(12) If a person is found guilty of tampering with the minutes of the proceedings of meeting, he shall be punishable with imprisonment for a term which may extend to two years and with fine which shall not be less than twenty-five thousand rupees but which may extend to one lakh rupees.

119. Inspection of minute-books of general meeting —

(3) If any inspection is refused, or if any copy required is not furnished within seven days of request and payment of charges, the company shall be liable to a penalty of twenty-five thousand rupees and **every officer of the company who is in default** shall be liable to a penalty of five thousand rupees for each such refusal or default, as the case may be.

120, , Rule 27 & Reg 9 - Maintenance and inspection of documents in electronic form —

121. Report in Form MGT-15 to Registrar by Listed Company on annual general meeting within thirty days of meeting.

> "(3) If the company fails to file the report such company shall be liable to a penalty of one lakh rupees and in case of continuing failure, with a further penalty of five hundred rupees for each day after the first during which such failure continues, subject to a maximum of five lakh rupees **and every officer of the company who is in default shall be liable to a penalty** which shall not be less than twenty-five thousand rupees and in case of continuing failure, with a further penalty of five hundred rupees for each day after the first during which such failure continues, subject to a maximum of one lakh rupees.".

{Mandatory} SS-2 SECRETARIAL STANDARD ON GENERAL MEETINGS {ICSI} [April 1, 2024}

INTRODUCTION

This Standard seeks to prescribe a set of principles for the convening and conducting of General Meetings and matters related thereto.

This Standard also deals with conduct of e-voting and postal ballot.

SCOPE

This Standard is applicable to all types of General Meetings of all companies incorporated under the Act except One Person

Company (OPC) and a company registered under Section 8 of the Companies Act, 2013 or corresponding provisions of any previous enactment thereof.

However, companies registered under Section 8 of the Companies Act, 2013 need to comply with the applicable provisions of the Act relating to General Meetings. The exemption to a company registered under Section 8 of the Companies Act, 2013 as referred above and the specific exemptions given to a private company and Government company in this Standard shall be available **only if it has not committed any default in filing its Financial Statements or Annual Return with the Registrar of Companies.**

The principles enunciated in this Standard for General Meetings of Members are applicable mutatis-mutandis to Meetings of debenture-holders and creditors. A Meeting of the Members or class of Members or debenture-holders or creditors of a company under the directions of the Court or the Company Law Board (CLB) or the National Company Law Tribunal (NCLT) or any other prescribed authority shall be governed by this Standard without prejudice to any rules, regulations and directions prescribed for and orders of, such courts, judicial forums and other authorities with respect to the conduct of such Meetings.

This Standard is in conformity with the provisions of the Act. However, if, due to subsequent changes in the Act, a particular Standard or any part thereof becomes inconsistent with the Act, the provisions of the Act shall prevail.

DEFINITIONS

The following terms are used in this Standard with the meaning specified:

- **"Act"** means the Companies Act, 2013 (Act No. 18 of 2013) or any previous enactment thereof, or any statutory modification thereto, or re-enactment thereof and includes any Rules and Regulations framed thereunder.

- **"Agency"** means agency approved or recognised by the Ministry of Corporate Affairs and appointed by the Board for providing and supervising electronic platform for voting.

- **"Chairman"** means the Chairman of the Board or the Chairman appointed or elected for a Meeting.

- **"Maintenance"** means keeping registers and records either in physical or electronic form, as may be permitted under any law for the time being in force, and includes the making of necessary entries therein, the authentication of such entries and the preservation of such physical or electronic records.

- **"Meeting"** or **"General Meeting"** or **"Annual General Meeting"** or **"Extra-Ordinary** General Meeting" means a duly convened, held and conducted Meeting of Members.

- **"Minutes"** means a formal written record, in physical or electronic form, of the proceedings of a Meeting.

- **"Minutes Book"** means a Book maintained in physical or in electronic form for the purpose of recording of Minutes.

- **"Ordinary Business"** means business to be transacted at an Annual General Meeting relating to

    (i)   the consideration of financial statements, consolidated financial statements, if any, and the reports of the Board of Directors and Auditors;

(ii)   the declaration of any dividend;

(iii)   the appointment of Directors in the place of those retiring; and

(iv)   the appointment and fixing of remuneration of the Auditors.

- **"Remote e-voting"** means the facility of casting votes by a member using an electronic voting system from a place other than venue of a general meeting.

- **"Secured Computer System"** means computer hardware, software, and procedure that – (a) are reasonably secure from unauthorized access and misuse;

    (b)   provide a reasonable level of reliability and correct operation;

    (c)   are reasonably suited to performing the intended functions; and

    (d)   adhere to generally accepted security procedures.

- **"Timestamp"** means the current time of an event that is recorded by a Secured Computer System and is used to describe the time that is printed to a file or other location to help keep track of when data is added, removed, sent or received.

- **"Voting by electronic means"** includes "remote e-voting" and voting at the general meeting through an electronic voting system which may be the same as used for remote e-voting.

- **"Voting by postal ballot"** means voting by ballot, by post or by electronic means.

1. Convening a Meeting

1.1 Authority

A General Meeting shall be convened by or on the authority of the Board. The Board shall, every year, convene or authorise convening of a Meeting of its Members called the Annual General Meeting to transact items of Ordinary Business specifically required to be transacted at an Annual General Meeting as well as Special Business, if any.

If the Board fails to convene its Annual General Meeting in any year, any Member of the company may approach the prescribed authority, which may then direct the calling of the Annual General Meeting of the company.

The Board may also, whenever it deems fit, call an Extra-Ordinary General Meeting of the company.

The Board shall, on the requisition of Members who hold, as on the date of the receipt of a valid requisition,

(a)   in the case of company having a share capital, not less than one-tenth of the paid-up share capital carrying Voting Rights or

(b)   in the case of a company not having share capital, not less than one-tenth of total voting power of the company, call an Extra-Ordinary General Meeting of the company. If, on receipt of a valid requisition having been made in this behalf, the Board, within twenty-one days from the date of such receipt, fails to call a Meeting on any day within forty-five days from the date of receipt of such requisition, the requisitionists may themselves call and hold the Meeting within three months from the date of requisition, in the same manner in which the Board should have called and held the Meeting.

Explanatory statement need not be annexed to the Notice of an Extra-Ordinary General Meeting convened by the requisitionists and the requisitionists may disclose the reasons for the Resolution(s) which they propose to move at the Meeting.

Such requisition shall not pertain to any item of business that is required to be transacted mandatorily through postal ballot.

1.2 Notice

1.2.1 Notice in writing of every Meeting shall be given to every Member of the company.

Such Notice shall also be given to the Directors and Auditors of the company, to the Secretarial Auditor, to Debenture Trustees, if any, and, wherever applicable or so required, to other specified persons.

In case of a Nidhi, Notice may be served individually only on Members who hold shares of more than one thousand rupees in face value or more than one percent of the total paid-up share capital of the company, whichever is less.

For other Members, Notice may be served by a public notice in newspaper circulated in the district where the Registered Office of the company is situated and by displaying the same on the Notice Board of the company. In the case of Members,

Notice shall be given at the address registered with the company or depository. In the case of shares or other securities held jointly by two or more persons, the Notice shall be given to the person whose name appears first as per records of the company or the depository, as the case may be.

In the case of any other person who is entitled to receive Notice, the same shall be given to such person at the address provided by him.

Where the company has received intimation of death of a Member, the Notice of Meeting shall be sent as under:

(a)   where securities are held singly, to the Nominee of the single holder;

(b)   where securities are held by more than one person jointly and any joint holder dies, to the surviving first joint holder;

(c)   where securities are held by more than one person jointly and all the joint holders die, to the Nominee appointed by all the joint holders;

In the absence of a Nominee, the Notice shall be sent to the legal representative of the deceased Member. In case of insolvency of a Member, the Notice shall be sent to the assignee of the insolvent Member.

In case the Member is a company or body corporate which is being wound up, Notice shall be sent to the liquidator.

1.2.2 Notice shall be sent by hand or by ordinary post or by speed post or by registered post or by courier or by facsimile or by e-mail or by any other electronic means. **'Electronic means'** means any communication sent by a company through its authorised and secured computer programme which is capable of producing confirmation and keeping record of such communication addressed to the person entitled to receive such communication at the last electronic mail address provided by the Member.

In case the Notice and accompanying documents are given by e-mail, these shall be sent at the Members' e-mail addresses, registered with the company or provided by the depository, in the manner prescribed under the Act.

The company shall ensure that it uses a system which produces confirmation of the total number of recipients e-mailed and a record of each recipient to whom the Notice has been sent and copy of such record and any Notices of any failed transmissions and subsequent re-sending shall be retained by or on behalf of the company as "proof of sending" for such period as decided by the Board, which shall not be less than three years from the date of the Meeting.

In case of the Directors, Auditors, Secretarial Auditors and others, if any, the Notice and accompanying documents shall be sent at the e-mail addresses provided by them to the company, if being sent by electronic means. Notice shall be sent to Members by registered post or speed post or courier or e-mail and not by ordinary post in the following cases:

(a)   if the company provides the facility of e-voting ;

(b)   if the item of business is being transacted through postal ballot. If a Member requests for delivery of Notice through a particular mode, other than the one followed by the company, he shall pay such fees as may be determined by the company in its Annual General Meeting and the Notice shall be sent to him in such mode.

Notice shall be sent to Members by registered post or speed post or e-mail if the Meeting is called by the requisitionists themselves where the Board had not proceeded to call the Meeting.

1.2.3 In case of companies having a website, the Notice shall simultaneously be hosted on the website till the conclusion of the Meeting. In case of a private company, the Notice shall be hosted on the website of the company, if any, unless otherwise provided in the Articles.

1.2.4 Notice shall specify the day, date, time and full address of the venue of the Meeting. Notice of Annual General Meeting shall also specify the serial number of the Meeting. Notice shall contain complete particulars of the venue of the Meeting including route map and prominent land mark, if any, for easy location, except in case of –

(i)   a company in which only its directors and their relatives are members;

(ii)   a wholly owned subsidiary. An Annual General Meeting and a Meeting called by the requisitionists shall be called during business hours, i.e., between 9 a.m. and 6 p.m., on a day that is not a National Holiday.

Annual General Meetings shall be held either at the registered office of the company or at some other place within the city, town or village in which the registered office of the company is situated.

However, Annual General Meetings of an unlisted company may be held at any place in, if prior consent is given by all the members either in writing or by Electronic Mode. Such consent shall be received before the Meeting. Extra-Ordinary General Meetings may be held at any place within India.

In case of a wholly owned subsidiary of a company incorporated outside India, Extra-Ordinary General Meetings may be held outside India.

A Meeting called by the requisitionists shall be held either at the registered office of the company or at some other place within the city, town or village in which the registered office of the company is situated.

In case of a Government company, the Annual General Meeting shall be held at its registered office or such other place within the city, town or village in which the registered office of the company is situated or such other place as the Central Government may approve in this behalf.

Notice of a company which has a share capital or the Articles of which provide for voting at a Meeting by Proxy, shall prominently contain a statement that a Member entitled to attend and vote is entitled to appoint a Proxy, or where that is allowed, one or more Proxies, to attend and vote instead of himself and that a Proxy need not be a Member.

In case of a private company, the Notice shall specify the entitlement of a member to appoint Proxy in accordance with this paragraph, unless otherwise provided in the Articles.

1.2.5 Notice shall clearly specify the nature of the Meeting and the business to be transacted thereat. In respect of items of Special Business, each such item shall be in the form of a Resolution and **shall be accompanied by an explanatory statement** which shall set out all such facts as would enable a Member to understand the meaning, scope and implications of the item of business and to take a decision thereon.

In respect of items of Ordinary Business, Resolutions are not required to be stated in the Notice.

The nature of the concern or interest (financial or otherwise), if any, of the following persons, in any special item of business or in a proposed Resolution, shall be disclosed in the explanatory statement:

(a)   Directors and Manager;

(b)   Other Key Managerial Personnel; and

(c)   Relatives of the persons mentioned above. In case any item of Special Business to be transacted at a Meeting of the company relates to or affects any other company, the extent of shareholding interest in that other company of every Promoter, Director, Manager and of every other Key Managerial Personnel of the first mentioned company shall, **if the extent of such shareholding is not less than two percent of the paid-up share capital of that company, also be stated in the explanatory statement.**

Where reference is made to any document, contract, agreement, the Memorandum of Association or Articles of Association, the relevant explanatory statement shall state that such documents are available for inspection and such documents shall be so made available for inspection in physical or in electronic form during specified business hours at the Registered Office of the company and copies thereof shall also be made available for inspection in physical or electronic form at the Head Office as well as Corporate Office of the company, if any, if such office is situated elsewhere, and also at the Meeting.

In case of a private company, explanatory statement shall comply with the above requirements, unless otherwise provided in the Articles.

In all cases relating to the appointment or re-appointment and/or fixation of remuneration of Directors including Managing Director or Executive Director or Whole - time Director or of Manager or variation of the terms of remuneration, details of each such Director or Manager, including age, qualifications, experience, terms and conditions of appointment or re-appointment along with details of remuneration sought to be paid and the remuneration last drawn by such person, if applicable, date of first appointment on the Board, shareholding in the company, relationship with other Directors, Manager and other Key Managerial Personnel of the company, the number of Meetings of the Board attended during the year and other Directorships, Membership/ Chairmanship of Committees of other Boards shall be given in the explanatory statement.

In case of appointment of Independent Directors, the justification for choosing the appointees for appointment as Independent Directors shall be disclosed and in case of re-appointment of Independent Directors, performance evaluation report of such Director or summary thereof shall be included in the explanatory statement.

1.2.6 Notice and accompanying documents shall be given at least twenty-one clear days in advance of the Meeting. For the purpose of reckoning twenty-one days clear Notice, the day of sending the Notice and the day of Meeting shall not be counted. Further in case the company sends the Notice by post or courier, an additional two days shall be provided for the service of Notice.

In case of a private company, the period of sending Notice including accompanying documents shall be as stated above, unless otherwise provided in the Articles. In case a valid special Notice under the Act has been received from Member(s), the company shall give Notice of the Resolution to all its Members at least seven days before the Meeting, exclusive of the day of dispatch of Notice and day of the Meeting, in the same manner as a Notice of any General Meeting is to be given.

Where this is not practicable, the Notice shall be published in a vernacular newspaper in the principal vernacular language of the district in which the registered office of the company is situated, and in an English newspaper in English language, both having a wide circulation in that district, at least seven days before the Meeting, exclusive of the day of publication of the Notice and day of the Meeting. In case of companies having a website, such Notice shall simultaneously be hosted on the website.

1.2.7 Notice and accompanying documents may be given at a **shorter period of time if the requisite consent of Members in writing** is accorded thereto, by physical or electronic means as under:

(i)   In case of an Annual General Meeting, **consent by not less than ninety-five percent of the Members entitled to vote at such Meeting.**

However, the Financial Statements and other documents required to be annexed thereto may be given at a shorter period of time if the requisite consent of Members in writing, by physical or electronic means, is accorded thereto:

(a)   if the company has a share capital, consent by the majority in number of members entitled to vote and represent not less than ninety-five per cent of such part of the paid-up share capital of the company as gives a right to vote at the Meeting;

(b) if the company has no share capital, consent by the Members having not less than ninety-five per cent of the total voting power exercisable at such Meeting.

(ii) In case of any other General Meeting –

(a) if the company has a share capital, consent by the majority in number of members entitled to vote and represent not less than ninety-five per cent of such part of the paid-up share capital of the company as gives a right to vote at the Meeting;

(b) if the company has no share capital, consent by the Members having not less than ninety-five per cent of the total voting power exercisable at such Meeting.

The request for consenting to shorter Notice and accompanying documents shall be sent together with the Notice and the Meeting shall be held only if the requisite consent of Members as stated above is received prior to the time fixed for the Meeting.

Where any Member of a company is entitled to vote only on some resolution or resolutions to be moved at a Meeting and not on the other, then vote of the Member with respect to shorter notice shall only be counted for the purpose of the resolution on which the Member can vote.

In addition, the company shall ensure compliance of provisions relating to appointment of Proxy unless all the Members entitled to vote at such Meeting, consent to holding of the General Meeting at shorter Notice.

In case of a private company, consent for shorter Notice shall be obtained from such number of Members as specified in this paragraph, unless otherwise provided in the Articles.

1.2.8 No business shall be transacted at a Meeting if Notice in accordance with this Standard has not been given.

However, any accidental omission to give Notice to, or the non-receipt of such Notice by any Member or other person who is entitled to such Notice for any Meeting shall not invalidate the proceedings of the Meeting.

1.2.9 No items of business other than those specified in the Notice and those specifically permitted under the Act shall be taken up at the Meeting.

A Resolution shall be valid only if it is passed in respect of an item of business contained in the Notice convening the Meeting or it is specifically permitted under the Act.

Items specifically permitted under the Act which may be taken up for consideration at the Meeting are:

(a)   Proposed Resolutions, the Notice of which has been given by Members;

(b)   Resolutions requiring special Notice, if received with the intention to move; (c) Candidature for Directorship, if any such Notice has been received.

Where special Notice is required of any Resolution and Notice of the intention to move such Resolution is received by the company from the prescribed number of Members, such item of business shall be placed for consideration at the Meeting after giving Notice of the Resolution to Members in the manner prescribed under the Act.

Any amendment to the Notice, including the addition of any item of business, can be made provided the Notice of amendment is given to all persons entitled to receive the Notice of the Meeting at least twenty-one clear days before the Meeting.

1.2.10 Notice shall be accompanied, by an attendance slip and a Proxy form with clear instructions for filling, stamping, signing and/ or depositing the Proxy form.

1.2.11 A Meeting convened upon due Notice shall not be postponed or cancelled. If, for reasons beyond the control of the Board, a Meeting cannot be held on the date originally fixed, the Board may reconvene the Meeting, to transact the same business as specified in the original Notice, after giving not less than three days intimation to the Members.

The intimation shall be either sent individually in the manner stated in this Standard or published in a vernacular newspaper in the principal vernacular language of the district in which the registered office of the company is situated, and in an English newspaper in English language, both having a wide circulation in that district.

2. Frequency of Meetings

2.1 Annual General Meeting

Every company shall, in each Calendar Year, hold a General Meeting called the Annual General Meeting.

Every company shall hold its first Annual General Meeting within nine months from the date of closing of the first financial year of the company and thereafter in each Calendar Year within six months of the close of the financial year, with an interval of not more than fifteen months between two successive Annual General Meetings.

The aforesaid period of six months or interval of fifteen months may be extended by a period not exceeding three months with the prior approval of the Registrar of Companies, in case of any Annual General Meeting other than the first Annual General Meeting.

If a company holds its first Annual General Meeting, as aforesaid, it shall not be necessary for the company to hold any Annual General Meeting in the Calendar Year of its incorporation.

2.2 Extra-Ordinary General Meeting

Items of business other than Ordinary Business may be considered at an Extra-Ordinary General Meeting or by means of a postal ballot, if thought fit by the Board.

3. Quorum

3.1 Quorum shall be present throughout the Meeting. Quorum shall be present not only at the time of commencement of the Meeting but also while transacting business.

Unless the Articles provide for a larger number, the Quorum for a General Meeting shall be:

(a)   in case of a public company, –

(i)   five Members personally present if the number of Members as on the date of Meeting is not more than one thousand;

(ii)   fifteen Members personally present if the number of Members as on the date of Meeting is more than one thousand but up to five thousand;

(iii)   thirty Members personally present if the number of Members as on the date of the Meeting exceeds five thousand;

(b)   in the case of a private company, two Members personally present. Where the Quorum provided in the Articles is higher than that provided under the Act, the Quorum shall conform to such higher requirement. Members need to be personally present at a Meeting to constitute the Quorum. Proxies shall be excluded for determining the Quorum.

3.2 A duly authorised representative of a body corporate or the representative of the President of India or the Governor of a State is deemed to be a Member personally present and enjoys all the rights of a Member present in person. One person can be an authorised representative of more than one body corporate. In such a case, he is treated as more than one Member present in person for the purpose of Quorum.

However, to constitute a Meeting, at least two individuals shall be present in person.

Thus, in case of a public company having not more than 1000 members with a Quorum requirement of five Members, an authorised representative of five bodies corporate cannot form a Quorum by himself but can do so if at least one more Member is personally present.

Members who have voted by Remote e-voting have the right to attend the General Meeting and accordingly their presence shall be counted for the purpose of Quorum.

A Member who is not entitled to vote on any particular item of business being a related party, if present, shall be counted for the purpose of Quorum.

The stipulation regarding the presence of a Quorum does not apply with respect to items of business transacted through postal ballot.

4. Presence of Directors and Auditors

4.1 Directors

4.1.1 If any Director is unable to attend the Meeting, the Chairman shall explain such absence at the Meeting.

The Chairman of the Audit Committee, Nomination and Remuneration Committee and the Stakeholders Relationship Committee, or any other Member of any such Committee authorised by the Chairman of the respective Committee to attend on his behalf, **shall attend the General Meeting.**

4.1.2 Directors who attend General Meetings of the company and the Company Secretary shall be seated with the Chairman. The Company Secretary shall assist the Chairman in conducting the Meeting.

4.2 Auditors

The Auditors, unless exempted by the company, shall, either by themselves or through their authorised representative, attend the

General Meetings of the company and shall have the right to be heard at such Meetings on that part of the business which concerns them as Auditors.

The authorised representative who attends the General Meeting of the company shall also be qualified to be an Auditor.

4.3 Secretarial Auditor

The Secretarial Auditor, unless exempted by the company shall, either by himself or through his authorised representative, attend the Annual General Meeting and shall have the right to be heard at such Meeting on that part of the business which concerns him as Secretarial Auditor.

The Chairman may invite the Secretarial Auditor or his authorised representative to attend any other General Meeting, if he considers it necessary. The authorised representative who attends the General Meeting of the company shall also be qualified to be a Secretarial Auditor.

5. Chairman

5.1 Appointment

The Chairman of the Board shall take the Chair and conduct the Meeting. If the Chairman is not present within fifteen minutes after the time appointed for holding the Meeting, or if he is unwilling to act as Chairman of the Meeting, or if no Director has been so designated, **the Directors present at the Meeting shall elect one of themselves to be the Chairman of the Meeting.**

If no Director is present within fifteen Minutes after the time appointed for holding the Meeting, or if no Director is willing to take the Chair, the **Members present shall elect, on a show of hands, one of themselves to be the Chairman of the Meeting, unless otherwise provided in the Articles**.

If a poll is demanded on the election of the Chairman, it shall be taken forthwith in accordance with the provisions of the Act and the Chairman elected on a show of hands shall continue to be the Chairman of the Meeting until some other person is elected as Chairman as a result of the poll, and such other person shall be the Chairman for the rest of the Meeting.

In case of a private company, appointment of the Chairman shall be in accordance with this paragraph, unless otherwise provided in the Articles.

The Chairman shall ensure that the Meeting is duly constituted in accordance with the Act and the Articles or any other applicable laws, before it proceeds to transact business.

The Chairman shall then conduct the Meeting in a fair and impartial manner and ensure that only such business as has been set out in the Notice is transacted. The Chairman shall regulate the manner in which voting is conducted at the Meeting keeping in view the provisions of the Act.

5.2 The Chairman shall explain the objective and implications of the Resolutions before they are put to vote at the Meeting.

The Chairman shall provide a fair opportunity to Members who are entitled to vote to seek clarifications and/or offer comments related to any item of business and address the same, as warranted.

5.3 In case of public companies, the Chairman shall not propose any Resolution in which he is deemed to

be concerned or interested nor shall he conduct the proceedings for that item of business.

If the Chairman is interested in any item of business, without prejudice to his Voting Rights on Resolutions, he shall entrust the conduct of the proceedings in respect of such item **to any Non -Interested Director or to a Member, with the consent of the Members present**, and resume the Chair after that item of business has been transacted.

6. Proxies

6.1 Right to Appoint

A Member entitled to attend and vote is entitled to appoint a Proxy, or where that is allowed, one or more Proxies, to attend and vote instead of himself and a Proxy need not be a Member.

A Proxy can act on behalf of Members not exceeding fifty and holding in the aggregate not more than ten percent of the total share capital of the company carrying Voting Rights.

However, a Member holding more than ten percent of the total share capital of the company carrying Voting Rights may appoint a single person as Proxy for his entire shareholding and such person shall not act as a Proxy for another person or shareholder.

If a Proxy is appointed for more than fifty Members, he shall choose any fifty Members and confirm the same to the company before the commencement of specified period for inspection.

In case, the Proxy fails to do so, the company shall consider only the first fifty Proxies received as valid.

In case of a private company, the Proxy shall be appointed in accordance with this paragraph, unless otherwise provided in the Articles.

6.2 Form of Proxy

6.2.1 An instrument appointing a Proxy shall be in the Form prescribed under the Act.

Such instrument shall not be questioned on the ground that it fails to comply with any special requirements specified by the Articles of a company.

The instrument of Proxy shall be signed by the appointer or his attorney duly authorised in writing, or if the appointer is a body corporate, be under its seal or be signed by an officer or an attorney duly authorised by it.

6.2.2 An instrument of Proxy duly filled, stamped and signed, is valid only for the Meeting to which it relates including any adjournment thereof.

6.3 Stamping of Proxies

An instrument of Proxy is valid only if it is properly stamped as per the applicable law. Unstamped or inadequately stamped Proxies or Proxies upon which the stamps have not been cancelled are invalid.

6.4 Execution of Proxies

6.4.1 The Proxy-holder shall prove his identity at the time of attending the Meeting.

6.4.2 An authorised representative of a body corporate or of the President of India or of the Governor of a State, holding shares in a company, may appoint a Proxy under his signature.

6.5 Proxies in Blank and Incomplete Proxies

6.5.1 A Proxy form which **does not state the name of the Proxy** shall not be considered valid.

6.5.2 Undated Proxy shall not be considered valid.

6.5.3 If a company receives multiple Proxies for the same holdings of a Member, the Proxy **which is dated last shall be considered valid**; if they are not dated or bear the same date without specific mention of time, all such multiple Proxies shall be treated as invalid.

6.6 Deposit of Proxies and Authorisations

6.6.1 Proxies shall be deposited with the company either in person or through post **not later than forty-eight hours** before the commencement of the Meeting in relation to which they are deposited and a Proxy shall be accepted even on a holiday if the last date by which it could be accepted is a holiday.

Any provision in the Articles of a company which specifies or requires a longer period for deposit of Proxy than forty-eight hours before a Meeting of the company shall have effect as if a period of forty-eight hours had been specified in or required for such deposit.

In case of a private company, the Proxy shall be deposited with the company in accordance with this paragraph, unless otherwise provided in the Articles.

6.6.2 If the Articles so provide, a Member who has not appointed a Proxy to attend and vote on his behalf at a Meeting may appoint a Proxy for any adjourned Meeting, not later than forty-eight hours before the time of such adjourned Meeting.

6.6.3 In case of remote e-voting:

(i)   the letter of appointment of representative(s) of the President of India or the Governor of a State; or

(ii)   the authorisation in respect of representative(s) of the Corporations; shall be received by the scrutiniser/company on or before close of e-voting.

In case of postal ballot such letter of appointment/ authorisation shall be submitted to the scrutiniser along with physical ballot form.

If the representative attends the Meeting in person to vote thereat, the letter of appointment / authorisation, as the case may be, shall be submitted before the commencement of Meeting.

6.7 Revocation of Proxies

6.7.1 If a Proxy had been appointed for the original Meeting and such Meeting is adjourned, any Proxy given for the adjourned Meeting revokes the Proxy given for the original Meeting.

6.7.2 A Proxy later in date revokes any Proxy/Proxies dated prior to such Proxy.

6.7.3 A Proxy is valid until written notice of revocation has been received by the company before the commencement of the Meeting or adjourned Meeting, as the case may be.

- An undated notice of revocation of Proxy shall not be accepted.

- A notice of revocation shall be signed by the same Member (s) who had signed the Proxy, in the case of joint Membership.

6.7.4 When a Member appoints a Proxy and both the Member and Proxy attend the Meeting, the Proxy stands **automatically revoked.**

6.8 Inspection of Proxies

6.8.1 Requisitions, if any, for inspection of Proxies shall be received in writing from a Member entitled to vote on any Resolution at least three days before the commencement of the Meeting.

6.8.2 Proxies shall be made available for inspection during the period beginning twenty-four hours before the time fixed for the commencement of the Meeting and ending with the conclusion of the Meeting.

Inspection shall be allowed between 9 a.m. and 6 p.m. during such period.

In case of a private company, inspection of Proxies shall be as stated above, unless otherwise provided in the Articles.

6.8.3 A fresh requisition, conforming to the above requirements, shall be given for inspection of Proxies in case the original Meeting is adjourned.

6.9 Record of Proxies

6.9.1 All Proxies received by the company shall be recorded chronologically in a register kept for that purpose.

6.9.2 In case any Proxy entered in the register is rejected, the reasons therefor shall be entered in the remarks column.

7. Voting

7.1 Proposing a Resolution at a Meeting

Every Resolution, except a Resolution which has been put to vote through Remote e-Voting or on which a poll has been demanded,

shall be proposed by a Member and seconded by another Member.

7.2 E-voting

7.2.1 Every company having its equity shares listed on a recognized stock exchange other than companies whose equity shares are listed on SME Exchange or on the Institutional Trading Platform and other companies as prescribed shall provide e-voting facility to their Members to exercise their Voting Rights.

Other companies presently prescribed are companies having not less than one thousand Members. Nidhis are not required to provide e-voting facility to their Members.

The facility of Remote e-voting does not dispense with the requirement of holding a General Meeting by the company.

7.2.2 Voting at the Meeting

Every company, which has provided e-voting facility to its Members, shall also put every Resolution to vote through a ballot process at the Meeting.

Ballot process may be carried out by distributing ballot/poll slips or by making arrangement for voting through computer or secure electronic systems.

Any Member, who has already exercised his votes through Remote e-voting, may attend the Meeting but is prohibited to vote at the Meeting and his vote, if any, cast at the Meeting shall be treated as invalid.

A Proxy can vote in the ballot process.

7.3 Show of Hands

Every company shall, at the Meeting, put every Resolution, except a Resolution which has been put to Remote e-voting, to vote on a show of hands at the first instance, unless a poll is validly demanded.

A Proxy cannot vote on a show of hands.

In case of a private company, the voting by show of hands shall be in accordance with this paragraph, unless otherwise provided in the Articles.

7.4 Poll

The Chairman shall order a poll upon receipt of a valid demand for poll either before or on the declaration of the result of the voting on any Resolution on show of hands.

Poll in such cases shall be through a Ballot process.

While a Proxy cannot speak at the Meeting, he has the right to demand or join in the demand for a poll.

The poll may be taken by the Chairman, on his own motion also. In case of a private company, the poll shall be conducted in accordance with this paragraph, unless otherwise provided in the Articles.

7.5 Voting Rights

7.5.1 Every Member holding equity shares and, in certain cases as prescribed in the Act, every Member holding preference shares, shall be entitled to vote on a Resolution.

Every Member entitled to vote on a Resolution and present in person shall, on a show of hands, have only one vote irrespective of the number of shares held by him.

A Member present in person or by Proxy shall, on a poll or ballot, have votes in proportion to his share in the paid up equity share capital of the company, subject to differential rights as to voting, if any, attached to certain shares as stipulated in the Articles or by the terms of issue of such shares.

Preference shareholders have a right to vote only in certain cases as prescribed under the Act.

In case of a private company, the Voting Rights shall be reckoned in accordance with this paragraph, unless otherwise provided in the Memorandum or Articles of the company.

In case of a Nidhi, no Member shall exercise Voting Rights on poll in excess of five percent of total Voting Rights of equity shareholders.

7.5.2 A Member who is a related party is not entitled to vote on a Resolution relating to approval of any contract or arrangement in which such Member is a related party, **except** in case of a company in which ninety percent or more Members, in number, are relatives of promoters or are related parties.

Further in case of wholly owned subsidiary, the resolution passed by the holding company shall be sufficient for the purpose of entering into the transactions between wholly owned subsidiary and holding company. In case of a private company, a member who is a related party is entitled to vote on such Resolution.

A member who is a related party is entitled to vote on a Resolution pertaining to approval of any contract or arrangement to be entered into by:

(a)   A Government company with any other Government company or with Central Government or any State

Government or any combination thereof; or (b) An unlisted Government company with the prior approval of competent authority, other than those contract or arrangements referred in clause (a).

7.6 Second or Casting Vote

Unless otherwise provided in the Articles, in the event of equality of votes, whether on show of hands or electronically or on a poll, the Chairman of the Meeting shall have a second or casting vote.

Where the Chairman has entrusted the conduct of proceedings in respect of an item in which he is interested to any Non-Interested Director or to a Member, a person who so takes the Chair shall have a second or casting vote.

8. Conduct of e-voting

8.1 Every company that is required or opts to provide e-voting facility to its Members shall comply with the provisions in this regard.

8.2 Every company providing e-voting facility shall offer such facility to all Members, irrespective of whether they hold shares in physical form or in dematerialised form.

8.3 The facility for Remote e-voting shall remain open for not less than three days. The voting period shall close at 5 p.m. on the day preceding the date of the General Meeting.

8.4 Board Approval

The Board shall:

(a)   appoint one or more scrutinisers for e-voting or the ballot process; The scrutiniser(s) may be a Company Secretary in Practice, a Chartered Accountant in Practice, a Cost Accountant in Practice, or an Advocate or any other person of repute who is not in the employment of the company and who can, in the opinion of the Board, scrutinise the e-voting process or the ballot process, as the case may be, in a fair and transparent manner.

The scrutiniser(s) so appointed may take assistance of a person who is not in employment of the company and who is well-versed with the e-voting system. Prior consent to act as a scrutiniser(s) shall be obtained from the scrutiniser(s) and placed before the Board for noting.

(b)   appoint an Agency;

(c)   decide the cut-off date for the purpose of reckoning the names of Members who are entitled to Voting Rights;

The cut-off date for determining the Members who are entitled to vote through Remote e-voting or voting at the meeting shall be a date not earlier than seven days prior to the date fixed for the Meeting.

Only Members as on the cut-off date, who have not exercised their Voting Rights through Remote e-voting, shall be entitled to vote at the Meeting.

8.5 Notice

8.5.1 Notice of the Meeting, wherein the facility of e-voting is provided, shall be sent either by registered post or speed post or by courier or by e-mail or by any other electronic means.

An advertisement containing prescribed details shall be published, immediately on completion of dispatch of Notices for Meeting but at least twenty one days before the date of the General Meeting, at least once in a vernacular newspaper in the principal vernacular language of the district in which the registered office of the company is situated and having a wide circulation in that district and at least once in English language in an English newspaper, having country-wide circulation, and specifying therein, inter-alia the following matters, namely:

(a)   A statement to the effect that the business may be transacted by e-voting;

(b)   The date and time of commencement of Remote e-voting;

(c)   The date and time of end of Remote e-voting;

(d)   The cut-off date as on which the right of voting of the Members shall be reckoned;

(e)   The manner in which persons who have acquired shares and become Members after the dispatch of Notice may obtain the login ID and password;

(f)   The manner in which company shall provide for voting by Members present at the Meeting;

(g)   The statement that:

(i)   Remote e-voting shall not be allowed beyond the said date and time;

(ii)   a Member may participate in the General Meeting even after exercising his right to vote through Remote e-voting but shall not be entitled to vote again; and

(iii)   a Member as on the cut-off date shall only be entitled for availing the Remote e-voting facility or vote, as the case may be, in the General Meeting;

(h)   Website address of the company, in case of companies having a website and Agency where Notice is displayed; and

(i)   Name, designation, address, e-mail ID and phone number of the person responsible to address the grievances connected with the e-voting.

Advertisement shall simultaneously be placed on the website of the company till the conclusion of Meeting, in case of companies having a website and of the Agency.

8.5.2 Notice shall simultaneously be placed on the website of the company, in case of companies having a website, and of the Agency. Such Notice shall remain on the website till the date of General Meeting.

8.5.3 Notice shall inform the Members about procedure of Remote e-voting, availability of such facility and provide necessary information thereof to enable them to access such facility.

Notice shall clearly state that the company is providing e-voting facility and that the business may be transacted through such voting. Notice shall describe clearly the Remote e-voting procedure and the procedure of voting at the General Meeting by Members who do not vote by Remote e-voting.

Notice shall also clearly specify the date and time of commencement and end of Remote e-voting and contain a statement that at the end of Remote e-voting period, the facility shall forthwith be blocked.

Notice shall also contain contact details of the official responsible to address the grievances connected with voting by electronic means.

Notice shall clearly specify that any Member, who has voted by Remote e-voting, cannot vote at the Meeting. Notice shall also specify the mode of declaration of the results of e-voting.

Notice shall also clearly mention the cut-off date as on which the right of voting of the Members shall be reckoned and state that a person who is not a Member as on the cut-off date should treat this Notice for information purposes only.

Notice shall provide the details about the login ID and the process and manner for generating or receiving the password and for casting of vote in a secure manner.

8.6 Declaration of results

8.6.1 The scrutiniser(s) shall submit his report within three days from the date of the Meeting to the Chairman or a person authorised by him, who shall countersign the same and declare the result of the voting forthwith with details of the number of votes cast for and against the Resolution, invalid votes and whether the Resolution has been carried or not.

8.6.2 The result of the voting, with details of the number of votes cast for and against the Resolution, invalid votes and whether the Resolution has been carried or not shall be displayed for at least three days on the Notice Board of the company at its Registered Office and its Head Office as well as Corporate Office, if any, if such office is situated elsewhere.

Further, the results of voting along with the scrutiniser's report shall also be placed on the website of the company, in case of companies having a website and of the Agency, immediately after the results are declared.

8.6.3 The Resolution, if passed by a requisite majority, shall be deemed to have been passed on the date of the relevant General Meeting.

8.7 Custody of scrutinisers' register, report and other related papers

The scrutinisers' register, report and other related papers received from the scrutiniser(s) shall be kept in the custody of the Company Secretary or any other person authorised by the Board for this purpose.

9. Conduct of Poll

9.1 When a poll is demanded on any Resolution, the Chairman shall get the validity of the demand verified and, if the demand is valid, shall order the poll forthwith if it is demanded on the question of appointment of the Chairman or adjournment of the Meeting and, in any other case, within forty-eight hours of the demand for poll.

9.2 In the case of a poll, which is not taken forthwith, the Chairman shall announce the date, venue and time of taking the poll to enable Members to have adequate and convenient opportunity to exercise their vote.

The Chairman may permit any Member who so desires to be present at the time of counting of votes.

If the date, venue and time of taking the poll cannot be announced at the Meeting, the Chairman shall inform the Members, the modes and the time of such communication, which shall in any case be within twenty four hours of closure of the Meeting.

A Member who did not attend the Meeting can participate and vote in the poll in such cases. In case of a private company, the demand and conduct of poll shall be as stated above, unless otherwise provided in the Articles.

9.3 Each Resolution put to vote by poll shall be put to vote separately.

One ballot paper may be used for more than one item.

9.4 Appointment of scrutinisers

The Chairman shall appoint such number of scrutinisers, as he deems necessary, who may include a Company Secretary in Practice, a Chartered Accountant in Practice, a Cost Accountant in Practice, an Advocate or any other person of repute who is not in the employment of the company, to ensure that the scrutiny of the votes cast on a poll is done in a fair and transparent manner.

In case of a private company, the appointment of scrutiniser(s) shall be in accordance with this paragraph, unless otherwise provided in the Articles.

9.5 Declaration of results

9.5.1 The scrutiniser(s) shall submit his report within seven days from the last date of the poll to the Chairman who shall countersign the same and declare the result of the poll within two days of the submission of report by the scrutiniser, with details of the number of votes cast for and against the Resolution, invalid votes and whether the Resolution has been carried or not. In case Chairman is not available, for such purpose, the report by the scrutiniser shall be submitted to a person authorised by the Chairman to receive such report, who shall countersign the scrutiniser's report on behalf of the Chairman.

The result shall be announced by the Chairman or any other person authorised by the Chairman in writing for this purpose. The Chairman of the Meeting shall have the power to regulate the manner in which the poll shall be taken and shall ensure that the poll is scrutinised in the manner prescribed under the Act.

In case of a private company, the declaration of result of poll shall be in accordance with this paragraph, unless otherwise provided in the Articles.

9.5.2 The result of the poll with details of the number of votes cast for and against the Resolution, invalid votes and whether the Resolution has been carried or not shall be displayed for at least three days on the Notice Board of the company at its Registered Office and its Head Office as well as Corporate Office, if any, if such office is situated elsewhere, and in case of companies having a website, shall also be placed on the website.

9.5.3 The result of the poll shall be deemed to be the decision of the Meeting on the Resolution on which the poll was taken.

10. Prohibition on Withdrawal of Resolutions

Resolutions for items of business which are likely to affect the market price of the securities of the company shall not be withdrawn.

Further, any resolution proposed for consideration through e-voting shall not be withdrawn.

11. Rescinding of Resolutions

A Resolution passed at a Meeting shall not be rescinded otherwise than by a Resolution passed at a subsequent Meeting.

12. Modifications to Resolutions

Modifications to any Resolution which do not change the purpose of the Resolution materially may be proposed, seconded and adopted by the requisite majority at the Meeting and, thereafter, the modified Resolution shall be duly proposed, seconded and put to vote.

No modification to any proposed text of the Resolution shall be made if it in any way alters the substance of the Resolution as set out in the Notice. Grammatical, clerical, factual and typographical errors, if any, may be corrected as deemed fit by the Chairman.

No modification shall be made to any Resolution which has already been put to vote by Remote e-voting before the Meeting.

13. Reading of Reports

13.1 The qualifications, observations or comments or other remarks, if any, mentioned in the Auditor's Report on the financial transactions, which have any adverse effect on the functioning of the company shall be read at the Annual General Meeting and attention of the Members present shall be drawn to the explanations / comments given by the Board of Directors in their report.

13.2 The qualifications, observations or comments or other remarks if any, mentioned in the Secretarial Audit Report issued by the Company Secretary in Practice, which have any material adverse effect on the functioning of the company, shall be read at the Annual General Meeting and attention of Members present shall be drawn to the explanations / comments given by the Board of Directors in their report.

14. Distribution of Gifts

No gifts, gift coupons, or cash in lieu of gifts shall be distributed to Members at or in connection with the Meeting.

15. Adjournment of Meetings

15.1 A duly convened Meeting shall not be adjourned unless circumstances so warrant.

The Chairman may adjourn a Meeting with the consent of the Members, at which a Quorum is present, and shall adjourn a Meeting if so directed by the Members.

Meetings shall stand adjourned for want of requisite Quorum.

The Chairman may also adjourn a Meeting in the event of disorder or other like causes, when it becomes impossible to conduct the Meeting and complete its business.

15.2 If a Meeting is adjourned sine-die or for a period of thirty days or more, a Notice of the adjourned Meeting shall be given in accordance with the provisions contained hereinabove relating to Notice.

15.3 If a Meeting is adjourned for a period of less than thirty days, the company shall give not less than three days' Notice specifying the day, date, time and venue of the Meeting, to the Members either individually or by publishing an advertisement in a vernacular newspaper in the principal vernacular language of the district in which the registered office of the company is situated, and in an English newspaper in English language, both having a wide circulation in that district.

However, if a Meeting is adjourned for a period not exceeding three days and where an announcement of adjournment has been made at the Meeting itself, giving in the details of day, date, time, venue and business to be transacted at the adjourned Meeting, **the company may also opt to give Notice of such adjourned Meeting either individually or by publishing an advertisement, as stated above.**

15.4 If a Meeting, other than an Annual General Meeting and a requisitioned Meeting, stands adjourned for want of Quorum, the adjourned Meeting shall be held on the same day, in the next week at the same time and place or on such other day or at such other time and place as may be determined by the Board.

If a Meeting is adjourned for want of a Quorum to the same day on the next week, at the same time and place or with a change of day, time or place, the company shall give not less than three days' Notice specifying the day, date, time and venue of the Meeting, to the Members either individually or by publishing an advertisement in a vernacular newspaper in the principal vernacular language of the district in which the registered office of the company is situated, and in an

English newspaper in English language, both having a wide circulation in that district.

If, at an adjourned Meeting, Quorum is not present within half an hour from the time appointed, the Members present, being not less than two in number, will constitute the Quorum.

An adjourned Annual General Meeting, adjourned for want of quorum or otherwise, shall not be held on a National Holiday, only if any item relating to filling up of vacancy of a director retiring by rotation is included in the agenda of such adjourned Meeting.

The company shall ensure compliance of the provisions of holding the Annual General Meeting every year, including adjournment thereof within a gap of not exceeding 15 months from the date of the previous Annual General Meeting or within such extended period permitted by the Registrar of Companies.

In case of a private company, the adjournment of Meeting for want of quorum shall be in accordance with this paragraph, unless otherwise provided in the Articles.

15.5 If, within half an hour from the time appointed for holding a Meeting called by requisitionists, a Quorum is not present, the Meeting shall stand cancelled.

In case of a private company, the requisitioned meeting shall stand cancelled in accordance with this paragraph, unless otherwise provided in the Articles.

15.6 At an adjourned Meeting, only the unfinished business of the original Meeting shall be considered.

Any Resolution passed at an adjourned Meeting would be deemed to have been passed on the date of the adjourned Meeting and not on any earlier date.

16. Passing of Resolutions by postal ballot

16.1 Every company, except a company having less than or equal to two hundred Members, shall transact items of business as prescribed, only by means of postal ballot instead of transacting such business at a General Meeting.

However, such item of business may be transacted at a General Meeting by a company which is required to provide e-voting facility to its Members.

The list of items of businesses requiring to be transacted only by means of a postal ballot is given below.

The Board may however opt to transact any other item of special business, not being any business in respect of which Directors or Auditors have a right to be heard at the Meeting, by means of postal ballot. Ordinary Business shall not be transacted by means of a postal ballot.

Annexure (Paragraph 16.1) Items of business which shall be passed only by postal ballot

1. Alteration of the objects clause of the Memorandum and in the case of the company in existence immediately before the commencement of the Act, alteration of the Main Objects of the Memorandum

2. Alteration of Articles of Association in relation to insertion or removal of provisions which are required to be included in the Articles of a company in order to constitute it a private company

3.   Change in place of Registered Office outside the local limits of any city, town or village

4.   Change in objects for which a company has raised money from public through prospectus and still has any unutilised amount out of the money so raised

5.   Issue of shares with differential rights as to voting or dividend or otherwise

6.   Variation in the rights attached to a class of shares or debentures or other securities

7.   Buy-back of shares by a company

8.   Appointment of a Director elected by Small Shareholders

9.   Sale of the whole or substantially the whole of an undertaking of a company or where the company owns more than one undertaking, of whole or substantially the whole of any of such undertakings

10.   Giving loans or extending guarantee or providing security in excess of the limit specified

11.   Any other Resolution prescribed under any applicable law, rules or regulations.

16.2 Every company having its equity shares listed on a recognised stock exchange other than companies whose equity shares are listed on SME Exchange or on the Institutional Trading Platform and other companies which are required to provide e-voting facility shall provide such facility to its Members in respect of those items, which are required to be transacted through postal ballot.

Other companies presently prescribed are companies having not less than one thousand Members.

Nidhis are not required to provide e-voting facility to their Members.

16.3 Board Approval

The Board shall:

(a)   identify the businesses to be transacted through postal ballot;

(b)   approve the Notice of postal ballot incorporating proposed Resolution(s) and explanatory statement thereto;

(c)   authorise the Company Secretary or where there is no Company Secretary, any Director of the company to conduct postal ballot process and sign and send the Notice along with other documents;

(d)   appoint one scrutiniser for the postal ballot; The scrutiniser may be a Company Secretary in Practice, a Chartered Accountant in Practice, a Cost Accountant in Practice, an Advocate or any other person of repute who is not in the employment of the company and, who can in the opinion of the Board, scrutinise the postal ballot process in a fair and transparent manner. The scrutiniser shall however not be an officer or employee of the company. The scrutiniser so appointed may take assistance of a person who is not in employment of the company and who is well-versed with the e-voting system. **Prior consent to act as a scrutiniser shall be obtained from the scrutiniser and placed before the Board for noting.**

(e)   appoint an Agency in respect of e-voting for the postal ballot;

(f)   decide the cut-off date for reckoning Voting Rights and ascertaining those Members to whom the Notice and postal ballot forms shall be sent. Only Members as on the cut-off date shall be entitled to vote on the proposed Resolution by postal ballot.

16.4 Notice

16.4.1 Notice of the postal ballot shall be given in writing to every Member of the company.

Such Notice shall be sent either by registered post or speed post, or by courier or by e-mail or by any other electronic means at the address registered with the company.

The Notice shall be accompanied by the postal ballot form with the necessary instructions for filling, signing and returning the same.

In case the Notice and accompanying documents are sent to Members by e-mail, these shall be sent to the Members' e-mail addresses, registered with the company or provided by the depository, in the manner prescribed under the Act.

Such Notice shall also be given to the Directors and Auditors of the company, to the Secretarial Auditor, to Debenture Trustees, if any, and, wherever applicable or so required, to other specified recipients.

An advertisement containing prescribed details shall be published at least once in a vernacular newspaper in the principal vernacular language of the district in which the registered office of the company is situated, and having a wide circulation in that district, and at least once in English language in an English newspaper having a wide circulation in that district, about having dispatched the Notice and the ballot papers.

16.4.2 In case of companies having a website, Notice of the postal ballot shall simultaneously be placed on the website. Such Notice shall remain on the website till the last date for receipt of the postal ballot forms from the Members.

16.4.3 Notice shall specify the day, date, time and venue where the results of the voting by postal ballot will be announced and the link of the website where such results will be displayed.

Notice shall also specify the mode of declaration of the results of the voting by postal ballot.

16.4.4 Notice of the postal ballot shall inform the Members about availability of e-voting facility, if any, and provide necessary information thereof to enable them to access such facility.

In case the facility of e-voting has been made available, the provisions relating to conduct of e-voting shall apply, mutatis mutandis, as far as applicable.

Notice shall describe clearly the e-voting procedure.

Notice shall also clearly specify the date and time of commencement and end of e-voting, if any and contain a statement that voting shall not be allowed beyond the said date and time.

Notice shall also contain contact details of the official responsible to address the grievances connected with the e-voting for postal ballot. Notice shall clearly specify that any Member cannot vote both by post and e-voting and if he votes both by post and e-voting, his vote by post shall be treated as invalid.

The advertisement shall, inter alia, state the following matters:

(a)   a statement to the effect that the business is to be transacted by postal ballot which may include voting by electronic means;

(b)   the date of completion of dispatch of Notices;

(c)   the date of commencement of voting (postal and e-voting);

(d)   the date of end of voting (postal and e-voting);

(e)   the statement that any postal ballot form received from the Member after thirty days from the date of dispatch of Notice will not be valid;

(f)   a statement to the effect that Member who has not received postal ballot form may apply to the company and obtain a duplicate thereof;

(g)   contact details of the person responsible to address the queries/grievances connected with the voting by postal ballot including voting by electronic means, if any; and

(h)   day, date, time and venue of declaration of results and the link of the website where such results will be displayed. Notice and the advertisement shall clearly mention the cut-off date as on which the right of voting of the Members shall be reckoned and state that a person who is not a Member as on the cut-off date should treat this Notice for information purposes only.

16.4.5 Each item proposed to be passed through postal ballot shall be in the form of a Resolution and shall be accompanied by an explanatory statement which shall set out all such facts as would enable a Member to understand the meaning, scope and implications of the item of business and to take a decision thereon.

16.5 Postal ballot forms

16.5.1 The postal ballot form shall be accompanied by a postage prepaid reply envelope addressed to the scrutiniser.

A single postal ballot form may provide for multiple items of business to be transacted.

16.5.2 The postal ballot form shall contain instructions as to the manner in which the form is to be completed, assent or dissent is to be recorded and its return to the scrutiniser.

The postal ballot form may specify instances in which such form shall be treated as invalid or rejected and procedure for issue of duplicate postal ballot forms.

16.5.3 A postal ballot form shall be considered invalid if:

(a)   A form other than one issued by the company has been used;

(b)   It has not been signed by or on behalf of the Member;

(c)   Signature on the postal ballot form doesn't match the specimen signatures with the company;

(d)   It is not possible to determine without any doubt the assent or dissent of the Member;

(e)   Neither assent nor dissent is mentioned;

(f)   Any competent authority has given directions in writing to the company to freeze the Voting Rights of the Member;

(g)   The envelope containing the postal ballot form is received after the last date prescribed;

(h)   The postal ballot form, signed in a representative capacity, is not accompanied by a certified copy of the relevant specific authority;

(i)   It is received from a Member who is in arrears of payment of calls;

(j)   It is defaced or mutilated in such a way that its identity as a genuine form cannot be established;

(k)   Member has made any amendment to the Resolution or imposed any condition while exercising his vote.

A postal ballot form which is otherwise complete in all respects and is lodged within the prescribed time limit but is undated shall be considered valid.

16.6 Declaration of results

16.6.1 The scrutiniser shall submit his report within seven days from the last date of receipt of postal ballot forms to the Chairman or a person authorised by him, who shall countersign the same and declare the result of the postal ballot on the date, time and venue specified in the Notice, with details of the number of votes cast for and against the Resolution, invalid votes and the final result as to whether the Resolution has been carried or not.

16.6.2 The result of the voting with details of the number of votes cast for and against the Resolution, invalid votes and whether the Resolution has been carried or not, along with the scrutiniser's report shall be displayed for at least three days on the Notice Board of the company at its Registered Office and its Head Office as well as Corporate Office, if any, if such office is situated elsewhere, and also be placed on the website of the company, in case of companies having a website.

16.6.3 The Resolution, if passed by requisite majority, shall be deemed to have been passed on the last date specified by the company for receipt of duly completed postal ballot forms or e-voting.

16.7 Custody of scrutiniser's registers, report and other related papers The postal ballot forms, other related papers, register and scrutiniser's report received from the scrutiniser shall be kept in the custody of the Company Secretary or any other person authorised by the Board for this purpose.

16.8 Rescinding the Resolution

A Resolution passed by postal ballot **shall not be rescinded otherwise than by a Resolution passed subsequently through postal ballot or passed at a General Meeting by a company** which is required to provide e-voting facility to its Members.

16.9 Modification to the Resolution

No amendment or modification shall be made to any Resolution circulated to the Members for passing by means of postal ballot.

17. Minutes

Every company shall keep Minutes of all Meetings.

Minutes kept in accordance with the provisions of the Act evidence the proceedings recorded therein.

Minutes help in understanding the deliberations and decisions taken at the Meeting.

17.1 Maintenance of Minutes

17.1.1 Minutes shall be recorded in books maintained for that purpose.

17.1.2 A distinct Minutes Book shall be maintained for Meetings of the Members of the company, creditors and others as may be required under the Act.

Resolutions passed by postal ballot shall be recorded in the Minutes book of General Meetings.

17.1.3 A company may maintain its **Minutes in physical or in electronic form.** Minutes may be maintained in electronic form in such manner as prescribed under the Act and as may be decided by the Board.

Minutes in electronic form shall be maintained with Timestamp.

A company shall, however, follow a uniform and consistent form of maintaining the Minutes.

Any deviation in such form of maintenance shall be authorised by the Board.

17.1.4 The pages of the Minutes Books shall be consecutively numbered. This shall be followed irrespective of a break in the Book arising out of periodical binding in case the Minutes are maintained in physical form.

This shall be equally applicable for maintenance of Minutes Book in electronic form with Timestamp.

In the event any page or part thereof in the Minutes Book is left blank, it shall be scored out and initialed by the Chairman who signs the Minutes.

17.1.5 Minutes shall not be pasted or attached to the Minutes Book, or tampered with in any manner.

17.1.6 Minutes of Meetings, if maintained in loose-leaf form, shall be bound periodically at least once in every three years.

There shall be a proper locking device to ensure security and proper control to prevent removal or manipulation of the loose leaves.

17.1.7 Minutes Books shall be kept at the Registered Office of the company.

17.2 Contents of Minutes

17.2.1 General Contents

17.2.1.1 Minutes shall state, at the beginning the Meeting, name of the company, day, date, venue and time of commencement of the Meeting. Minutes of Annual General Meeting shall also state the serial number of the Meeting. In case a Meeting is adjourned, the Minutes shall be entered in respect of the original Meeting as well as the adjourned Meeting. In respect of a Meeting convened but adjourned for want of Quorum a statement to that effect shall be recorded by the Chairman or any Director present at the Meeting in the Minutes.

17.2.1.2 Minutes shall record the names of the Directors and the Company Secretary present at the Meeting.

The names of the Directors shall be listed in alphabetical order or in any other logical manner, but in either case starting with the name of the person in the Chair.

17.2.2 Specific Contents

17.2.2.1 Minutes shall, inter alia, contain:

(a)   The Record of election, if any, of the Chairman of the Meeting.

(b)   The fact that certain registers, documents, the Auditor's Report and Secretarial Audit Report, as prescribed under the Act were available for inspection.

(c)   The Record of presence of Quorum.

(d)   The number of Members present in person including representatives.

(e)   The number of Proxies and the number of shares represented by them.

(f)   The presence of the Chairmen of the Audit Committee, Nomination and Remuneration Committee and Stakeholders Relationship Committee or their authorised representatives.

(g)   The presence if any, of the Secretarial Auditor, the Auditors, or their authorised representatives, the Court/Tribunal appointed observers or scrutinisers.

(h)   Summary of the opening remarks of the Chairman.

     (i)   Reading of qualifications, observations or comments or other remarks on the financial transactions, which have any adverse effect on the functioning of the company, as mentioned in the report of the Auditors.

     (ii)   Reading of qualifications, observations or comments or other remarks, which have any material adverse effect on the functioning of the company, as mentioned in the report of the Secretarial Auditor.

(iii)   Summary of the clarifications provided on various Agenda Items.

(iv)   In respect of each Resolution, the type of the Resolution, the names of the persons who proposed and seconded and the majority with which such Resolution was passed. Where a motion is moved to modify a proposed Resolution, the result of voting on such motion shall be mentioned. If a Resolution proposed undergoes modification pursuant to a motion by shareholders, the Minutes shall contain the details of voting for the modified Resolution.

(v)   In the case of poll, the names of scrutinisers appointed and the number of votes cast in favour and against the Resolution and invalid votes.

(vi)   If the Chairman vacates the Chair in respect of any specific item, the fact that he did so and in his place some other Director or Member took the Chair.

(vii)   The time of commencement and conclusion of the Meeting.

17.2.2.2 In respect of Resolutions passed by e-voting or postal ballot, **a brief report on the e-voting or postal ballot conducted including the Resolution proposed**, the result of the voting thereon and the summary of the scrutiniser's report shall be recorded in the Minutes Book and signed by the Chairman or in the event of death or inability of the Chairman, by any Director duly authorised by the Board for the purpose, **within thirty days from the date of passing of Resolution by e-voting or postal ballot.**

17.3 Recording of Minutes

17.3.1 Minutes shall **contain a fair and correct summary** of the proceedings of the Meeting.

The Company Secretary shall record the proceedings of the Meetings. Where there is no Company Secretary, any other person authorised by the Board or by the Chairman in this behalf shall record the proceedings.

The Chairman shall ensure that the proceedings of the Meeting are correctly recorded.

> **The Chairman has absolute discretion to exclude from the Minutes, matters which in his opinion are or could reasonably be regarded as defamatory of any person, irrelevant or immaterial to the proceedings or which are detrimental to the interests of the company.**

17.3.2 Minutes shall be written in clear, concise and plain language.

Minutes shall be written in third person and past tense. Resolutions shall however be written in present tense. Minutes need not be an exact transcript of the proceedings at the Meeting.

17.3.3 Each item of business taken up at the Meeting shall be numbered. Numbering shall be in a manner which would enable ease of reference or cross-reference.

17.4 Entry in the Minutes Book

17.4.1 Minutes shall be entered in the Minutes Book within thirty days from the date of conclusion of the Meeting.

In case a Meeting is adjourned, the Minutes in respect of the original Meeting as well as the adjourned Meeting shall

be entered in the Minutes Book within thirty days from the date of the respective Meetings.

17.4.2 The date of entry of the Minutes in the Minutes Book shall be recorded by the Company Secretary. Where there is no Company Secretary, it shall be entered by any other person authorised by the Board or the Chairman.

17.4.3 Minutes, once entered in the Minutes Book, shall not be altered.

17.5 Signing and Dating of Minutes

17.5.1 Minutes of a General Meeting shall be signed and dated by the Chairman of the Meeting or in the event of death or inability of that Chairman, by any Director who was present in the Meeting and duly authorised by the Board for the purpose, within thirty days of the General Meeting.

17.5.2 The Chairman shall initial each page of the Minutes, sign the last page and append to such signature the date on which and the place where he has signed the Minutes.

Any blank space in a page between the conclusion of the Minutes and signature of the Chairman shall be scored out. If the Minutes are maintained in electronic form, the Chairman shall sign the Minutes digitally.

17.6 Inspection and Extracts of Minutes

17.6.1 Directors and Members are entitled to inspect the Minutes of all General Meetings including Resolutions passed by postal ballot.

Minutes of all General Meetings shall be open for inspection by any Member during business hours of the company, without charge, subject to such reasonable restrictions as the company may, by its Articles or in General Meeting, impose, so, however, that not less than two hours in each business day are allowed for inspection.

The Company Secretary in Practice appointed by the company, the Secretarial Auditor, the Statutory Auditor, the Cost Auditor or the Internal Auditor of the company can inspect the Minutes as he may consider necessary for the performance of his duties.

Inspection of Minutes Book may be provided in physical or in electronic form.

While providing inspection of Minutes Book, the Company Secretary or the official of the company authorised by the Company Secretary to facilitate inspection shall take all precautions to ensure that the Minutes Book is not mutilated or in any way tampered with by the person inspecting.

17.6.2 Extract of the Minutes shall be given only after the Minutes have been duly signed. However, any Resolution passed at a Meeting may be issued even pending signing of the Minutes, provided the same is certified by the Chairman or any Director or the Company Secretary.

When a Member requests in writing for a copy of any Minutes, which he is entitled to inspect, the company shall furnish the same within seven working days of receipt of his request, subject to payment of such fee as may be specified in the Articles of the company.

In case a Member requests for the copy of the Minutes in electronic form, in respect of any previous General Meetings held during a period immediately preceding

three financial years, the company shall furnish the same on payment of such fee as prescribed under the Act.

Copies of the Minutes or the extracts thereof as requisitioned by the Member, duly certified by the Company Secretary or where there is no Company Secretary, an officer duly authorised by the Board in this behalf, may be provided in physical or electronic form.

18. Preservation of Minutes and other Records

18.1 Minutes of all Meetings shall be preserved permanently in physical or in electronic form with Timestamp.

Where, under a scheme of arrangement, a company has been merged or amalgamated with another company,

Minutes of all Meetings of the transferor company, as handed over to the transferee company, shall be preserved permanently by the transferee company, notwithstanding that the transferor company might have been dissolved.

18.2 Office copies of Notices, scrutiniser's report and related papers shall be preserved in good order in physical or in electronic form for as long as they remain current or for eight financial years, whichever is later and may be destroyed thereafter with the approval of the Board.

Office copies of Notices, scrutiniser's report and related papers of the transferor company, as handed over to the transferee company, shall be preserved in good order in physical or electronic form for as long as they remain current or for eight financial years, whichever is later and may be destroyed thereafter with the approval of the Board and permission of the Central Government, where applicable.

18.3 Minutes Books shall be kept in the custody of the Company Secretary. Where there is no Company Secretary, Minutes shall be kept in the custody of any Director duly authorised for the purpose by the Board.

19. Report on Annual General Meeting

Every listed public company shall prepare a report on Annual General Meeting in the prescribed form, including a confirmation that the Meeting was convened, held and conducted as per the provisions of the Act.

Such report which shall be a fair and correct summary of the proceedings of the Meeting shall contain:

(a)   the day, date, time and venue of the Annual General Meeting;

(b)   confirmation with respect to appointment of Chairman of the Meeting; (c) number of Members attending the Meeting;

(d)   confirmation of Quorum;

(e)   confirmation with respect to compliance of the Act and Standards with respect to calling, convening and conducting the Meeting;

(f)   business transacted at the Meeting and result thereof with a brief summary of the discussions;

(g)   particulars with respect to any adjournment, postponement of Meeting, change in venue; and

(h)   any other points relevant for inclusion in the report.

Such report shall be filed with the Registrar of Companies within thirty days of the conclusion of the Annual General Meeting.

20. Disclosure

The Annual Return of a company shall disclose the date of Annual General Meeting held during the financial year.

Chapter VIII

Declaration and Payment of Dividend under Companies Act, 2313; Companies (Declaration and Payment of Dividends (Rules, 2014 and Recommendatory Secretarial Standards on Dividends (SS-3) by ICSI

A. Companies Act, 2013

123. Declaration of dividend.

Reg 12- Payment of dividend or interest or redemption or repayment.

The listed entity shall use any of the electronic mode of payment facility approved by the Reserve Bank of India, in the manner specified in Schedule I, for the payment of the following:

(a)   dividends;

(b)   interest;

(c)   redemption or repayment amounts:

Provided that where it is not possible to use electronic mode of payment, 'payable-at-par' warrants or cheques may be issued:

Provided further that where the amount payable as dividend exceeds one thousand and five hundred rupees, the 'payable-at-par' warrants or cheques shall be sent by speed post.

124. Unpaid Dividend Account —

(3) If any default is made in transferring the total amount referred of unpaid dividends or any part thereof to the Unpaid Dividend Account of the company, it shall pay, from the date of such default, interest on so much of the amount as has not been transferred to the said account, at the rate of twelve per cent. per annum and the interest accruing on such amount shall ensure to the benefit of the members of the company in proportion to the amount remaining unpaid to them.

"(7) If a company fails to comply with any of the requirements of this section, such company shall be liable to a penalty of one lakh rupees and in case of continuing failure, with a further penalty of five hundred rupees for each day after the first during which such failure continues, subject to a maximum of ten lakh rupees and **every officer of the company who is in default shall be liable** to a penalty of twenty-five thousand rupees and in case of continuing failure, with a further penalty of one hundred rupees for each day after the first during which such failure continues, subject to a maximum of two lakh rupees.

125. Investor Education and Protection Fund —

126. Right to dividend, rights shares and bonus shares to be held in abeyance pending registration of transfer of shares —

127. Punishment for failure to distribute dividends —

Where a dividend has been declared by a company but has not been paid or the warrant in respect thereof has not been posted within thirty days from the date of declaration to any shareholder entitled to the payment of the dividend, **every director of the company shall, if he is knowingly a party to the default, be punishable with imprisonment** which may extend to two years and with fine which shall not be less than one thousand rupees for every day during which such default continues and the company shall be liable to pay simple interest at the rate of eighteen per cent. per annum during the period for which such default continues:

B. Companies Declaration and Payment of Dividends Rules, 2014

Rule 3: Declaration of Dividends out of Reserves

Payment of Dividend; Interim Dividend (Sec 123(3); Procedure of Declaration and Payment of Dividend

C. **Reg. of SEBI (LODR) 2015.**

D. **Reg 43: Dividends.**

(1)   The listed entity shall declare and disclose the dividend on per share basis only.

(2)   The listed entity shall not forfeit unclaimed dividends before the claim becomes barred by law and such forfeiture, if effected, shall be annulled in appropriate cases.

Reg 43A: Dividend Distribution Policy.

(1)   The top 1000 listed entities based on market capitalization (calculated as on March 31 of every financial year) shall

formulate a dividend distribution policy **which shall be disclosed on the website** of the listed entity and a web-link shall also be provided in their annual reports].

(2) The dividend distribution policy shall include the following parameters:

(a) the circumstances under which the **shareholders of the listed entities may or may not expect dividend**;

(b) the **financial parameters** that shall be considered while declaring dividend;

(c) **internal and external factors that shall be considered** for declaration of dividend;

(d) policy as to **how the retained earnings shall be utilized**; and

(e) **parameters** that shall be adopted with regard to **various classes of shares:**

Provided that if the listed entity proposes to declare dividend on the basis of parameters in addition to clauses (a) to (e) or proposes to change such additional parameters or the dividend distribution policy contained in any of the parameters, it shall disclose such changes along with the rationale for the same in its annual report and on its website.

(3) The listed entities other than those specified at sub-regulation (1) of this regulation may disclose their dividend distribution policies on a voluntary basis on their websites and provide a web-link in their annual reports.

E. **SS-3- Secretarial Standards on Dividend {Recommendatory}**

1. Ascertainment of amount available for payment/ distribution as Dividend.

1.1 Out of profits

1.1.2 A company shall not declare Dividend on its equity shares in case of non-compliance of provisions relating to the acceptance of deposits under the Act, till such time the deposits accepted have been repaid with interest in accordance with the terms and conditions of the agreement entered with the depositors.

A company shall also not declare any Dividend, if it has defaulted in –

(a)   Redemption of debentures or payment of interest thereon or creation of debenture redemption reserve,

(b)   Redemption of preference shares or creation of capital redemption reserve,

(c)   Payment of Dividend declared in the current or previous financial year(s), or

(d)   Repayment of any term loan to a bank or financial institution or interest thereon, till such time the default is subsisting.

No Dividend shall be declared by the company during the extended time, if any, granted by the Tribunal/Court for repayment of above liabilities.

1.1.3 Dividend shall not be declared out of the Securities Premium Account or the Capital Redemption Reserve or Revaluation

Reserve or Amalgamation Reserve or out of profits on re-issue of forfeited shares or out of profits earned prior to incorporation of the company.

1.2 Out of Free Reserves

1.2.2 Interim Dividend shall not be declared out of Free Reserves. In the event of a loss or inadequacy of profits during a financial year, no Interim Dividend shall be declared/ paid out of Free Reserves.

2. Declaration of Dividend

2.1 Dividend shall be declared only on the recommendation of the Board, made at a meeting of the Board.

Unless the Dividend has been recommended by the Board, Members in Annual General Meeting cannot on their own declare any Dividend.

Where a company has an Audit Committee, this Committee shall consider the annual financial statements before submission to the Board.

Dividend shall be recommended by the Board after consideration and approval of said financial statements.

All requisite approvals shall be obtained before declaration of Dividend.

Dividend shall not be declared subject to any condition such as the approval of financial institutions/ banks or foreign collaborators or compliance with any other contractual obligation.

2.2 Dividend shall be declared only at an Annual General Meeting. Dividend shall relate to a financial year and shall be declared by the Members at the Annual General Meeting of the company after adoption of the financial statements of the company. Members may declare a lower rate of Dividend than the rate recommended by the Board but have no power to increase the amount or rate of Dividend recommended by the Board.

The Members may also decide not to declare the Dividend recommended by the Board. The Dividend, if declared, should be disclosed on per share basis.

2.4 Interim Dividend shall be declared at a meeting of the Board.

While Final Dividend is recommended by the Board and declared by the Members, approval of Members is not required for declaration of Interim Dividend.

Where a company has an Audit Committee, this Committee shall consider the financial results which shall thereafter be submitted to the Board for its consideration and declaration of Interim Dividend.

3. Entitlement to Dividend

4. Dividend in Abeyance

5. Payment of Dividend

5.1 Dividend shall be deposited in a separate bank account within five days from the date of declaration and shall be paid within thirty days of declaration.

The intervening holidays, if any, falling during such period shall be included.

The amount deposited in such bank account shall be utilised only for the payment of Dividend or for transfer to Unpaid Dividend Account/Investor Education and Protection Fund and for no other purpose.

The requirement of deposit of Dividend amount in a separate bank account within five days from the date of its declaration, shall not apply to a Government Company in which the entire paid up share capital is held by the Central Government or State Government(s) or jointly by both or by one or more Government Company.

6. Unpaid Dividend

6.1 The amount of Dividend which remains unpaid or unclaimed after thirty days from the date of its declaration shall be transferred to a special bank account titled as 'Unpaid Dividend Account' to be opened by the company in that behalf with any scheduled bank. Such transfer shall be made within seven days from the date of expiry of the thirty days period from the date of declaration of Dividend.

The company shall within a period of ninety days of transferring such amount to 'Unpaid Dividend Account' prepare a statement containing the names, last known addresses and the amount of Dividend to be paid to each of the Members. Such statement shall be uploaded on the website of the company, if any, and also on the website specified by the Central Government for this purpose.

Such statement shall remain on the website(s) till such time the unpaid or unclaimed Dividend is transferred to the Investor Education and Protection Fund (the Fund) and be updated by the company at regular intervals.

Any person claiming to be entitled to any amount transferred to the Unpaid Dividend Account may apply to the company for payment of such amount. In case of a Nidhi company, any Dividend payable in cash may be paid by crediting the same to the account of the Member, if the Dividend is not claimed within 30 days from the date of declaration of the Dividend.

6.2 Any amount in the Unpaid Dividend Account of the company which remains unpaid or unclaimed for a period of seven years from the date of transfer of such amount to the Unpaid Dividend Account, along with interest accrued, if any, shall be transferred to the **Investor Education and Protection Fund.**

Any transfer to the Fund shall be made within thirty days from the expiry of seven years from the date of transfer of unpaid or unclaimed Dividend to the Unpaid Dividend Account.

7. Revocation of Dividend

7.1 Dividend, once declared, becomes a debt and shall not be revoked.

8. Preservation of Dividend Cheques, Warrants and Dividend Registers

Additional compliances applicable to Listed Companies

A Listed Company shall conform to the following:

(i)   The equity shares allotted by the company shall rank pari passu with the existing equity shares for the purpose of payment of Dividend, if the same are in existence as on the record date/ book closure.

(ii)   The company shall not issue shares in any manner which may confer on any person, superior rights as to voting or Dividend vis-à-vis the rights on equity shares that are already listed.

(iii)   The company shall give prior intimation to the Stock Exchange(s) about the Board Meeting in which Dividend is proposed to be recommended / declared, at least two working days in advance excluding the date of the meeting and the date of the intimation.

(iv)   The company shall intimate the Stock Exchange(s), the record date fixed for the purpose of payment of Dividend at least seven working days in advance excluding the date of the intimation and the record date.

(v)   The company shall recommend or declare Dividend at least five working days before the record date fixed for the purpose. The said period of five working days is excluding the date of declaration/recommendation of Dividend and the record date fixed for the purpose.

(vi)   The company shall disclose the outcome of the Board Meeting held to consider the Dividend matters, to the Stock Exchange(s) within 30 minutes of closure of the meeting. In case of recommendation / declaration of Dividend, the intimation shall also include the date on which such Dividend shall be paid or Dividend warrant shall be dispatched.

(vii)   In case of payment of Dividend through warrant or cheque payable at par, if the amount of Dividend exceeds one thousand and five hundred rupees, the company shall dispatch such

Dividend warrant or cheque by speed post to the concerned Member at the registered address.

(viii)   The company shall declare and disclose Dividend on per share basis only.

(ix)   The company shall not forfeit unclaimed Dividends before the claim becomes barred by law and such forfeiture, if effected, shall be annulled in appropriate cases.

(x)   Top five hundred Listed Companies based on market capitalisation as on 31st March every financial year, shall formulate a Dividend Distribution Policy covering the prescribed parameters by Securities and Exchange Board of India (SEBI). Such policy shall be disclosed in the Annual Report of the company and also be placed on its website.

(xi)   The company shall disclose in its Corporate Governance Report the Dividend payment date under the General Shareholder Information Section.

Chapter IX

Accounts of Companies & Companies (Accounts) Rules, 2014; Financial Statements & Boards's Report

128. Books of account and other relevant books, papers and financial statements to be kept by company —

(1) Every company shall prepare and keep at its registered office books of account and other relevant books and papers and financial statement for every financial year **which give a true and fair view of the state of the affairs of the company,** including that of its branch office or offices, if any, and explain the transactions effected both at the registered office and its branches and such books shall be kept on accrual basis and according to the double entry system of accounting:

Provided that all or any of the books of account aforesaid and other relevant papers **may be kept at such other place in India as the Board of Directors may decide and** where such a decision is taken, the company shall, within seven days thereof, file with the Registrar a notice in writing giving the full address of that other place:

Provided further that the company may keep such books of account or other relevant papers in electronic mode in such manner prescribed under Rule 3.

(3) The books of account and other books and papers maintained by the company within India shall be **open for inspection** at the registered office of the company or at such other place in India **by any director during business hours,** and in the case of financial information, if any, maintained outside the country, copies of such financial information shall be maintained and produced for inspection by any director subject to such conditions as may be prescribed:

Provided that the inspection in respect of any **subsidiary of the company** shall be done only by the person authorized in this behalf by a resolution of the Board of Directors.

(5) The books of account of every company relating to a period of **not less than eight financial years immediately preceding a financial year,** or where the company had been in existence for a period less than eight years, in respect of all the preceding years together with the vouchers relevant to any entry in such books of account shall be kept in good order:

Provided that where an investigation has been ordered in respect of the company under Chapter XIV, the Central Government may direct that the books of account may be kept for such longer period as it may deem fit.

(6) If the managing director, the whole-time director in charge of finance, the Chief Financial Officer or any other person of a company charged by the Board with the duty of complying with the provisions of this section,

contravenes such provisions, such managing director, whole-time director in charge of finance, Chief Financial officer or such other person of the company shall be punishable with fine which shall not be less than fifty thousand rupees but which may extend to five lakh rupees.

Rule 3: Manner of books of account to be kept in electronic mode.-

(5) There shall be a **proper system for storage, retrieval, display or printout** of the electronic records **as the Audit Committee, if any, or the Board may deem appropriate** and such records shall not be disposed of or rendered unusable, unless permitted by law:

Provided that the back-up of the books of account and other books and papers of the company maintained in electronic mode, including at a place outside India, if any, shall be kept in servers physically located in India on a periodic basis.

4. Conditions regarding maintenance and inspection of certain financial information maintained outside India by directors.-

129. Financial statement —

(1) The financial statements shall give a true and fair view of the state of affairs of the company or companies, comply with the accounting standards notified under section 133 and shall be in the form or forms as may be provided for different class or classes of companies in Schedule III:

Provided that the items contained in such financial statements shall be in accordance with the accounting standards:

Provided further that nothing contained in this sub-section shall apply to any insurance or banking company or any company engaged in the generation or supply of electricity, or to any other class of company for which a form of financial statement has been specified in or under the Act governing such class of company:

(3) Where a company has one or more subsidiaries, it shall, in addition to financial statements, prepare a consolidated financial statement of the company and of all the subsidiaries in the same form and manner as that of its own which shall also be laid before the annual general meeting of the company along with the laying of its financial statement.

Provided that the company shall also attach along with its financial statement, a separate statement containing the salient features of the financial statement of its subsidiary or subsidiaries in such form as may be prescribed:

(4) The provisions of this Act applicable to the preparation, adoption and audit of the financial statements of a holding company shall, mutatis mutandis, apply to the consolidated financial statements.

(5) where the financial statements of a company do not comply with the accounting standards, the company shall disclose in its financial statements, the deviation from the accounting standards, the reasons for such deviation and the financial effects, if any, arising out of such deviation.

(7) If a company contravenes the provisions of this section, the managing director, the whole-time director in charge of finance, the Chief Financial Officer **or any other person charged by the Board with the duty of complying**

with the requirements of this section and in the absence of any of the officers mentioned above, all the directors shall be punishable with imprisonment for a term which may extend to one year or with fine which shall not be less than fifty thousand rupees but which may extend to five lakh rupees, or with both.

Rule 5. Form of Statement containing salient features of financial statements of subsidiaries

Rule 6.Manner of consolidation of accounts

"129A. Periodical Financial Results, approval of the BOD and filing within thirty days with Registrar.

134. Financial statement, Board's report, etc —

(1)   The financial statement, including consolidated financial statement, if any, shall be approved by the Board of Directors before they are signed on behalf of the Board at least by the chairperson of the company where he is authorised by the Board or by two directors out of which one shall be managing director and the Chief Executive Officer, if he is a director in the company, the Chief Financial Officer and the company secretary of the company, wherever they are appointed, or in the case of a One Person Company, only by one director, for submission to the auditor for his report thereon.

(2)   The auditors' report shall be attached to every financial statement.

(3)   There shall be attached to statements laid before a company in general meeting, a report by its Board of Directors, which shall include—

(a)   the extract of the annual return as provided under sub-section (3) of section 92;

(b)   number of meetings of the Board;

(c)   Directors' Responsibility Statement;

(ca)   details in respect of frauds reported by auditors under sub-section (12) of section 143 other than those which are reportable to the Central Government;

(d)   a statement on declaration given by independent directors under sub-section (6) of section 149;

(e)   in case of a company covered under sub-section (1) of section 178, company's policy on directors' appointment and remuneration including criteria for determining qualifications, positive attributes, independence of a director and other matters provided under sub-section (3) of section 178;

(f)   explanations or comments by the Board on every qualification, reservation or adverse remark or disclaimer made—

       (i)   by the auditor in his report; and

       (ii)   by the company secretary in practice in his secretarial audit report;

(g)   particulars of loans, guarantees or investments under section 186;

(h)   particulars of contracts or arrangements with related parties referred to in sub-section (1) of section 188 in the prescribed form;

(i)   the state of the company's affairs;

(j)   the amounts, if any, which it proposes to carry to any reserves;

(k)   the amount, if any, which it recommends should be paid by way of dividend;

(l)   material changes and commitments, if any, affecting the financial position of the company which have occurred between the end of the financial year of the company to which the financial statements relate and the date of the report;

(m)   the conservation of energy, technology absorption, foreign exchange earnings and outgo, in such manner as may be prescribed;

(n)   a statement indicating development and implementation of a risk management policy for the company including identification therein of elements of risk, if any, which in the opinion of the Board may threaten the existence of the company;

(o)   the details about the policy developed and implemented by the company on corporate social responsibility initiatives taken during the year;

(p)   in case of a listed company and every other public company having such paid-up share capital as may be prescribed, a statement indicating the manner in which formal annual evaluation has been made by the Board of its own performance and that of its committees and individual directors;

    (q)   such other matters as may be prescribed. **{Rule 8-Matters to be included in Board's report}.-**

(4)   The report of the Board of Directors to be attached to the financial statement under this section shall, in case of a One Person Company, mean a report containing explanations or comments by the Board on every qualification, reservation or adverse remark or disclaimer made by the auditor in his report.

(5)   The Directors' Responsibility Statement referred to in clause (c) of sub-section (3) shall state that—

    (a)   in the preparation of the annual accounts, the applicable accounting standards had been followed along with proper explanation relating to material departures;

    (b)   the directors had selected such accounting policies and applied them consistently and made judgments and estimates that are reasonable and prudent so as to give a true and fair view of the state of affairs of the company at the end of the financial year and of the profit and loss of the company for that period;

    (c)   the directors had taken proper and sufficient care for the maintenance of adequate accounting records in accordance with the provisions of this Act for safeguarding the assets of the company and for preventing and detecting fraud and other irregularities;

    (d)   the directors had prepared the annual accounts on a going concern basis; and

    (e)   the directors, in the case of a listed company, had laid down internal financial controls to be followed by the company and that such internal financial controls are adequate and were operating effectively.

Explanation — For the purposes of this clause, the term —internal financial controls— means the policies and procedures adopted by the company for ensuring the orderly and efficient conduct of its business, including adherence to company's policies, the safeguarding of its assets, the prevention and detection of frauds and errors, the accuracy and completeness of the accounting records, and the timely preparation of reliable financial information;

(5)(f)   the directors had devised proper systems to ensure compliance with the provisions of all applicable laws and that such systems were adequate and operating effectively.

(6)   The Board's report and any annexures thereto under sub-section (3) shall be signed by its chairperson of the company if he is authorised by the Board and where he is not so authorised, shall be signed by at least two directors, one of whom shall be a managing director, or by the director where there is one director.

(7)   A signed copy of every financial statement, including consolidated financial statement, if any, shall be issued, circulated or published along with a copy each of—

(a)   any notes annexed to or forming part of such financial statement;

(b)   the auditor's report; and

(c)   the Board's report referred to in sub-section (3).

"(8)   If a company is in default in complying with the provisions of this section, the company shall be liable to a penalty of three lakh rupees and every officer of the company who is in default shall be liable to a penalty of fifty thousand rupees.".

135. Corporate Social Responsibility —

(1)   Every company having net worth of rupees five hundred crore or more, or turnover of rupees one thousand crore or more or a net profit of rupees five crore or more during any financial year shall constitute a Corporate Social Responsibility Committee of the Board consisting of three or more directors, out of which at least one director shall be an independent director.

(2)   The Board's report shall disclose the composition of the Corporate Social Responsibility Committee.

(3)   The Corporate Social Responsibility Committee shall,—

   (a)   formulate and recommend to the Board, a Corporate Social Responsibility Policy which shall indicate the activities to be undertaken by the company as specified in Schedule VII;

   (b)   recommend the amount of expenditure to be incurred on the activities referred to in clause (a); and

   (c)   monitor the Corporate Social Responsibility Policy of the company from time to time.

(4)   The Board of every company referred to in sub-section (1) shall,—

   (a)   after taking into account the recommendations made by the Corporate Social Responsibility Committee,

> > approve the Corporate Social Responsibility Policy for the company and disclose contents of such Policy in its report and also place it on the company's website, if any, in such manner as may be prescribed; and
>
> > (b) ensure that the activities as are included in Corporate Social Responsibility Policy of the company are undertaken by the company.

(5) The Board of every company referred to in sub-section (1), shall ensure that the company spends, in every financial year, at least two per cent. of the average net profits of the company made during the three immediately preceding financial years "or where the company has not completed the period of three financial years" since its incorporation, during such immediately preceding financial years,, in pursuance of its Corporate Social Responsibility Policy: CAA 2019

Provided that the company shall give preference to the local area and areas around it where it operates, for spending the amount earmarked for Corporate Social Responsibility activities:

Provided further that if the company fails to spend such amount, "and, unless the unspent amount relates to any ongoing project referred to in sub-section (6), transfer such unspent amount to a Fund specified in Schedule VII, within a period of six months of the expiry of the financial year" the Board shall, in its report made under clause (o) of sub-section (3) of section 134, specify the reasons for not spending the amount.

"Provided also that if the company spends an amount in excess of the requirements provided under this sub-section, such company may set off such excess amount against the requirement to spend under this sub-section for such number of succeeding financial years and in such manner, as may be prescribed.";

"(6) Any amount remaining unspent, pursuant to any ongoing project, fulfilling such conditions as prescribed, undertaken by a company in pursuance of its Corporate Social Responsibility Policy, shall be transferred by the company within a period of thirty days from the end of the financial year to a special account to be opened by the company in that behalf for that financial year in any scheduled bank to be called the **Unspent Corporate Social Responsibility Account**, and such amount shall be spent by the company in pursuance of its obligation towards the Corporate Social Responsibility Policy within a period of three financial years from the date of such transfer, failing which, the company shall transfer the same to a Fund specified in Schedule VII, within a period of thirty days from the date of completion of the third financial year.

(7) If a company is in default in complying with the provisions of sub-section (5) or sub-section (6), the company shall be liable to a penalty of twice the amount required to be transferred by the company to the Fund specified in Schedule VII or the Unspent Corporate Social Responsibility Account, as the case may be, or one crore rupees, whichever is less, **and every officer of the company who is in default** shall be liable to a penalty of one-tenth of the amount required to be transferred by the company to such Fund specified in Schedule VII, or the Unspent Corporate Social Responsibility Account, as the case may be, or two lakh rupees, whichever is less.";

"(9) Where the amount to be spent by a company does not exceed fifty lakh rupees, the requirement under sub-section (1) for constitution of the Corporate Social Responsibility

Committee shall not be applicable and the functions of such Committee provided under this section shall, in such cases, be discharged by the Board of Directors of such company.

Rule 9. Disclosures about CSR Policy.-

The disclosure of contents of Corporate Social Responsibility Policy in the Board's report and on the company's website, if any, shall be as per annexure attached to the Companies (Corporate Social Responsibility Policy) Rules, 2014.

136. Right of member, every trustee for the debenture-holder, and to all such other persons so entitled, **to copies of audited financial statement** not less than twenty-one days before the date of the meeting:

Provided that in the case of a listed company, the provisions of this sub-section shall be deemed to be complied with, if the copies of the documents are made available for inspection at its registered office during working hours for a period of twenty-one days before the date of the meeting and a statement containing the salient features of such documents in Form AOC-3 or copies of the documents, as the company may deem fit, is sent to every member of the company and to every trustee for the holders of any debentures issued by the company not less than twenty-one days before the date of the meeting unless the shareholders ask for full financial statements:

(2) A company shall allow every member or trustee of the holder of any debentures issued by the company to inspect the documents stated under sub-section (1) at its registered office during business hours.

(3) If any default is made in complying with the provisions of this section, the company shall be liable to a penalty of twenty-five

thousand rupees **and every officer of the company who is in default** shall be liable to a penalty of five thousand rupees.

137. Copy of financial statement to be filed with Registrar shall be filed with the Registrar within thirty days of the date of annual general meeting in such manner, with such fees or additional fees as may be prescribed within the time specified under section 403:

Provided that where the financial statements are not adopted at annual general meeting or adjourned annual general meeting, such **unadopted financial statements along with the required documents shall be filed with the Registrar** within thirty days of the date of annual general meeting and the Registrar shall take them in his records as provisional till the financial statements are filed with him after their adoption in the adjourned annual general meeting for that purpose:

Provided further that **financial statements adopted in the adjourned annual general meeting** shall be filed with the Registrar within thirty days of the date of such adjourned annual general meeting with such fees or such additional fees as may be prescribed within the time specified under section 403:

Provided also that a company shall, along with its financial statements to be filed with the Registrar, **attach the accounts of its subsidiary or subsidiaries** which have been incorporated outside India and which have not established their place of business in India.

(2) Where the **annual general meeting of a company for any year has not been held,** the financial statements along with the documents required to be attached under sub-section

(1), duly signed along with the statement of facts and reasons for not holding the annual general meeting shall be filed with the Registrar within thirty days of the last date before which the annual general meeting should have been held and in such manner, with such fees or additional fees as may be prescribed within the time specified, under section 403.

(3) If a company fails to file the copy of the financial statements, as the case may be, before the expiry of the period specified in section 403, the company shall be punishable with fine of ten thousand rupees and in case of continuing failure, with a further penalty of one hundred rupees for each day during which such failure continues, subject to a maximum of two lakh rupees, **and the managing director and the Chief Financial Officer of the company, if any, and, in the absence of the managing director and the Chief Financial Officer, any other director who is charged by the Board with the responsibility of complying with the provisions of this section, and, in the absence of any such director, all the directors of the company, shall be punishable with imprisonment for a term which may extend to six months or with fine which shall not be less than** ten thousand rupees **but which may extend to** fifty thousand rupees", or with both.

138. & Rule 13 Internal audit —

(1)   The following class of companies shall be required to appoint an internal auditor firm of internal auditors, namely: –

   (a)   every listed company;

   (b)   every unlisted public company having-

(i)   paid up share capital of fifty crore rupees or more during the preceding financial year; or

(ii)   turnover of two hundred crore rupees or more during the preceding financial year; or

(iii)   outstanding loans or borrowings from banks or public financial institutions exceeding one hundred crore rupees or more at any point of time during the preceding financial year; or

(iv)   outstanding deposits of twenty five crore rupees or more at any point of time during the preceding financial year; and

(c)   every private company having-

(i)   turnover of two hundred crore rupees or more during the preceding financial year; or

(ii)   outstanding loans or borrowings from banks or public financial institutions exceeding one hundred crore rupees or more at any point of time during the preceding financial year:

Chapter X

Audit and Auditors & The Companies (Audit & Auditors) Rules, 2014

139. Appointment of auditors —

(1) Appointment at first annual general meeting either an individual or a firm as an auditor who shall hold office **from the conclusion of that meeting till the conclusion of its sixth annual general meeting and thereafter till the conclusion of every sixth meeting** as per **Rule 3.**

Provided that the company shall place the matter relating to such **appointment for ratification by members at every annual general meeting:**

(9) A retiring auditor may be **re-appointed** at an annual general meeting, if—

(a)   he is not disqualified for re-appointment;

(b)   he has not given the company a notice in writing of his unwillingness to be re-appointed; and

(c)   a special resolution has not been passed at that meeting appointing some other auditor or providing expressly that he shall not be re-appointed.

(10) Where at any annual general meeting, **no auditor is appointed or re-appointed**, the existing auditor shall continue to be the auditor of the company.

(11) Where a company is required to constitute an **Audit Committee** under section 177, all appointments, including the filling of a casual vacancy of an auditor under this section shall be made after taking into account the **recommendations of such committee**.

140. Removal, resignation of auditor and giving of special notice —

141. Eligibility, qualifications and disqualifications of auditors —

142. Remuneration of auditors —

143. Powers and duties of auditors and auditing standards —

(1)   Every auditor of a company shall have a right of access at all times to the books of account and vouchers of the company, whether kept at the registered office of the company or at any other place and shall be entitled to require from the officers of the company such information and explanation as he may consider necessary for the performance of his duties as auditor and amongst other matters inquire into the following matters, namely:—

(a)   whether **loans and advances** made by the company on the basis of security have been **properly secured** and whether the **terms on which they have been made are prejudicial to the interests of the company** or its members;

(b)   whether transactions of the company which are represented **merely by book entries are prejudicial to the interests of the company**;

(c)   where the company not being an investment company or a banking company, whether so much of the assets of the company as consist of **shares, debentures and other securities have been sold at a price less than that at which they were purchased by the company**;

(d)   whether **loans and advances made by** the company have been **shown as deposits**; (e) whether **personal expenses** have been **charged to revenue account**;

(f)   where it is stated in the books and documents of the company that any shares have been allotted for cash, **whether cash has actually been received in respect of such allotment,** and if no cash has actually been so received, whether the position as stated in the account books and the balance sheet is correct, regular and not misleading:

Provided that the auditor of a company which is a holding company shall also have the right of access to the records of all its subsidiaries in so far as it relates to the consolidation of its financial statements with that of its subsidiaries.

(2)   The auditor shall make a report to the members of the company on the accounts examined by him and on every financial statements which are required by or under this Act to be laid before the company in general meeting and the report shall after taking into account the provisions of

this Act, the accounting and auditing standards and matters which are required to be included in the audit report and to the best of his information and knowledge, the said accounts, financial statements give a true and fair view of the state of the company's affairs as at the end of its financial year and profit or loss and cash flow for the year and such other matters as may be prescribed.

(3)   The auditor's report shall also state—

(a)   whether he has sought and obtained all the information and explanations which to the best of his knowledge and belief were necessary for the purpose of his audit and if not, the details thereof and the effect of such information on the financial statements;

(b)   whether, in his opinion, proper books of account as required by law have been kept by the company so far as appears from his examination of those books and proper returns adequate for the purposes of his audit have been received from branches not visited by him;

(c)   whether the report on the accounts of any branch office of the company audited by a person other than the company's auditor has been sent to him under the proviso to that sub-section and the manner in which he has dealt with it in preparing his report;

(d)   whether the company's balance sheet and profit and loss account dealt with in the report are in agreement with the books of account and returns;

(e)   whether, in his opinion, the financial statements comply with the accounting standards;

(f)   the observations or comments of the auditors on financial transactions or matters which have any adverse effect on the functioning of the company;

(g)   **whether any director is disqualified from being appointed as a director under sub-section (2) of section 164;**

(h)   any qualification, reservation or adverse remark relating to the maintenance of accounts and other matters connected therewith;

(i)   **whether the company has adequate internal financial controls system in place and the operating effectiveness of such controls;**

(j)   such other matters as may be prescribed. (4) Where any of the matters required to be included in the audit report under this section is answered in the negative or with a qualification, the report shall state the reasons therefor.

(9) Every auditor shall comply with the auditing standards.

(12) Notwithstanding anything contained in this section, if an auditor {including cost accountant or company secretary} of a company, in the course of the performance of his duties as auditor, **has reason to believe that an offence involving fraud is being or has been committed against the company by officers or employees of the company, he shall immediately report the matter to the Central Government as provided under Rule 13.**

RULE 13

Reporting of frauds by auditor.-

(1)   For the purpose of sub-section (12) of section 143, in case the auditor has sufficient reason to believe that an offence involving fraud, is being or has been committed against the company by officers or employees of the company, he shall report the matter to the Central Government immediately but **not later than sixty days of his knowledge** and after following the procedure indicated herein below:

(i)   auditor shall forward his report to the Board or the Audit Committee, as the case may be, immediately after he comes to knowledge of the fraud, seeking their reply or observations within forty-five days;

(ii)   on receipt of such reply or observations the auditor shall forward his report and the reply or observations of the Board or the Audit Committee along with his comments (on such reply or observations of the Board or the Audit Committee) to the Central Government **within fifteen days of receipt of such reply or observations;**

(iii)   in case the auditor fails to get any reply or observations from the Board or the Audit Committee within the stipulated period of forty-five days, he shall forward his report to the Central Government along with a note containing the details of his report that was earlier forwarded to the Board or the Audit Committee for which he failed to receive any reply or observations within the stipulated time.

(2)   The report shall be sent to the Secretary, Ministry of Corporate Affairs in a sealed cover by Registered Post with Acknowledgement Due or by Speed post followed by an e-mail in confirmation of the same.

(3)   The report shall be on the letter-head of the auditor containing postal address, e-mail address and contact number and be signed by the auditor with his seal and shall indicate his Membership Number.

(4)   The report shall be in the form of a statement as specified in **Form ADT-4.**

(5)   The provision of this rule shall also apply, mutatis mutandis, to a cost auditor and a secretarial auditor during the performance of his duties under section 148 and section 204 respectively.

144. Auditor not to render certain services —

An auditor appointed under this Act shall provide to the company only such other services as are approved by the Board of Directors or the audit committee, as the case may be, but which shall not include any of the following services (whether such services are rendered directly or indirectly to the company), or its holding company or subsidiary company, namely:—

(a)   accounting and book keeping services;

(b)   internal audit;

(c)   design and implementation of any financial information system;

(d)   actuarial services;

(e)   investment advisory services;

(f)   investment banking services;

(g)   rendering of outsourced financial services;

(h)   management services; and

(i)   any other kind of services as may be prescribed:

Explanation — For the purposes of this sub-section, the term —directly or indirectly— shall include rendering of services by the auditor,—

(i)   in case of auditor being an individual, either himself or through his relative or any other person connected or associated with such individual or through any other entity, whatsoever, in which such individual has significant influence or control, or whose name or trade mark or brand is used by such individual;

(ii)   in case of auditor being a firm, either itself or through any of its partners or through its parent, subsidiary or associate entity or through any other entity, whatsoever, in which the firm or any partner of the firm has significant influence or control, or whose name or trade mark or brand is used by the firm or any of its partners.

147. Punishment for contravention —

(1)   If any of the provisions of **sections 139 to 146** (both inclusive) is contravened, the company shall be punishable with fine which shall not be less than twenty-five thousand rupees but which may extend to five lakh rupees and **every officer of the company who is in default shall**

be punishable with fine which shall not be less than ten thousand rupees but which may extend to one lakh rupees.

(2)   If an auditor of a company contravenes any of the provisions of section 139, section 143, section 144 or section 145, the auditor shall be punishable with fine which shall not be less than twenty-five thousand rupees but which may extend to five lakh rupees:

Provided that if an auditor has contravened such provisions knowingly or willfully with the intention to deceive the company or its shareholders or creditors or tax authorities, he shall be punishable with imprisonment for a term which may extend to one year and with fine which shall not be less than one lakh rupees but which may extend to twenty-five lakh rupees.

148. Central Government to specify audit of items of cost in respect of certain companies —

(6) A company shall within thirty days from the date of receipt of a copy of the cost audit report prepared furnish the Central Government with such report along with full information and explanation on every reservation or qualification contained therein.

(7) If, after considering the cost audit report and explanation furnished by the company, the Central Government is of the opinion that any further information or explanation is necessary, it may call for such further information and explanation and the company shall furnish the same within such time as may be specified by that Government.

(8) If any default is made in complying with the provisions of this section,—

(a)   **the company and every officer of the company** who is in default shall be punishable in the manner as provided in sub-section (1) of section 147;

(b)   the cost auditor of the company who is in default shall be punishable in the manner as provided in section 147.

204. Secretarial audit for bigger companies —

(1) Every listed company, every public company having a paid-up share capital of fifty crore rupees or more; or every public company having a turnover of two hundred fifty crore rupees or more. shall annex with its Board's report a secretarial audit report in Form No. MR.3. given by a company secretary in practice.

(4) If a company or **any officer of the company** or the company secretary in practice, contravenes the provisions of this section, the company, every officer of the company or the company secretary in practice, who is in default, shall be liable to a penalty of two lakh rupees.

Chapter XI

Appointment and Remuneration of Managerial Personnel & The Companies (Appointment and Remuneration of Managerial Personnel) Rules, 2014 & Schedule V

196. Appointment of managing director, whole-time director or manager —

(2) No company shall **appoint or re-appoint** any person as its managing director, whole-time director or manager **for a term exceeding five years at a time**:

Provided that no re-appointment shall be made earlier than one year before the expiry of his term.

(3) **No company shall appoint or continue the employment of any person as managing director, whole-time director or manager** who —

(a)   is below the **age of twenty-one years or has attained the age of seventy years**: Provided that appointment of a person who has attained the age of **seventy years may be made by passing a special resolution** in which case the explanatory statement annexed to the notice for such motion shall indicate the justification for appointing such person;

(b)   is an **undischarged insolvent** or has at any time been adjudged as an insolvent;

(c)   has at any time **suspended payment to his creditors** or makes, or has at any time made, a composition with them; or

(d)   has at **any time been convicted by a court** of an offence and sentenced for a period of **more than six months.**

(4) Subject to the provisions of section 197 and Schedule V, a managing director, whole-time director or manager shall be appointed and the **terms and conditions of such appointment and remuneration payable be approved by the Board of Directors at a meeting which shall be subject to approval by a resolution at the next general meeting of the company and by the Central Government in case such appointment is at variance to the conditions specified in that Schedule:**

Provided that a notice convening Board or general meeting for considering such appointment shall **include the terms and conditions of such appointment, remuneration payable and such other matters including interest, of a director or directors in such appointments,** if any:

Provided further that **a return in form MR-1 shall be filed within sixty days of such appointment with the Registrar.**

(5) Subject to the provisions of this Act, where an appointment of a managing director, whole-time director or manager is not approved

by the company at a general meeting, any act done by him before such approval shall not be deemed to be invalid.

197. Overall maximum managerial remuneration and managerial remuneration in case of absence or inadequacy of profits —

(1)   The total managerial remuneration payable by a public company, to its directors, including managing director and whole-time director, and its manager in respect of any financial year **shall not exceed eleven per cent. of the net profits** of that company for that financial year computed in the manner laid down in section 198 except that the remuneration of the directors shall not be deducted from the gross profits:

Provided that the **company in general meeting may, with the approval of the Central Government, authorise the payment of remuneration exceeding eleven per cent. of the net profits of the company, subject to the provisions of Schedule V:**

Provided further that, **except with the approval of the company in general meeting,—**

(a)   the remuneration payable **to any one managing director; or whole-time director or manager shall not exceed five per cent.** of the net profits of the company and if there is **more than one such director remuneration shall not exceed ten per cent. of the net profits** to all such directors and manager taken together;

(b)   the remuneration payable to directors who are **neither managing directors nor whole-time directors shall not exceed,—**

(A) **one per cent. of the net profits of the company, if there is a managing or whole-time director or manager;**

(B) **three per cent. of the net profits in any other case.**

(2)   The percentages aforesaid shall be exclusive of any fees payable to directors under sub-section (5).

(3)   Notwithstanding anything contained in sub-sections (1) and (2), **but subject to the provisions of Schedule V, if, in any financial year, a company has no profits or its profits are inadequate, the company shall not pay to its directors, including any managing or whole-time director or manager, "or any other non-executive director, including an independent director by way of remuneration any sum exclusive of any fees payable to directors under sub-section (5) hereunder except in accordance with the provisions of Schedule V and if it is not able to comply with such provisions, with the previous approval of the Central Government.**

(4)   The remuneration payable to the directors of a company, including any managing or whole-time director or manager, **shall be determined, in accordance with and subject to the provisions of this section, either by the articles of the company, or by a resolution or, if the articles so require, by a special resolution, passed by the company in general meeting** and the remuneration payable to a director determined aforesaid shall be inclusive

of the remuneration payable to him for the services rendered by him in any other capacity:

Provided that **any remuneration for services rendered** by any such director in other capacity **shall not be so included** if—

(a) the services rendered are of a professional nature; and

(b) in the opinion of the Nomination and Remuneration Committee, or the Board of Directors, as the case may be, the director possesses the requisite qualification for the practice of the profession.

(5) A director may receive remuneration by way of fee for attending meetings of the Board or Committee thereof or for any other purpose whatsoever as may be decided by the Board:

Provided that the amount of such fees shall not exceed one lakh rupees per meeting:

Provided further for Independent Directors and Women Directors, the sitting fee shall not be less than the sitting fee payable to other directors.

{Rule 4}.

(6) A director or manager may be paid remuneration either by way of a monthly payment or at a specified percentage of the net profits of the company or partly by one way and partly by the other.

(11) In cases where Schedule V is applicable on grounds of no profits or inadequate profits, any provision relating to the remuneration of any director which purports to increase or has

the effect of increasing the amount thereof, whether the provision be contained in the company's memorandum or articles, or in an agreement entered into by it, or in any resolution passed by the company in general meeting or its Board, **shall not have any effect unless such increase is in accordance with the conditions specified in that Schedule and if such conditions are not being complied, the approval of the Central Government had been obtained.**

(12) Every listed company shall disclose in the Board's report, the ratio of the remuneration of each director to the median employee's remuneration and such other details as prescribed under Rule 5.

(13) Where any insurance is taken by a company on behalf of its managing director, whole-time director, manager, Chief Executive Officer, Chief Financial Officer or Company Secretary for indemnifying any of them against any liability in respect of any negligence, default, misfeasance, breach of duty or breach of trust for which they may be guilty in relation to the company, the premium paid on such insurance shall not be treated as part of the remuneration payable to any such personnel: Provided that if such person is proved to be guilty, the premium paid on such insurance shall be treated as part of the remuneration.

(14) Subject to the provisions of this section, any director who is in receipt of any commission from the company and who is a managing or whole-time director of the company shall not be disqualified from receiving any remuneration or commission from any holding company or subsidiary company of such company subject to its disclosure by the company in the Board's report.

"(15) **If any person makes any default in complying with the provisions** of this section, he shall be liable to a penalty of one lakh rupees and where any default has been made by a company, the company shall be liable to a penalty of five lakh rupees.".

198. Calculation of profits —

203. Appointment of key managerial personnel —

(1) **Every listed company and every other public company having a paid-up share capital of ten crore rupees or more shall have whole-time key managerial personnel. {Rule 8}**

Provided that **an individual shall not be appointed or reappointed as the chairperson of the company, in pursuance of the articles of the company, as well as the managing director or Chief Executive Officer of the company at the same time** after the date of commencement of this Act unless,—

(a) the articles of such a company provide otherwise; or

(b) the company does not carry multiple businesses:

Provided further that nothing contained in the first proviso shall apply to such class of companies engaged in multiple businesses and which has appointed one or more Chief Executive Officers for each such business as may be notified by the Central Government.

(2) Every whole-time key managerial personnel of a company shall be appointed by means of a resolution of the Board containing the terms and conditions of the appointment including the remuneration.

(3)   A whole-time, key managerial personnel shall not hold office in more than one company except in its subsidiary company at the same time: Provided that nothing contained in this sub-section shall disentitle a key- managerial personnel from being a director of any company with the permission of the Board:

Provided also that **a company may appoint or employ a person as its managing director, if he is the managing director or manager of one, and of not more than one,** other company and such appointment or employment is made or approved by a resolution passed at a meeting of the Board with the consent of all the directors present at the meeting and of which meeting, and of the resolution to be moved thereat, specific notice has been given to all the directors then in India.

(4)   If the office of any whole-time key managerial personnel is **vacated**, the resulting vacancy shall be filled-up by the Board at a meeting of the Board **within a period of six months from the date of such vacancy.**

"(5)   If any company makes any default in complying with the provisions of this section, such company shall be liable to a penalty of five lakh rupees **and every director and key managerial personnel of the company who is in default** shall be liable to a penalty of fifty thousand rupees and where the default is a continuing one, with a further penalty of one thousand rupees for each day after the first during which such default continues but not exceeding five lakh rupees.".

Schedule V

(See sections 196 and 197)

PART I

Conditions to be fulfilled for the Appointment of a Managing or Whole-time Director or a Manager without the approval of the Central Government Appointments

No person shall be eligible for appointment as a managing or whole-time director or a manager (hereinafter referred to as managerial person) of a company unless he satisfies the following conditions, namely:—

(a)   he had **not been sentenced to imprisonment** for any period, or to a fine exceeding one thousand rupees, for the conviction of an offence **under any of the following Acts,** namely:—

    (i)   the Indian Stamp Act, 1899 (2 of 1899);

    (ii)   the Central Excise Act, 1944 (1 of 1944);

    (iii)   the Industries (Development and Regulation) Act, 1951 (65 of 1951);

    (iv)   the Prevention of Food Adulteration Act, 1954 (37 of 1954);

    (v)   the Essential Commodities Act, 1955 (10 of 1955);

    (vi)   the Companies Act, 2013 (18 of 2013) or any previous company law;

    (vii)   the Securities Contracts (Regulation) Act, 1956 (42 of 1956);

(viii)   the Wealth-tax Act, 1957 (27 of 1957);

(ix)   the Income-tax Act, 1961 (43 of 1961);

(x)   the Customs Act, 1962 (52 of 1962);

(xi)   the Competition Act, 2002 (12 of 2003);

(xii)   the Foreign Exchange Management Act, 1999 (42 of 1999);

(xiii)   the Sick Industrial Companies (Special Provisions) Act, 1985 (1 of 1986);

(xiv)   the Securities and Exchange Board of India Act, 1992 (15 of 1992);

(xv)   the Foreign Trade (Development and Regulation) Act, 1922 (22 of 1922);

(xvi)   the Prevention of Money-Laundering Act, 2002 (15 of 2003);

(xvii)   the Insolvency and Bankruptcy Code, 2016 (31 of 2016);

(xviii)   the Goods and Services Tax Act, 2017 (12 of 2017);

(xix)   the Fugitive Economic Offenders Act, 2018 (17 of 2018).

(b) he had not been detained for any period under the **Conservation of Foreign Exchange and Prevention of Smuggling Activities Act, 1974** (52 of 1974):

Provided that where the Central Government has given its approval to the appointment of a person convicted or detained under sub-paragraph (a) or sub-paragraph (b), as the case may be, no further approval of the Central Government shall be necessary for the subsequent appointment of that person if he had not been so convicted or detained subsequent to such approval.

(c) he has completed the age of twenty-one years and has not attained the age of seventy years:

Provided that where he has attained the age of seventy years; and where his **appointment is approved by a special resolution** passed by the company in general meeting, **no further approval of the Central Government shall be necessary** for such appointment;

(d) where he is a managerial person in more than one company, he draws remuneration from one or more companies subject to the ceiling provided in section V of Part II;

(e) he is resident of India.

Explanation I — For the purpose of this Schedule, resident in India includes a person who has been staying in India for a continuous period of not less than twelve months immediately preceding the date of his appointment as a managerial person and who has come to stay in India,—

(i) for taking up employment in India; or

(ii) for carrying on a business or vacation in India.

Explanation II — This condition shall not apply to the companies in Special Economic Zones as notified by Department of Commerce from time to time:

Provided that a person, being a non-resident in India shall enter India only after obtaining a proper Employment Visa from the concerned Indian mission abroad. For this purpose, such person shall be required to furnish, along with the visa application form, profile of the company, the principal employer and terms and conditions of such person's appointment.

PART II REMUNERATION

Section I. — Remuneration payable by companies having profits:

Subject to the provisions of section 197, a company having profits in a financial year may pay remuneration to a managerial person or persons or other director or directors not exceeding the limits specified in such section.

Section II. — Remuneration payable by companies having no profit or inadequate profit

Where in any financial year during the currency of tenure of a managerial person or other director, a company has no profits or its profits are inadequate, **it may, pay remuneration to the managerial person or other director not exceeding the limits under (A) and (B) given below:—**

A.

1	2	3	
Sl. No.	Where the effective capital (in rupees) is	Limit of yearly remuneration payable shall not exceed (in Rupees) in case of a managerial person	Limit of yearly remuneration payable shall not exceed (in rupees) in case of Other director
(i)	Negative or less than 5 crores.	60 lakhs	12 lakhs
(ii)	5 crores and above but less than 100 crores.	84 lakhs	17 lakhs
(iii)	100 crores and above but less than 250 crores	120 lakhs	24 lakhs
(iv)	100 crores and above but less than 250 crores	120 lakhs plus 0.01% of the effective capital in excess of Rs. 250 crores:	24 Lakhs plus 0.01% of the effective capital in excess of Rs. 250 crores:

Provided that the **remuneration in excess of above limits may be paid if the resolution passed by the shareholders is a special resolution.**

Explanation — It is hereby clarified that for a period less than one year, the limits shall be pro-rated.

(B) In case of a **managerial person who is functioning in a professional capacity**, remuneration as per item (A) may be paid], if such managerial person **is not having any interest in the capital** of the company or its holding company or any of its subsidiaries directly or indirectly or through any other statutory structures and not having any direct or indirect interest or related to the directors or promoters of the company or its holding company or any of its subsidiaries **at any time during the last two years** before or on or after the date of appointment **and possesses graduate level qualification with expertise and specialised knowledge in the field in which the company operates**:

Provided that any employee of a company holding shares of the company not exceeding 0.5% of its paid up share capital under any scheme formulated for allotment of shares to such employees including Employees Stock Option Plan or by way of qualification shall be deemed to be a person not having any interest in the capital of the company:

Provided further that the limits specified under items (A) and (B) of this section shall apply, if-

(i)   payment of remuneration is approved by a **resolution passed by the Board** and, in the case of a company covered under sub-section (1) of section 178 also **by the Nomination and Remuneration Committee;**

(ii)   the company **has not committed any default in payment of dues to** any bank or public financial institution or non-convertible debenture holders or any other secured creditor, and in case of default, the prior approval of the bank or public financial institution concerned or the non-convertible debenture holders or other secured creditor, as the case may be, shall be obtained by the company before obtaining the approval in the general meeting;

(iii) **an ordinary resolution or a special resolution**, as the case may be, has been passed for payment of remuneration as per item (A) or a special resolution has been passed for payment of remuneration as per item (B), at the general meeting of the company for a period not exceeding three years.

(iv) a statement along with a notice calling the general meeting referred to in clause (iii) is given to the shareholders containing the following information, namely:-

I. General information:

(1)   Nature of industry

(2)   Date or expected date of commencement of commercial production

(3)   In case of new companies, expected date of commencement of activities as per project approved by financial institutions appearing in the prospectus

(4)   Financial performance based on given indicators

(5)   Foreign investments or collaborations, if any.

II. Information about the appointee:

(1)   Background details

(2)   Past remuneration

(3)   Recognition or awards

(4)   Job profile and his suitability

(5)   Remuneration proposed

(6)   Comparative remuneration profile with respect to industry, size of the company, profile of the position and person (in case of expatriates the relevant details would be with respect to the country of his origin)

(7)   Pecuniary relationship directly or indirectly with the company, or relationship with the managerial personnel, if any.

III. Other information:

(1)   Reasons of loss or inadequate profits

(2)   Steps taken or proposed to be taken for improvement

(3)   Expected increase in productivity and profits in measurable terms

IV. Disclosures:

The following disclosures shall be mentioned in the Board of Director's report under the heading "Corporate Governance", if any, attached to the financial statement:

(i)   all elements of remuneration package such as salary, benefits, bonuses, stock options, pension, etc., of all the directors;

(ii)   details of fixed component and performance linked incentives along with the performance criteria; (iii) service contracts, notice period, severance fees; and

(iv)   stock option details, if any, and whether the same has been issued at a discount as well as the period over which accrued and over which exercisable.

Explanation: For the purposes of Section II of this part, "Statutory Structure" means any entity which is entitled to hold shares in any company formed under any statute.

Section III. — Remuneration payable by companies having no profit or inadequate profit in certain special circumstances:

In the following circumstances a **company may, pay remuneration to a managerial person or other director in excess of the amounts provided in Section II above:—**

(a)   where the remuneration in excess of the limits specified in Section I or Section II **is paid by any other company and that other company is either a foreign company or has got the approval of its shareholders in general meeting to make such payment,** and treats this amount as managerial remuneration for the purpose of section 197 and the total managerial remuneration payable by such other company to its managerial persons including such amount or amounts is within permissible limits under section 197.

(b)   where the company—

(i)   is a **newly incorporated company, for a period of seven years from the date of its incorporation,** or (ii) is a **sick company, for whom a scheme of revival or rehabilitation has been ordered** by the Board for Industrial and Financial Reconstruction **for a period of five years from the date of sanction of scheme** of revival, or

(iii)   is a **company in relation to which a resolution plan has been approved** by the National Company

Law Tribunal under the Insolvency and Bankruptcy Code, 2016 (31 of 2016) **for a period of five years** from the date of such approval,

it may pay any remuneration to its managerial persons or other directors.

(c)   where remuneration of a managerial person or other director exceeds the limits in Section II but the remuneration has been fixed by the Board for Industrial and Financial Reconstruction or the National Company Law Tribunal:

Provided that the limits under this Section shall be applicable subject to meeting all the conditions specified under Section II and the following additional conditions:—

(i)   except as provided in para (a) of this Section, **the managerial person is not receiving remuneration from any other company;**

(ii)   the auditor or Company Secretary of the company or where the company has not appointed a Secretary, a Secretary in whole-time practice, **certifies that all secured creditors and term lenders have stated in writing that they have no objection** for the appointment of the managerial person or other director as well as the quantum of remuneration and such certificate is filed along with the return as prescribed under sub-section (4) of section 196.

(iii)   the auditor or Company Secretary or where the company has not appointed a secretary, a secretary in whole-time practice **certifies that there is no default on payments to any creditors, and all dues to deposit holders are being settled on time.**

Explanation — For the purposes of Section I, Section II and Section III, the term "or other director" shall mean a non-executive director or an independent director.

Section IV — Perquisites not included in managerial remuneration:

1. A managerial person shall be eligible for the following perquisites **which shall not be included in the computation of the ceiling on remuneration** specified in Section II and Section III:—

    (a) contribution to provident fund, superannuation fund or annuity fund to the extent these either singly or put together are not taxable under the Income-tax Act, 1961(43 of 1961);

    (b) gratuity payable at a rate not exceeding half a month's salary for each completed year of service; and (c) encashment of leave at the end of the tenure.

2. In addition to the perquisites specified in paragraph 1 of this section, **an expatriate managerial person (including a non-resident Indian) shall be eligible** to the following perquisites which shall not be included in the computation of the ceiling on remuneration specified in Section II or Section III—

    (a) Children's education allowance: In case of children studying in or outside India, an allowance limited to a maximum of Rs. 12,000 per month per child or actual expenses incurred, whichever is less. Such allowance is admissible up to a maximum of two children.

(b) Holiday passage for children studying outside India or family staying abroad: Return holiday passage once in a year by economy class or once in two years by first class to children and to the members of the family from the place of their study or stay abroad to India if they are not residing in India, with the managerial person.

(c) Leave travel concession: Return passage for self and family in accordance with the rules specified by the company where it is proposed that the leave be spent in home country instead of anywhere in India.

Explanation I — For the purposes of Section II of this Part, "effective capital" means the aggregate of the paid-up share capital (excluding share application money or advances against shares); amount, if any, for the time being standing to the credit of share premium account; reserves and surplus (excluding revaluation reserve); long-term loans and deposits repayable after one year (excluding working capital loans, overdrafts, interest due on loans unless funded, bank guarantee, etc., and other short-term arrangements) as reduced by the aggregate of any investments (except in case of investment by an investment company whose principal business is acquisition of shares, stock, debentures or other securities),accumulated losses and preliminary expenses not written off.

Explanation II —

(a) Where the appointment of the managerial person is made in the year in which company has been incorporated, the effective capital shall be calculated as on the date of such appointment;

(b)		In any other case the effective capital shall be calculated as on the last date of the financial year preceding the financial year in which the appointment of the managerial person is made.

Explanation III — For the purposes of this Schedule, "family" means the spouse, dependent children and dependent parents of the managerial person.

Explanation IV — The Nomination and Remuneration Committee while approving the remuneration under Section II or Section III, shall—

(a)		take into account, financial position of the company, trend in the industry, appointee's qualification, experience, past performance, past remuneration, etc.;

(b)		be in a position to bring about objectivity in determining the remuneration package while striking a balance between the interest of the company and the shareholders.

Explanation V — For the purposes of this Schedule, "negative effective capital" means the effective capital which is calculated in accordance with the provisions contained in Explanation I of this Part is less than zero.

Explanation VI —	For the purposes of this Schedule:) "Remuneration" means remuneration as defined in clause (78) of section 2 and includes reimbursement of any direct taxes to the managerial person.

Section V.— Remuneration payable to a managerial person in two companies:

Subject to the provisions of sections I to IV, a managerial person shall draw remuneration from one or both companies, **provided**

that the total remuneration drawn from the companies does not exceed the higher maximum limit admissible from any one of the companies of which he is a managerial person.

PART III Provisions applicable to Parts I and II of this Schedule 1.

The appointment and remuneration referred to in Part I and Part II of this Schedule **shall be subject to approval by a resolution of the shareholders in general meeting.**

2. The auditor or the Secretary of the company or where the company is not required to appointed a Secretary, a Secretary in whole-time practice **shall certify that the requirement of this Schedule have been complied with and such certificate shall be incorporated in the return filed with the Registrar under subsection (4) of section 196.**

PART IV

The Central Government may, by notification, exempt any class or classes of companies from any of the requirements contained in this Schedule.

Regulation 17 (6) (a) (b) of (SEBI LODR), 2015

(a)   The board of directors shall recommend all fees or compensation, if any, paid to non-executive directors, **including independent directors and shall require approval of shareholders** in general meeting.

(b)   The requirement of obtaining **approval of shareholders in general meeting shall not apply to payment of sitting fees to non-executive directors, if made within the limits prescribed under the Companies Act, 2013** for payment of sitting fees without approval of the Central Government.

(c)   The approval of shareholders mentioned in clause (a), shall specify the limits for the maximum number of stock options that may be granted to non-executive directors, in any financial year and in aggregate.

(ca) The **approval of shareholders by special resolution shall be obtained every year, in which the annual remuneration payable to a single non-executive director exceeds fifty per cent** of the total annual remuneration payable to all non-executive directors, giving details of the remuneration thereof.

(d)   Independent directors **shall not be entitled to any stock option.**

(e)   The fees or compensation payable to executive directors who are promoters or members of the promoter group, **shall be subject to the approval of the shareholders by special resolution in general meeting, if-**

   (i)   the annual remuneration payable to such executive director exceeds rupees 5 crore or 2.5 per cent of the net profits of the listed entity, whichever is higher; or

     (ii)   where there is more than one such director, the aggregate annual remuneration to such directors exceeds 5 per cent of the net profits of the listed entity:

Provided that the approval of the shareholders under this provision shall be valid only till the expiry of the term of such director.

Potential Areas of Risks to be guarded by NEDs, non-promoter; non-whole-time directors for not being classified as an "Officer of the Company who is in Default"

3. Formation of company —

(1) A company may be formed for any lawful purpose by—

(a)   seven or more persons, where the company to be formed is to be a public company;

(b)   two or more persons, where the company to be formed is to be a private company; or

(c)   one person, where the company to be formed is to be One Person Company that is to say, a private company, by subscribing their names or his name to a memorandum and complying with the requirements of this Act in respect of registration:

Rule 5: If One Person Company or **any officer of such company contravenes** these rules, One Person Company or any officer of the One Person Company shall be **punishable** with fine which may extend to ten thousand rupees and with a further fine which may extend to one thousand rupees for every day after the first during which such contravention continues.

4. Memorandum —

5. Articles —

(1) The articles of a company shall contain the regulations for management of the company.

(6) The articles of a company shall be in respective forms specified in Tables, F, G, H, I and J in Schedule I as may be applicable to such company.

6. Act to override memorandum, articles, etc —

7. Incorporation of company —

(1)   There shall be filed with the Registrar in Form DIR-12 within whose jurisdiction the registered office of a company is proposed to be situated, the following documents and information for registration, namely:—

(a)   the memorandum and articles of the company duly signed by **all the subscribers** to the memorandum in the manner prescribed under **Rule 13**;

(b)   a declaration in the INC-8 form by an advocate, a chartered accountant, cost accountant or company secretary in practice, who is engaged in the formation of the company, and by a **person named in the**

articles as a director, manager or secretary of the company, that all the requirements of this Act and the rules made thereunder in respect of registration and matters precedent or incidental thereto have been complied with;

(c)   an affidavit in Form INC-9 from each of the subscribers to the memorandum and from persons **named as the first directors,** if any, in the articles that he is not convicted of any offence in connection with the promotion, formation or management of any company, or that he has not been found guilty of any fraud or misfeasance or of any breach of duty to any company under this Act or any previous company law during the preceding five years and that all the documents filed with the Registrar for registration of the company contain information that is correct and complete and true to the best of his knowledge and belief;

(d)   the address for correspondence till its registered office is established;

(e)   the particulars of name, including surname or family name, residential address, nationality and such other particulars **of every subscriber to the memorandum** along with proof of identity, as may be prescribed, and in the case of a subscriber being a body corporate, such particulars as prescribed under Rule 16;

(f)   the particulars of the persons mentioned in the articles as the first directors of the company, their names, including surnames or family names, **the Director Identification Number,** residential address, nationality and such other particulars including proof of identity as may prescribed under Rule 16; and

(g) the **particulars of the interests of the persons mentioned in the articles as the first directors** of the company in other firms or bodies corporate along with their consent to act as directors of the company in such form and manner as prescribed under Rule 17.

(3) On and from the date mentioned in the certificate of incorporation issued, the Registrar shall allot to the company a corporate identity number, which shall be a distinct identity for the company and which shall also be included in the certificate.

(4) The company shall maintain and preserve at its registered office copies of all documents and information as originally filed till its dissolution under this Act.

(5) **If any person furnishes any false or incorrect particulars of any information or suppresses any material information, of which he is aware in any of the documents filed with the Registrar in relation to the registration of a company, he shall be liable for action under section 447.**

(6) Without prejudice to the provisions of sub-section (5) where, at any time after the incorporation of a company, it is proved that the company has been got incorporated by furnishing any false or incorrect information or representation or by

suppressing any material fact or information in any of the documents or declaration filed or made for incorporating such company, or by any fraudulent action, the **promoters, the persons named as the first directors of the company and the persons making declaration under clause (b) of subsection (1) shall each be liable for action under section 447.**

8. Formulation of companies with charitable objects, etc —

(11) If a company makes any default in complying with any of the requirements laid down in this section, the company shall, without prejudice to any other action under the provisions of this section, be punishable with fine which shall not be less than ten lakh rupees but which may extend to one crore rupees and **the directors and every officer of the company who is in default** shall be punishable with fine which shall not be less than twenty-five thousand rupees but which may extend to twenty-five lakh rupees.

Provided that when it is proved that the affairs of the company were conducted fraudulently, **every officer in default shall be liable for action under section 447.**

10A Commencement of business, etc.

(1)   A company incorporated after the commencement of the Companies (Amendment) Act, 2019 and having a share capital shall not commence any business or exercise any borrowing powers unless—

    (a)   a declaration is filed by a director within a period of one hundred and eighty days of the date of incorporation of the company in form **INC-21** and verified in such manner as prescribed (Rule 24), with the Registrar that every subscriber to the memorandum has paid the value of the shares agreed to be taken by him on the date of making of such declaration; and

(b)   the company has filed with the Registrar a verification of its registered office in **Form-25**,as provided in sub-section (2) of section 12.

(2)   If any default is made, the company shall be liable to a penalty of fifty thousand rupees and **every officer who is in default** shall be liable to a penalty of one thousand rupees for each day during which such default continues but not exceeding an amount of one lakh rupees.

(3)   Where no declaration has been filed with the Registrar within a period of one hundred and eighty days of the date of incorporation of the company and the Registrar has reasonable cause to believe that the company is not carrying on any business or operations, he may, without prejudice to the provisions of sub-section (2), initiate action for the **removal of the name of the company** from the register of companies under Chapter XVIII.".

12. Registered office of company —

(1)   A company shall, on and from the fifteenth day of its incorporation **and at all times thereafter**, have a registered office capable of receiving and acknowledging all communications and notices as may be addressed to it.

(2)   The company shall furnish to the Registrar verification of its registered office within thirty days of its incorporation by filing **Form INC-22,** as prescribed.

(5) Except on the authority of a **special resolution** passed by a company, the registered office of the company shall not be changed,—

(a)(b): in the case of a company, **outside the local limits** of any city, town or village where such office is situated by virtue of a special resolution passed by the company; and

Provided that no company shall change the place of its **registered office from the jurisdiction of one Registrar to the jurisdiction of another Registrar within the same State unless such change is confirmed by the Regional Director** on an application made in this behalf by the company in Form No. INC-23. {Rule 28}.

(8) If any default is made in complying with the requirements of this section, the company and **every officer who is in default** shall be liable to a penalty of one thousand rupees for every day during which the default continues but not exceeding one lakh rupees.

13. Alteration of memorandum —

(1) Save as provided in section 61, a company may, by a special resolution and after complying with the procedure specified in this section, alter the provisions of its memorandum.

(4) **The alteration of the memorandum relating to the place of the registered office from one State to another shall not have any effect unless it is approved by the**

Central Government on an application in form INC-24 as prescribed. {Rule 29}

Rule 29: (1) The change of name shall not be allowed to a company which has defaulted in filing its annual returns or financial statements or any document due for filing with the Registrar or which has defaulted in repayment of matured deposits or debentures or interest on deposits or debentures.

(10) No alteration made under this section shall have any effect until it has been registered in accordance with the provisions of this section. 32

14. Alteration of articles —

(1)   Subject to the provisions of this Act and the conditions contained in its memorandum, if any, a company may, **by a special resolution,** alter its articles.

"Provided further that any alteration having the effect of conversion of a public company into a private company shall not be valid unless it is approved by an order of the Central Government on an application made in such form and manner as may be prescribed:

(2)   Every alteration of the articles under this section and a copy of the order of the Central Government approving the alteration **shall be filed with the Registrar**, together with a printed copy of the altered articles, within a period of fifteen days.

15. Alteration of memorandum or articles to be noted in every copy —

(2)   If a company makes any default the company and **every officer who is in default shall be liable** to a penalty of

one thousand rupees for every copy of the memorandum or articles issued without such alteration.

17. Copies of memorandum, articles, agreement, resolution referred to in Sec 117 , to be given to member. within seven days of the request.

(2)   For default in compliance, the company and **every officer of the company who is in default shall be liable** for each default, to a penalty of one thousand rupees for each day during which such default continues or one lakh rupees, whichever is less.

23. Public offer and private placement —

(1)   A public company may issue securities—

   (a)   to public through prospectus (herein referred to as "public offer") by complying with the provisions of this Part; or

   (b)   through private placement by complying with the provisions of Part II of this Chapter; or

   (c)   through a rights issue or a bonus issue in accordance with the provisions of this Act and in case of a listed company or a company which intends to get its securities listed also with the provisions of the Securities and Exchange Board of India Act, 1992 (15 of 1992) and the rules and regulations made thereunder.

(2)   A private company may issue securities—

   (a)   by way of rights issue or bonus issue in accordance with the provisions of this Act; or

(b)   through private placement by complying with the provisions of Part II of this Chapter.

"(3) Such class of public companies may issue such class of securities for the purposes of listing on permitted stock exchanges in permissible foreign jurisdictions or such other jurisdictions, as may be prescribed.

25. Document containing offer of securities for sale to be deemed prospectus — and all enactments and rules of law as to the contents of prospectus and as to liability in respect of mis-statements, in and omissions from, prospectus, or otherwise relating to prospectus, shall apply.

26. & Rule 3 Companies (Prospectus and Allotment of Securities) Rules, 2014 related **Matters to be stated in prospectus** — Inter alia:

(iii)   a **statement by the Board of Directors about the separate bank account** where all monies received out of the issue are to be transferred and disclosure of details of all monies including utilised and unutilised monies out of the previous issue in the prescribed manner;

Rule 3:

(1)(c) a **declaration which shall be made by the Board or the Committee** authorised by the Board in the prospectus that the allotment letters shall be issued or application money shall be refunded within fifteen days from the closure of the issue or such lesser time as may be specified by Securities and Exchange Board or else the application money shall be refunded to the applicants forthwith, failing which interest shall be due to be paid to the applicants at the rate of fifteen per cent. per annum for the delayed period. (d) a statement given by the Board that all monies received out of the issue shall be transferred to a separate bank account maintained with a Scheduled Bank;

(5) The **details of directors** including their appointment and remuneration, **and particulars of the nature and extent of their interests in the company** shall be disclosed in the following manner, namely:-

(i)   the name, designation, Director Identification Number (DIN), age, address, period of directorship, details of other directorships;

(ii)   the remuneration payable or paid to the director by the issuer company, its subsidiary and associate company; shareholding of the director in the company including any stock options; shareholding in subsidiaries and associate companies; appointment of any relatives to an office or place of profit;

(iii)   the full particulars of the nature and extent of interest, if any, of every director:

    (a)   in the promotion of the issuer company; or

    (b)   in any immoveable property acquired by the issuer company in the two years preceding the date of the Prospectus or any immoveable property proposed to be acquired by it.

(iv)   where the interest of such a director consists in being a member of a firm or company, the nature and extent of his interest in the firm or company, with a statement of all sums paid or agreed to be paid to him or to the firm or company in cash or shares or otherwise by any person either to induce him to become, or to help him qualify as a director, or otherwise for services rendered by him or by the firm or company, in connection with the promotion or formation of the issuer company shall be disclosed.

(v)   **consent of the directors,** auditors, bankers to the issue, expert's opinion, if any, and of such other persons, as prescribed;

Rule 5 Companies (Prospectus and Allotment of Securities) Rules, 2014

(4) The aggregate number of securities of the issuer company and its subsidiary companies purchased or sold by the promoter group and **by the directors of the company which is a promoter of the issuer company and by the directors of the issuer company and their relatives within six months** immediately preceding the date of filing the prospectus with the Registrar of Companies shall be disclosed.

(8) The **details of any inquiry, inspections or investigations** initiated or conducted under the Companies Act or any previous companies law in the last five years immediately preceding the year of issue of prospectus in the case of company and all of its subsidiaries; and if there were any prosecutions filed (whether pending or not); fines imposed or compounding of offences done in the last five years immediately preceding the year of the prospectus for the company and all of its subsidiaries.

(9) The details of acts of **material frauds committed against the company** in the last five years, if any, and if so, the action taken by the company.

Sec 26. Matters to be stated in Prospectus

(4) No prospectus shall be issued by or on behalf of a company or in relation to an intended company unless on or before the date of its publication, there has been delivered to the Registrar for "filing", a copy thereof **signed by every person who is named therein as a director or proposed director** of the company or by his duly authorised attorney.

(8) No prospectus **shall be valid if it is issued more than ninety days** after the date on which a copy thereof is delivered to the Registrar.

(9) If a prospectus is issued in contravention of the provisions of this section, the company shall be punishable with fine which shall not be less than fifty thousand rupees but which may extend to three lakh rupees and **every person who is knowingly a party to the issue of such prospectus** shall be punishable with fine which shall not be less than fifty thousand rupees but which may extend to three lakh rupees,

34. Criminal liability for mis-statements in prospectus —

Where a prospectus, issued, circulated or distributed under this Chapter, includes any statement which is untrue or misleading in form or context in which it is included or where any inclusion or omission of any matter is likely to mislead, every person who

authorises the issue of such prospectus shall be liable under section 447:

Provided that nothing in this section shall apply to a person if he proves that such statement or omission was immaterial or that he had reasonable grounds to believe, and did up to the time of issue of the prospectus believe, that the statement was true or the inclusion or omission was necessary.

35. Civil liability for mis-statements in prospectus —

(1)   Where a person has subscribed for securities of a company acting on any statement included, or the inclusion or omission of any matter, in the prospectus which is misleading **and has sustained any loss or damage** as a consequence thereof, the company and every person who—

    (a)   is a director of the company at the time of the issue of the prospectus;

    (b)   has authorised himself to be named and is named in the prospectus as a director of the company, or has agreed to become such director, either immediately or after an interval of time;

    (c)   is a promoter of the company;

    (d)   has authorised the issue of the prospectus; and

    (e)   is an expert referred to in sub-section (5) of section 26, shall, without prejudice to any punishment to which any person may be liable under section 36, be liable to pay compensation to every person who has sustained such loss or damage.

(3)   Notwithstanding anything contained in this section, where it is proved that a prospectus has been issued with intent to defraud the applicants for the securities of a company or any other person or for any fraudulent purpose, **every person referred to in subsection (1) shall be personally responsible, without any limitation of liability, for all or any of the losses or damages that may have been incurred by any person who subscribed to the securities on the basis of such prospectus.**

39. Allotment of securities by company —

(1) No allotment of any securities of a company offered to the public for subscription shall be made unless the amount stated in the prospectus as **the minimum amount (5% of nominal amount) has been subscribed** and the sums payable on application for the amount so stated have been paid to and received by the company by cheque or other instrument.

(4) Whenever a company having a share capital makes any allotment of securities, it **shall file with the Registrar a return of allotment in PAS-3** Form within thirty days of allotment.(Rule 12}.

(5) In case of any default under sub-section (3) or sub-section (4), the company and **its officer who is in default shall be liable** to a penalty, for each default, of one thousand rupees for each day during which such default continues or one lakh rupees, whichever is less.

40. Permission for Securities to be dealt with in stated stock exchanges —

(3) All monies received on application from the public for subscription to the securities shall be kept in a separate bank account in a scheduled bank and shall not be utilised for any purpose other than—

(a)   for adjustment against allotment of securities where the securities have been permitted to be dealt with in the stock exchange or stock exchanges specified in the prospectus; or

(b)   for the repayment of monies within the time specified by the Securities and Exchange Board, received from applicants in pursuance of the prospectus, where the company is for any other reason unable to allot securities.

(5) If a default is made in complying with the provisions of this section, the company shall be punishable with a fine which shall not be less than five lakh rupees but which may extend to fifty lakh rupees and **every officer of the company who is in default** shall be punishable with fine which shall not be less than fifty thousand rupees but which may extend to three lakh rupees,

42. & Rule 14. Offer or invitation for subscription of securities on private placement —

(5) All monies payable towards subscription of securities under this section shall be paid through cheque or demand draft or other banking channels but not by cash.

(6) A company making an offer or invitation under this section shall allot its securities **within sixty days** from the date of

receipt of the application money for such securities and **if the company is not able to allot the securities** within that period, it shall repay the application money to the subscribers within fifteen days from the date of completion of sixty days and if the company fails to repay the application money within the aforesaid period, it shall be liable to repay that money with interest at the rate of twelve per cent. per annum from the expiry of the sixtieth day:

(7) All offers covered under this section shall be made only to such persons whose names are recorded by the company prior to the invitation to subscribe, and that such persons shall receive the offer by name, and that a complete record of such offers shall be kept by the company in form **PAS-5** and complete information about such offer shall be filed with the Registrar in **PAS_4** form within a period of thirty days of circulation of relevant private placement offer letter.

(9) Whenever a company makes any allotment of securities under this section, it shall file with the Registrar a return of allotment in such manner as may be prescribed, including the complete list of all security-holders, with their full names, addresses, number of securities allotted and such other relevant information as may be prescribed.

(10) If a company makes an offer or accepts monies in contravention of this section, the company, its promoters **and directors shall be liable for a penalty** which may extend to the amount involved in the offer or invitation or two crore rupees, whichever is higher, and the company shall also refund all monies to subscribers within a period of thirty days of the order imposing the penalty.

53. Prohibition on issue of shares at discount —(1) Except as provided in section 54, a company shall not issue shares at a discount.

(2) Any share issued by a company at a discounted price shall be void.

"(3) Where any company **fails to comply** with the provisions of this section, such company and **every officer who is in default** shall be liable to a penalty which may extend to an amount equal to the amount raised through the issue of shares at a discount or five lakh rupees, whichever is less, and the company shall also be liable to refund all monies received with interest at the rate of twelve per cent. per annum from the date of issue of such shares to the persons to whom such shares have been issued."

Companies (Share Capital & Debentures) Rules, 2014

- **Rule 4:** Issue of Shares with Differential Rights

- **Rule 5:** Certificate of shares where shares are not in de-mat form)

- **Rule 6:** Issue of Renewed or Duplicate Share Certificates

- **Rule 7: Maintenance of Share Certificate Forms and Related Books and Documents**

- **Sec 54: Rule 8: Issue of Sweat Equity Shares**

- **Sec 55: Rule 9: Issue and Redemption of Preference Shares**

- **Rule 10: Issue and Redemption of Preference Shares by Infrastructure Project Company**

- **Sec 56: Rule 11: Instrument of Transfer**

(4)   Every company shall, unless prohibited by any provision of law or any order of Court, Tribunal or other authority, deliver the certificates of all securities allotted, transferred or transmitted—

> (a)   within a period of two months from the date of incorporation, in the case of subscribers to the memorandum;

> (b)   within a period of two months from the date of allotment, in the case of any allotment of any of its shares;

> (c)   within a period of one month from the date of receipt by the company of the instrument of transfer under sub-section (1) or, as the case may be, of the intimation of transmission under subsection (2)   in the case of a transfer or transmission of securities;

> (d)   within a period of six months from the date of allotment in the case of any allotment of debenture:

Provided that where the securities are dealt with in a depository, the company shall intimate the details of allotment of securities to depository immediately on allotment of such securities.

(5)   The transfer of any security or other interest of a deceased person in a company made by his legal representative shall, even if the legal representative is not a holder thereof, be valid as if he had been the holder at the time of the execution of the instrument of transfer.

"(6)   Where any default is made in complying with the provisions of sub-sections (1) to (5), the company **and every officer of the company who is in default** shall be liable to a penalty of fifty thousand rupees.".

Rule 12: Issue of Employees Stock Options

Sec 62: Rule 13: Issue of Shares on Preferential Basis

Sec 63: Rule 14: Issue of Bonus Shares

Sec 64: Rule 15: Notice to Registrar for alteration of share capital

"(2) Where any company fails to comply with the provisions of sections 61. 62, , such company and **every officer who is in default** shall be liable to a penalty of one thousand rupees for each day during which such default continues, or five lakh rupees whichever is less.".

Rule 16: Provision of money by company for purchase of its own shares by employees or by trustees for the benefit of employees.-

Rule 17: Buy-back of Shares or Other Securities

Sec 71: Rule 18: Debentures

60. Publication of authorised, subscribed and paid-up capital —

(1)   Where any notice, advertisement or other official publication, or any business letter, billhead or letter paper of a company contains a statement of the amount of the authorised capital of the company, such notice, advertisement or other official publication, or such letter, billhead or letter paper shall also

Sec 74 (3) If a company fails to repay the deposit or part thereof or any interest thereon within of deposits outstanding as on April 1, 2014 or such further time as may be allowed by the Tribunal, the company shall, in addition to the payment of the amount of deposit or part thereof and the interest due, be punishable with fine which shall not be less than one crore ru-0-0pees but which may extend to ten crore rupees and **every officer of the company who is in default shall be punishable** with imprisonment which may extend to seven years or with fine which shall not be less than twenty-five lakh rupees but which may extend to two crore rupees, or with both.

Rule 17. Penal rate of interest.- Every company shall pay a penal rate of interest of eighteen per cent. per annum for the overdue period in case of deposits, whether secured or unsecured, matured and claimed but remaining unpaid.

Rule 21. Punishment for contravention.-

If any company referred to in sub-section (2) of section 73 or any eligible company inviting deposits or any other person contravenes any provision of these rules for which no punishment is provided in the Act, the company and **every officer of the company who is in default shall be punishable** with fine which may extend to five thousand rupees and where the contravention is a continuing one, with a further fine which may extend to five hundred rupees for every day after the first day during which the contravention continues.

75. Damages for fraud —

(1)   Where a company fails to repay the deposit or part thereof or any interest thereon referred to in section 74 and it is

proved that the deposits had been accepted with intent to defraud the depositors or for any fraudulent purpose, **every officer of the company who was responsible for the acceptance of such deposit shall, without prejudice to the provisions contained in subsection (3) of that section and liability under section 447, be personally responsible,** without any limitation of liability, for all or any of the losses or damages that may have been incurred by the depositors.

(2)   Any suit, proceedings or other action may be taken by any person, group of persons or any association of persons who had incurred any loss as a result of the failure of the company to repay the deposits or part thereof or any interest thereon.

76A. Punishment for contravention of section 73 or section 76 —

(a) the company shall, in addition to the payment of the amount of deposit or part thereof and the interest due, be punishable with fine which shall not be less than one crore rupees but which may extend to ten crore rupees; and

(b) **every officer of the company who is in default shall be punishable** with imprisonment which may extend to seven years or with fine which shall not be less than twenty-five lakh rupees but which may extend to two crore rupees, or with both:

Provided that **if it is proved that the officer of the company who is in default,** has contravened such provisions knowingly or willfully with the intention to deceive the company or its shareholders or depositors or creditors or tax authorities, he shall be liable for action under section 447.

86. Punishment for contravention —

(1) If **any person willfully** furnishes any false or incorrect information or knowingly suppresses any material information, required to be registered in accordance with the provisions of section 77, he shall be liable for action under section 447.

"(2) If any company is in default in complying with any of the provisions of this Chapter, the company shall be liable to a penalty of five lakh rupees **and every officer of the company who is in default** shall be liable to a penalty of fifty thousand rupees.".

206. Power to call for information, inspect books and conduct inquiries —

(4) If the Registrar is satisfied on the basis of information available with or furnished to him or on a representation made to him by any person that the business of a company is being carried on for a fraudulent or unlawful purpose or not in compliance with the provisions of this Act or if the grievances of investors are not being addressed, the Registrar may, after informing the company of the allegations made against it by a written order, call on the company to furnish in writing any information or explanation on matters specified in the order within such time as he may specify therein and carry out such inquiry as he deems fit after providing the company a reasonable opportunity of being heard:

Provided further that where business of a company has been or is being carried on for a fraudulent or unlawful purpose, every officer of the company who is in default shall be punishable for fraud in the manner as provided in section 447.

(5) Without prejudice to the foregoing provisions of this section, the Central Government may, if it is satisfied that the circumstances so warrant, direct inspection of books and papers of a company by an inspector appointed by it for the purpose.

(7) If a company fails to furnish any information or explanation or produce any document required under this section, the company **and every officer of the company, who is in default** shall be punishable with a fine which may extend to one lakh rupees and in the case of a continuing failure, with an additional fine which may extend to five hundred rupees for every day after the first during which the failure continues.

207. Conduct of inspection and inquiry —

(4) **(i) If any director or officer of the company disobeys the direction** issued by the Registrar or the inspector under this section, the director or the officer shall be punishable with imprisonment which may extend to one year and with fine which shall not be less than twenty-five thousand rupees but which may extend to one lakh rupees.

(ii) If a director or an officer of the company has been convicted of an offence under this section, the director or the officer shall, on and from the date on which he is so convicted, be deemed to have vacated his office as such and on such vacation of office, shall be disqualified from holding an office in any company.

209. Search and seizure where it is believed that the books and papers of a company, or relating to the key managerial personnel **or any director** or auditor or company secretary in practice if the company has not appointed a company secretary, are likely to be destroyed, mutilated, altered, falsified or secreted, after obtaining an order from the Special Court.

210. Investigation into affairs of company —

212. Investigation into affairs of Company by Serious Fraud Investigation Office —

(8) If any officer not below the rank of Assistant Director of Serious Fraud Investigation Office authorised in this behalf by the Central Government by general or special order, has on the basis of material in his possession reason to believe (the reason for such belief to be recorded in writing) **that any person has been guilty of any offence punishable,** he may arrest such person and shall, as soon as may be, inform him of the grounds for such arrest.

"(14A) Where the report states that fraud has taken place in a company and due to such fraud **any director, key managerial personnel, other officer of the company or any other person or entity, has taken undue advantage or benefit,** whether in the form of any asset, property or cash or in any other manner, the Central Government may file an application before the Tribunal for appropriate orders with regard to disgorgement of such asset, property or cash and also for holding such director, key managerial personnel, other officer or any other person liable personally without any limitation of liability.".

213. Investigation into company's affairs by the Tribunal in other cases —

if after investigation it is proved that—

(i)   the business of the company is being conducted with intent to defraud its creditors, members or any other persons or otherwise for a fraudulent or unlawful purpose, or that the company was formed for any fraudulent or unlawful purpose; or

(ii)   any person concerned in the formation of the company or the management of its affairs have in connection therewith been guilty of fraud, then, every officer of the company who is in default and the person or persons concerned in the formation of the company or the management of its affairs shall be punishable for fraud in the manner as provided in section 447.

217. Procedure, powers, etc., of inspectors —

(6) (i) If any director or officer of the company disobeys the direction issued by the Registrar or the inspector under this section, the director or the officer shall be punishable with imprisonment which may extend to one year and with fine which shall not be less than twenty-five thousand rupees but which may extend to one lakh rupees.

(ii)   If a director or an officer of the company has been convicted of an offence under this section, the director or the officer shall, on and from the date on which he is so convicted, be deemed to have vacated his office as such and on such vacation of office, shall be disqualified from holding an office in any company.

(7) The notes of any examination under sub-section (4) shall be taken down in writing and shall be read over to, or by, and signed by, the person examined, and may thereafter be used in evidence against him.

(8) If any person fails without reasonable cause or refuses—

(a)   to produce to an inspector or any person authorised by him in this behalf any book or paper which is his duty under sub-section (1) or sub-section (2) to produce;

(b)   to furnish any information which is his duty under sub-section (2) to furnish;

(c)   to appear before the inspector personally when required to do so under subsection (4) or to answer any question which is put to him by the inspector in pursuance of that sub-section; or

(d)   to sign the notes of any examination,

he shall be punishable with imprisonment for a term which may extend to six months and with fine which shall not be less than twenty-five thousand rupees but which may extend to one lakh rupees, and also with a further fine which may extend to two thousand rupees for every day after the first during which the failure or refusal continues.

218. Protection of employees during investigation —

219. Power of inspector to conduct investigation into affairs of related companies, etc —

221. Freezing of assets of company on inquiry and investigation —

(2) In case of any removal, transfer or disposal of funds, assets, or properties of the company in contravention of the order of the Tribunal under sub-section (1), the company shall be punishable with fine which shall not be less than one lakh rupees but which

may extend to twenty-five lakh rupees **and every officer of the company who is in default** shall be punishable with imprisonment for a term which may extend to three years or with fine which shall not be less than fifty thousand rupees but which may extend to five lakh rupees, or with both.

222. Imposition of restrictions upon securities —

(2) Where securities in any company are issued or transferred or acted upon in contravention of an order of the Tribunal under sub-section (1), the company shall be punishable with fine which shall not be less than one lakh rupees but which may extend to twenty-five lakh rupees **and every officer of the company who is in default shall be punishable with imprisonment** for a term which may extend to six months or with fine which shall not be less than twenty-five thousand rupees but which may extend to five lakh rupees, or with both.

229. Penalty for furnishing false statement, mutilation, destruction of documents —

he shall be punishable for fraud in the manner as provided in section 447.

232. Merger and amalgamation of companies —

(5) Every company in relation to which the order is made shall cause a certified copy of the order to be filed with the Registrar for registration within thirty days of the receipt of certified copy of the order.

"(8) If a company fails to comply with sub-section (5), the company **and every officer of the company who is in default** shall be liable to a penalty of twenty thousand rupees, and where the failure is a continuing one, with a further penalty of one thousand rupees for each day after the first during which such failure continues, subject to a maximum of three lakh rupees.".

241. Application to Tribunal for relief in cases of oppression

242. Powers of Tribunal —

(3) A certified copy of the order of the Tribunal under sub-section (1) shall be filed by the company with the Registrar within thirty days of the order of the Tribunal.

(5) Where an order of the Tribunal under sub-section (1) makes any alteration in the memorandum or articles of a company, then, notwithstanding any other provision of this Act, **the company shall not have power**, except to the extent, if any, permitted in the order, to make, without the leave of the Tribunal, any alteration whatsoever which is inconsistent with the order, either in the memorandum or in the articles.

(8) If a company contravenes the provisions of sub-section (5), the company shall be punishable with fine which shall not be less than one lakh rupees but which may extend to twenty-five lakh rupees **and every officer of the company who is in default** shall be punishable with imprisonment for a term which may extend to six months or with fine which shall not be less than twenty-five thousand rupees but which may extend to one lakh rupees.

243. Consequences of termination or modification of certain agreements —

(2) Any person who knowingly acts as a managing director or other director or manager of a company

in contravention of clause (b) of sub-section (1) or sub-section (1A) **and every other director of the company who is knowingly a party to such contravention,** shall be punishable with imprisonment for a term which may extend to six months or with fine which may extend to five lakh rupees, or with both.

two or more persons jointly, they shall be counted only as one member.

(2) Where any members of a company are entitled to make an application under subsection (1), any one or more of them having obtained the consent in writing of the rest, may make the application on behalf and for the benefit of all of them.

245. Class action —

(1) Such number of member or members, depositor or depositors or any class of them, as the case may be, as prescribed in sub-section (3) may, if they are of the opinion that the management or conduct of the affairs of the company are being conducted in a manner prejudicial to the interests of the company or its members or depositors, file an application before the Tribunal on behalf of the members or depositors for seeking appropriate orders.

(7) Any company which fails to comply with an order passed by the Tribunal under this section shall be punishable with fine which shall not be less than five lakh rupees but which may extend to twenty-five lakh rupees **and every officer of the company who is in default** shall be punishable with imprisonment for a term which may extend to three years and with fine which shall not be less than twenty-five thousand rupees but which may extend to one lakh rupees.

246. Application of certain provisions to proceedings under section 241 and section 245 — The provisions of sections 337 to 341 (both inclusive) shall apply mutatis mutandis, in relation to an application made to the Tribunal under section 241 or section 245.

Chapter XVIII Removal of Names of Companies from the Register of Companies

248. Power of Registrar to remove name of company from register of companies —

251. Fraudulent application for removal of name —

(1)   Where it is found that an application by a company under section 248 has been made with the object of evading the liabilities of the company or with the intention to deceive the creditors or to defraud any other persons, the **persons in charge of the management of the company** shall, notwithstanding that the company has been notified as dissolved—

    (a)   be jointly and severally liable to any person or persons who had incurred loss or damage as a result of the company being notified as dissolved; and

    (b)   be punishable for fraud in the manner as provided in section 447.